Cavalry Experiences

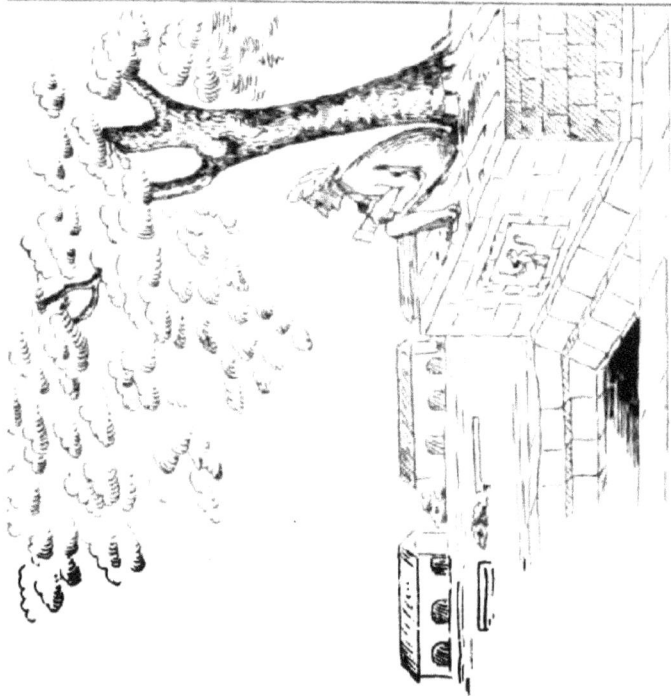

A LITTLE CHIT (LETTER)

AND ITS CONSEQUENCE

Cavalry Experiences

Letters & Journals of a British Cavalry Officer
During the Second Sikh War & Indian Mutiny

Henry Aimé Ouvry

LEONAUR

Cavalry Experiences
Letters & Journals of a British Cavalry Officer
During the Second Sikh War & Indian Mutiny
by Henry Aimé Ouvry

First published under the title
Cavalry Experiences and Leaves From My Journal

Leonaur is an imprint of Oakpast Ltd

Copyright in this form © 2012 Oakpast Ltd

ISBN: 978-0-85706-882-8 (hardcover)
ISBN: 978-0-85706-883-5 (softcover)

http://www.leonaur.com

Contents

Preface

Need hardly say these letters and journals were never intended for publication; this may easily be seen from internal evidence. My family, however, kept all my letters and papers, which were sent back to me some ten or twelve years ago and, as they contain accounts and remarks on military matters and cavalry experiences, I have thought that sufficient time has elapsed when they may appear in print.

I was some sixteen years in the army before I saw any active service, all of which time I had served in the infantry; but, having met with a severe accident while serving in the 68th Light Infantry in Canada, whereby I sustained a compound fracture of the right leg, I was pronounced unfit for further service in the infantry, by a medical board.

I was on detachment duty with part of a company at Riviere du Loup, a small place on the River St. Lawrence, when I was ordered to the headquarters of the regiment at Lake Tamisquata, to attend on a court-martial. On my return I was upset from a cart and my leg was broken. The Medical Board reported that I had received an injury, on service, nearly equal to the loss of a limb, and the Secretary of State awarded me what he considered a compensation for such an injury to a lieutenant, *viz.* £50.

After I, in a measure, recovered, I found that the Medical Board were in the right, so I purchased into the 3rd, or King's Own Light Dragoons, who were then stationed at Umballa, in the East Indies, and in this Regiment I first saw actual service in the Second Sikh war.

The Duke of Wellington said, justly, "*A battle is like a ball:*" we know all about our own adventures, but we cannot possibly see all that occurs. Hence half a dozen pens each give a different account of the same event from their own point of view, and from this results the very different accounts of the same affair which we meet in various so-called histories of wars.

Thirty-five years have flown since the great Mutiny in India, and now in my old age I think very differently as to our conduct, as well as the part which I took, individually, with regard to its suppression.

Russell, the *Times* correspondent, remarks in his diary that there were men who had lived so long among Asiatics as to have imbibed their worst feelings and to have forgotten the sentiments of civilization and religion.—

> As cruel as covenanters, without their faith; as relentless as inquisitors, without their fanaticism; these sanguinary creatures, from the safe seclusion of their desks, utter stridulous cries as they plunge their pens into the seething ink, and shout out 'Blood! more blood!' with the energy and thirst of Marat or St. Just 'We want vengeance!' they cry, 'we must have it full, we care not if it be indiscriminate. We are not Christians now, because we are dealing with those who are not of our faith.'

Of course there was great provocation. Russell says:

> Mylne told me that he had no doubt two women were blown from guns, and some children had been placed against the targets on the practice ground as marks, by the men of the 10th and 41st B. N. I.

But this was no excuse for our side having put men to the torture before killing them. The Asiatics were, so to say, in a state of barbarism; we, on the contrary, at any rate, pretended to have arrived at a higher degree of civilization. Was it the act of civilized Christians when— again to quote Russell:

> We hung a relative of the Nawab of Furruckabad, under circumstances of the most disgusting indignity, whilst a chaplain stood by among the spectators? It is actually true that the miserable man entertained one or two officers of a British Regiment in his palace the day before his death, and that he believed his statements with respect to his innocence were received; but in a few hours after he had acted as host to a colonel in our army, he was pounced upon by the civil power, and hanged in a way which excited the displeasure of everyone who saw it, and particularly of Sir William Peel. All these kinds of vindictive, unchristian, Indian torture, such as sewing Mahomedans in pigskins; smearing them with pork-fat before execution; burning their bodies, and forcing Hindoos to defile themselves; are dis-

graceful, and ultimately recoil on ourselves. They are spiritual and mental tortures to which we have no right to resort, and which we dare not perpetrate in the face of Europe.

But it is very easy to reason in cold blood. The provocation was great, and revenge is a passion implanted in the breast of man by human nature, but when exercised without limit, as described above, it is always followed by unavailing regret— as I myself now experience, although I cannot reproach myself with any of the atrocities as described by Mr. Russell in his most interesting diary.

Possibly the Nana Sahib may have studied our Bible through some missionary translation; at any rate, he did not outdo Moses, if we are to accept the account (Numbers' xxxi, 14—18) as historical. Human nature remains the same now as it always has been from the first. When the lower propensities are not kept in subjection by the Divine spark, the bestial instinct gains the ascendency, and man becomes worse than the brute creation, because his intellect gives him greater power to do evil.

It is all very well to preach that vengeance to God alone belongs; but vengeance, is one of the strongest feelings which Nature has implanted in the breast of man. I admit that I was under its influence in common with all the rest, if it had been otherwise, we should not have been human beings. So far from being divine is nature, that we find it generally cruel in the extreme. Aristotle remarks that nature is rather diabolical than divine; and those who preach that God is love should recollect that:

Nature red in tooth and claw
With ravine shrieks against your creed.

Either God rules this world or He does not; if He does so, He must have decreed that it should be as it is. *Deus ita desiderat hunc mundum, qualis est; si meliorem vellet, meliorem haberet.* Thus wrote Vanini, whom it was much easier to burn alive than to refute.

Thirty-five years have flown since the Mutiny, (as at time of first publication)—as we call it, but which after-ages may consider as an effort of a subjugated nation to cast off' the yoke of its oppressors—has been suppressed, and how stand we now?

The brilliant author of an episode in that great calamity writes:

The January sun of 1857 had looked down on the dominions of the Honourable the East India Company. The January sun of

9

1887 looks down on the empire of Victoria, Queen of England and Empress of India. It looks down on a great empire, greatly administered. It looks down on a changed and transformed India—on a new India. It looks down on great changes—great improvements, for great canals and railroads now traverse the land; the railroad and telegraph have annulled its vast intervening distances It looks down on fine new cities—on the old ones made sweeter and brighter. It looks down on innumerable schools and colleges—on a new generation of educated natives; the stream of human learning which for so many generations had flowed backward and forward, between Europe and Western Asia has now reached further from west to east, and is flowing in full tide into India. It looks down on a people among whom has been an enormous diffusion of wealth—an enormous increase in the comforts of life. It looks down on a land in which peace and security, order and quiet, law and justice, prevail in an eminent degree.

This is indeed a very optimistic view of the case. But what does the sun of 1891 really look down on, if there be any reality in the graphic account of the situation in India by C. B. Norman, late 90th L. I. in the *United Service Magazine* for December, 1891? This is what he says:

Enemies, as we learnt in '57, and again in the spring of this year, are to be found within our gates. The spread of false education, the freedom—nay, the license of the press, the ill-judged agitation fostered by notoriety-hunting nonentities, have all tended to spread disaffection in the land. What happened at Manipur last March may well happen in other States tomorrow. It is not only on the borders of far-off Assam that discontented native princes are to be met with. In India we live, as it were, in a powder magazine. Misplaced leniency, construed into weakness, may set the whole country in a blaze; for there is no disguising the fact, that never, since the mutiny, has India been in a more critical position than at present We sleep on contentedly, as we did in the spring of '57, but those who know India best, know too, that our hold on the country is not one whit more secure than it was then, and that *we are as cordially hated* throughout the length and breadth of the land as we were in those far distant days.

The only matter that I have thought fit to suppress in my journal

10

are my remarks on the operations after the arrival of Sir Colin Campbell, as I consider them to touch on matters which may be best discussed hereafter, and besides not suited to my gossiping letters which, if they afford the amusement to my readers which they have given me thirty- five years after they were written, I shall feel great satisfaction.

With regard to the illustrations scratched by me in my letters, chiefly when I was at the siege of Delhi, there is one in the frontispiece which is not described in the text, as it appears the letter has been lost in which it was mentioned.

The holy man sitting under the trees, was well known to me for years before the mutiny. After the troops had marched from Umballa for Delhi, he was observed to be continually writing; he was watched by means of a telescope and then suddenly seized *en flagrant delit* with a pen in his hand.

The nature of his letter, addressed, I believe, to the Nana Sahib, was to this effect—

> May it appear good to your most excellent mind, the seat of all that is great, that the Feringhi troops having left the station, the opportunity occurs for exterminating all the Christians in the place, etc.

He was immediately hanged, a lady's music stool being used for him to stand upon, the rope breaking once as shown in the sketch. I had several times talked with the culprit and he appeared a highly excellent and religious man. Doubtless he considered it a very praiseworthy act to destroy Christians—*Tantum Religio potuit suadere malorum.*

Voyage to Bombay

On the 3rd, November 1846, I left Southampton docks in the Oriental Steam Navigation Company's ship *Achilles*—Captain Wilson—at three o'clock, p.m. We had a bad passage, the wind being dead an end against us across the Bay of Biscay. On the 9th November at 6 p.m. we reached Gibraltar.

To a stranger, Gibraltar appears a dull comfortless place: inns very wretched; and, as at this time of the year the weather is very rainy, the streets were choaked with mud and slush. I tried to get a warm bath, but after waiting half-an-hour only succeeded in getting a tepid one in a cold bath room; the towels were also cold and coarse, so that, on the whole, my dip did me more harm than good. I got up at 6 a.m. and walked through the town as far as the Almeida or promenade. The town is a very poor place, no good public buildings, and I had no time to inspect the rock or fortifications. I felt very glad on sailing at 9 a.m. that I did not belong to the garrison.

We continued our voyage, and on November 12th we passed within a mile of Algiers, which rose like an amphitheatre from the bay. I had seen a picture of it, and it appeared quite familiar to me. The houses were all white and appeared to be built of sandstone.

13th November. Passed by Bona, a fortified place. Very beautiful weather, sailing ten knots; all the ladies on deck in their finest feathers.

14th November. Wind shifted to the eastward; bad weather coming on. About midnight we Were caught in a regular northeaster, or as they call it here a *gregáli*.[1] What a change! from a beautiful smooth sea like a vast lake without a ripple on the water, suddenly a raging sea

1. This word is apparently an Italian nautical term for *Greco Levante*, a north-east wind; it most probably should be written *Grecali*.

sprung up, which made a clean breach over the vessel Nothing being prepared, there was a great smash of crockery glass, etc., plenty of fear among the ladies and among some gentlemen likewise, of course without there being any danger. The *Achilles* was heavily laden and hardly made any headway, certainly not more than one knot an hour.

Sunday, 15th. No dinner put on the table, a huge bowl of lobscouse being placed in one corner of the cabin, those who were out of their berths helped themselves as best they could. As for the sea-sick passengers they must have come off second best. As we approached the island of Pantalaria the head engineer reported the engine out of order, so to the disgust of all on board, we were obliged to make sail and stop the engines. It took three hours to repair the damage, after which the gale abated a little and we were enabled to make some way. We were now off Malta. A north-east wind blows right into the harbour, so we put up our helm and ran between the batteries—a most imposing sight; they were crowded with the inhabitants and military. In a few minutes we were in smooth water snugly moored to a buoy.

With regard to this wind, I am inclined to think that it was a *gregáli* that wrecked St. Paul; there is a place pointed out at this very spot called St Paul's Bay. Now St. Paul says that the wind in which his ship made such bad weather was called "*Euroclydon.*" But what is the meaning of that word? It would appear that there was something south in it; but then if it had been a south or south-west wind, he could not have been wrecked on that side of the island; and the other side must have been quite out of the question, both from his description of his course and from the nature of the shore: so I feel inclined to think that St. Paul made a mistake or was misinformed by his captain. *Euroclydon* cannot possibly mean a northeaster.[2]

There are no venomous snakes in the island; the inhabitants say that St. Paul sent them all out of the place because one of them bit him. Something like the story of St. Patrick charming the snakes out of Ireland.

Gozo, Calypso's Island, is an islet separated from Malta by a channel; it abounds in many curious fossil remains. I bought some fossil shark's teeth for a few shillings, very interesting on account of their great age and size, they must have belonged to a fish full forty feet in length.

I should like to have stayed a few days at Malta and to have vis-

---

2. Liddell Scott's lexicon inclines to the belief that it does mean a N. E. wind.

ited Gozo. The church with the tombs of the Grand Masters was the principal object of attraction—the Mosaic pavements, the sculptured monuments, together with the whole interior structure, formed an elaborate example of workmanship, industry, and art, such as superstition or enthusiasm has rarely exceeded.

A stranger might pass an agreeable week at Malta, but he had better avoid it in the hot season. Here we left the *Achilles* and embarked on board the *Ariel*. The *Ariel* was an iron boat; a splendid vessel in fine weather, but a shockingly bad sea-boat. We put to sea, the same gale constantly blowing, which was a very rare occurrence, as these *gregáli* seldom last more than three days; this one held on for nine days.

On the 19th November the wind slackened and again we saw the blue sky, and the next day towards evening we arrived at Alexandria. Contrary to all expectation and to my extreme disgust, we were hurried away at 9 p.m. the same night, so that I had no opportunity of seeing the *pasha's* palace which was all that there was worth seeing. Pompey's Pillar was very distinct before we disembarked.

(Several letters are here missing as I find the next letter at my disposition is dated—"Atalanta, at sea, lat. 19. 13. N. long. 71. 20. E. 14th December.")

My Dear Mim,

We are now within four and twenty hours of Bombay, where we most probably shall arrive tomorrow which is the very day that the mail leaves for England, therefore I shall barely have time, perhaps, to throw this letter on board the mail steamer. Had we made an ordinary passage we should have been at Bombay about a week ago.

I have not got much news to tell you. We have been in a state of utter discomfort ever since we embarked at Aden. We started with beautiful prospects, sea as calm as a mill pond, and the Indian officers on board all said that the calm weather would continue the whole voyage. On the second day of our departure it came on to blow dead an end against us and it has never ceased since. Now that we are approaching the land, the sea has become smoother, but the wind still continues contrary. I do sincerely advise nobody to come out to India by the so called "Overland." The misery is beyond expression, and I have wished a thousand times that I had gone round the Cape.

There are no beds; we lie all night on the deck and are roused

15

out at half-past four by the cry of "Hands wash decks." Then we lounge about till 7 a.m., when a servant brings about half a tumbler of dirty water to wash with; and to add to the mess, on going down to breakfast, there is nothing you can eat: that is to say nothing any civilized person can eat. The bread is so bad as to be totally unfit for consumption; the tea is undrinkable; no butter, and in fact the only thing really eatable is rice and curry. I stuff myself with this wretched food on the same principle as the savages, who eat dirt to stave off the pangs of hunger. Strange to say, notwithstanding all this, I feel much better, and that my health has improved by the voyage

From all I can learn, I shall have to get up to Umballa by land, and even if I could get up the Indus, I am told I should be at least three months on the voyage. Steamboats run up as far as Sukkur. There is one of Ch. Delamain's regiment on board, he is going to Sukkur, and of course I shall go with him if I take the Indus route. He seems a good fellow, but I should say his health is ruined by the climate, as, although only twenty-five years old, he looks forty, his name is Olfield, he says that his regiment is in a very unhealthy place, I am quite delighted with all the accounts I hear of Umballa, it is the best station in India, and if you are unwell, the hills are within six hours *dak* journey.

The servants on board speak no English, and I have already made some progress in Hindustani which must be learnt by ear as I find my books of little use. The natives speak a corrupt jargon, and I shall not take much trouble to study it; Persian is the correct thing to learn and would be of use to me afterwards. The captain says that they will delay the mail twenty-four hours for us, so I will tell you my plans after I have seen the adjutant-general when we arrive. One poor lady has nearly died of sea-sickness, today she is out of danger, but had the gale continued a few hours longer, it would have been all up with her, I got out my medicine chest to find some essence of ginger for her as they had none on board; I found many of the bottles broken, and the whole was in a pretty mess.

Tuesday 10th. 10 a. m.

My Dear Mim,

We are now only five miles from Bombay. Yesterday after finishing my letter to you I went to bed, that is to say I laid me down

16

on the deck thinking that all our troubles were over, when suddenly it came on to blow a gale when we were within six. hours sail of Bombay. A furious sea got up and swept the deck fore and aft, wetting me through, and my medicine chest rolled over me completely smashed. However we shall now shortly be at anchor in Bombay Harbour.

Bombay, Wednesday, 16th December, 8 a. m. At last here I am, the mail closes at 10 a.m., so I am afraid I shall not be able to tell you anything of my plans. The expense of travelling by Palanquin is dearer than posting in England, so most probably I shall march. I shall then have to buy horses, camels, ponies, etc. The Indus route is out of the question, so I will leave a letter at Bombay when I start on my journey, which you will get next mail; after that it will be some time before you hear from me again.

Goodbye, and love to you all.

Your affectionate son, Henry.

Bombay, 20th December, 1846.

My Dear Mim

I have taken the best advice and shall march. Bombay is a very expensive, place; horses are horribly dear, a good Arab charger would cost from £230 to £300. I am told that the reason of this is that two cavalry regiments have just passed through Bombay—the 10th Hussars—all looking out for horses have raised the prices so. I have bought three small Arabs to mount myself and servants on; I gave £40 each for them, and I have since bought one charger for £100. I got these horses chosen by a proper person, as I was no judge of Arabs myself. I have got six servants in all, which is all I intend to have; most people have a cook but I intend to do without one. I shall march about twenty miles a day and with halts it will take me two months to reach Umballa.

I am living at the Hope Hall Hotel, about three miles from the Fort of Bombay. It is a nice cool place, and I sleep in a tent in the garden. I pay twelve shillings a day for board and lodging, which does not include beer or wine; a Palanquin costs ten shillings a day. Yesterday I went to the governor's public breakfast which takes place every Saturday, and is a kind of levee. I was in full uniform and found it very stupid. I shall keep this letter open and make additions to it, from time to time, as anything crops up that may interest you.

Nassuck, January 3rd, 1847.

My Dear Mim,

I have advanced thus far on my journey; my route is Bombay, Tannah, Bheundy, Nassuck, Mulligaum, Mhow, Indore, Neemuch, Kishnaghur, Jeypore, Agra, Dehli, Umballa, these are the principal places; of course I have not put down the minor stages. Thus on the 1st January, I halted at Kassara till evening and then went on at 4 p.m. to the *dak* bungalow at Egapoora. The road was hilly; the natives brought in a lynx, which they had shot; it was a fearful looking animal much resembling a large wolf, it had evidently been first caught in a trap as the mark on its leg plainly shewed.

January 2nd. Marched at daybreak; found a bullock by the side of the road, which had evidently sunk from fatigue; it was abandoned, and vultures were eating it alive; these horrible birds had torn out both its eyes and had otherwise lacerated it terribly. I dismounted and put an end to its misery by a pistol shot in the forehead.

*January 3r*d. Marched at 6 a.m. and halted at Warrewarra at 9 a.m. sent on my tents six miles on the Nassick road, where I went to sleep, picketing my horses by the roadside. I am now, as you see, at Nassuck in the *dak* Bangalow.

January 4th. Still halted at Nassuck, or as some write it Nassick. Went and visited the celebrated Rock Temples; these cave-temples were first discovered and mentioned by Captain Delamain; the inscriptions in ancient Devanagari have been deciphered; they date at about 1600 or 1800 years ago. Very interesting old Buddhist Monument here in the *dak* bungalow. I found some of my fellow passengers who were on board with me: a Roman Catholic priest, the Revd. Father Dodo, and with him some nuns. One of them was dying of dysentery and no wonder, this ignorant fellow travels during the heat of the day and he has no provisions or money. He has also a young girl with him who is also ill, the doctor here says that if they go on, the women will all die.

The Revd. Father Dodo is a low uneducated Frenchman, and

he is taking the nuns to a convent at Agra; he ought to be imprisoned as a madman or hung for murder. He could not pay the government tax for the *dak* bungalow, and I saw he had written in the bungalow book "vary insolent for the *passagere*," this was because the nigger who kept the house asked him to pay. On the march I saw the first snake, my horse trod upon it, the servants told me that it was a very venomous one called the whip snake. I also passed a large encampment belonging to a native princess.

Biora, lat. 24, 10. N. Long. 77. 30. E.
8th February.

My Dear Mim,

My last letter was from Nassick, since which I have been constantly marching. Since I last wrote from Nassick everything has gone well with me, though I have not got rid of my rheumatism which troubles me at times. It has been intensely cold, and I wish I had brought my Canadian coat. No such weather has been known, I am told, for the last forty years; I saw ice as thick as a half-crown piece I have been told that the native princess that I mentioned in my last letter was the Baisabhae, I do not know whether I spell it correctly, but Her Highness has about three thousand followers, nine pieces of artillery, several hundred horse and I do not know how many elephants; she was going to Bombay. I have shot some flying foxes or vampire bats; it is not true that they suck men's blood, but they do a great deal of mischief in the gardens.

I find that the gun Fred gave me shoots beautifully with ball. I shot an antelope and a *nyl-gye*. The word means "blue cow".

I feel very much annoyed at times with the people I meet, I mean the English missionaries in particular; they are ten times worse than the natives, many of whom have really good intellects. All missionaries should be prohibited and sent out of the country. They bring discredit on the English name by their folly. I am now within eighteen marches of Agra.

Gonah, February, 13. I have made up my mind never to be astonished at anything. *"Nil Admirari."* Today, the thermometer being 88° in the shade, I got off my horse to shoot a peacock, when suddenly a heavy shower of hail mixed with snow came down and wetted me to the skin; the hailstones were as large as peas, it lasted half an hour. I shot a magnificent peacock and have preserved the feathers. I have now been six weeks on the march, and having an opportunity, I shall send this letter off, and write again from Agra.

Yours affectionately, Henry.

Umballa, March 29, 1847.

My Dear Mim,

You see I am at Umballa. I had no opportunity of writing from Agra. The hot weather is just commencing. I have not yet visited the native town which is two miles from my present residence in cantonments. I have got very good rooms in a large bungalow at £1 a month. The great advantage of this station is its vicinity to the hills.

I find that I shall only be allowed two months leave this season; but next year I can have six months, which will enable me to visit Cashmere. My expenses will be about three hundred *rupees* a month. Our mode of life here is somewhat as follows. We get up early in the morning and ride, and go out driving in the evening.

The tone of society is decidedly low in India; I have seen very few that would be called ladies in England. In fact, people are what circumstances make them; what astonishes me is that there are men out here who have private fortunes; but I do not think they stay long. You know that I commenced studying Persian on the voyage out, and have made some progress. I shall conclude this letter by giving you a specimen of one of the odes of Hafiz. I should have said that I was sorry to hear that Uncle John had been suffering; as for dying that is what we must all do, and he has passed the ordinary life of man; why does he not take morphia?

Umballa, April 13th, 1847.

My Dear Francisca,

They say that you should always look for the most important part of a lady's letter in the postscript. You tell me of the death of my uncle; I never expected to see him again, neither do I expect to see my aunt any more. She, like, my late uncle, has passed the ordinary term of human life. I see also that the Duke of Northumberland has passed away, he was saved a few short years of suffering. I myself sincerely hope that I shall die when any of my faculties have become so deranged, either by accident or any other cause, so as to render life no longer worth living.

The hot weather has just set in and the thermometer stands at 98° in the shade. This is the state of things here. There are about a dozen gentlemen mixed up with some five thousand men and two hundred women (no ladies) You will feel astonished at my saying this, but I can assure you that it is too true; the beautiful description in the last chapter of proverbs comes most forcibly to my mind. That not one real lady-like person should be found among so many is a most unfortunate truth. And then the wretched state of disunion that prevails; the vice and ill-nature of these wretched women makes India ten times worse than it otherwise would be.

I have been at two balls since I have been here, and I never intend to go to another. My ordinary life is this. There is no drill going on during the hot weather. I get up at 6 a.m. and ride out the same dull round; from 7 a.m. till 9 a.m. I read Persian; then I dress and have breakfast; after that I lie down and doze over a book till 4 p.m.; I then write till 5 p.m.; and at 6 p.m. go out and hear the band play and take a ride till dinner time at 7.30 p.m.; at 9 p.m. I go to bed, and this will be my life for the next six months.

I have written to Johnny Delamain but he has returned no answer. I only hope that he will pass through this fiery ordeal of India without being utterly ruined. I have heard nothing yet of my lathe but I am anxiously expecting it by every mail. A small mess bill amounting to 19s. 3d. and a wine bill of 17s. 1d. from my old regiment the 68th Light Infantry, has been sent to me here, will you send the money to the paymaster, his name is Campbell.

This morning the hills did not look more than five miles off, while they are full thirty, so that if I fall ill I can get into a climate like England in a few hours. Very strange, is it not, that it should be so hot here? Will you get Peter to go to the Horse Guards and enquire about this regiment, as they say that we are to go home next year, I am sorry old O—— has made such an ass of himself. My love to you all.

Your affectionate brother, Henry.

My Dear Mother,

I have very little news to tell you, the affairs at Lahore are quite quiet, and all those who can get away have gone to the hills. They say that John Company are pressed for money and that we are to go home in order to save expense, but I do not believe it. I have had a letter from Johnny Delamain, and only conceive, he will have to pass the hot weather in tents, he however seems in good spirits and does not appear to mind it a bit. How cadets get on in this country is difficult to imagine, their pay is so small and their wants are so great. Johnny had about £100 to begin with, and his tents alone cost £70, he has about £18 a month to live on, and how he can buy and keep horses and pay house rent out of this, it is impossible to imagine.

I find that on arriving in this country cadets generally borrow money at 15 *p.c.* interest from the banks, which they endeavour to pay off at the rate of fifty *rupees* a month till the debt is liquidated, thus they really have next to nothing to live upon, and great numbers fall victims to brandy-and-water, smoking, and idleness; they are outcasts, as it were from all society, and what then can be expected from them? In our cantonments there are two or three regiments of native infantry. I do not know one officer among them and, if I were to be here for the next ten years, I should be no better acquainted with them. The civilians all hold themselves aloof and consider themselves as a kind of aristocracy simply because they have more pay.

We have a lieutenant of native infantry attached to my regiment. There is not a subaltern among us who is capable of acting as interpreter. The pay is 100 *rupees* a month and a captain is not eligible; otherwise I should like to take the post myself. I am pretty well in health but I always feel so thirsty; however, I drink no wine but plenty of beer, which agrees with me very well. My three horses are quite well and I have sent the two ponies to be sold as they are of no use to me now.

29th April, 1847. The weather still continues cool and most delightful in the mornings, which is owing to rain having fallen in the hills. Lord Hardinge is at Simla, and there is to be a grand fancy ball on the 10th June. I am sorry to say that my leg does not get better. I removed another piece of bone yesterday and can feel that there is a great deal more to come away before it heals up. There is no inflammation or pain and thus it is not of much consequence to me. I still continue my Persian, and like it as an amusement. Although nothing can be more quiet than everything in India is at the present time, still I think we shall have something to do in the cold season. People felt quite as secure just before the late affairs.

The papers look as if we should have a war with France and I feel convinced that it would be the best thing that could happen for both countries. The long peace has over- stocked everything and no employment is to be got. Now, a war with France would put an end to all this—those who got killed would want nothing, and those who escaped would have enough.

I send you an Arabic Inscription which I copied, it means "*God is God and Mohammed is the Prophet of God.*"

My love to all,

Your affectionate Henry.

Umballa, 5th May, 1847.

My Dear Fanny,

The hot season has now set in in earnest, the wind blows like that of a blast furnace, and most people begin to feel ill. I, however, never was better. Of course I always stay indoors, as the heat of the sun causes liver complaint. We buried a lieutenant of the 61st Regiment yesterday, who went off in a few days with liver complaint. I suspect there must have been something else wrong with him, as I do not think that I should get the disease even if I were to expose myself to the sun; however, I should rather not try. In a French work that I have, I find the following.

> *Jacquemont a son arrivée au Bengale s'eloigne du monde, suit les loix de l'hygiéne le plus stricte, et malgré ses travaux et ses fatigues il echappe à l'influence meurtrière du climat; mais apres deux ans de prudence, l'example l'entraine, la table de ses amis Anglais lui porte le premier coup; trop confident dans ses forces, il brave une chaleur de 40° les marais empestées de l'isle Salsette font le reste, et il secombe à une maladie du foie.*

Now we have here a greater heat than 104° so I suspect that the "*marais empestées*" had more to do with his death than the heat or the "*table de ses amis Anglais.*" This however is certain, that the

English are more careless and intemperate than they would be in England; I suppose it is the heat that makes them reckless. The better order of people here are not so superstitious as in England. Sunday is hardly observed, and the generality of the clergy are of two kinds: those who lead irregular lives and who have no real religion, and the opposite extreme: the narrow no-minded furious fanatics.

They make few or, indeed, no converts to Christianity; and the greatest rascals in India, are those who have been nominally converted. The returns sent home by the missionaries of the number of their converts are simply false; some wretched children inscribe their names as converts for a small sum of money, and are then called "converts." The missionaries also are of two sorts: the rogues and the fools, they ought to be abolished by an enlightened government.

With regard to the native troops, the English are kept in total ignorance. I saw a speech by a Sir something Hogg a few days ago in the papers. He said that:

> . . . . the untiring perseverance under hardships of the *sepahis* was only equalled by their gallantry in the field.

Now he knew very well that he was lying, but he also knew full well that the English are a gullible race, and it was to his purpose not to undeceive them. The truth is they are all, cavalry as well as infantry, incurable natural cowards; and this is known full well to all who have ever served with them. If we were to leave India, the Sikhs, with a few hill tribes, would have posses-sion of India in as short a time as it would take them to march through it. The *sepahis* are capital soldiers for everything except one, and that is fighting, and well for us that such is the case, for if they were brave, how long should we be able to hold India? The *sepahis* behaved very ill in all the late actions; the dispatches were garbled and false; whole regiments gave way without fir-ing a shot. Regiments ordered to charge, went a little way and then dispersed; in fact the whole of the fighting was done by the Europeans. Whenever you see in the papers that the "*sepoys*" as they call them, have behaved well, you may set it down as a pious fraud; a flock of sheep never attack a troup of wolves. You may recollect some private soldier having written home about killing men in what is called 'cold blood.' It was brought up in the House of Commons, and there met with a positive denial. The truth is, numbers were shot or bayoneted in what people at home call 'cold blood,' but it was anything but this. The men were exasperated, and I have it from an officer, an eyewitness, that every man that could be found was unhesitatedly killed. Everybody agrees that the Sikhs are fine fellows, and shewed a perfect indifference to life.

If we have a European war, we should probably lose India if the European force were not materially augmented; we should then require at least 30,000 more English troops. I feel inclined to think that the Hindus are the primitive race of men; they must have developed from monkeys, for monkeys they are and monkeys they will remain, without any doubt. I still go on with my Persian, I am not fagging hard, but merely making an amusement of it. Hafiz says:

> .... alas youth has gone and thou hast not gathered the rose; let all take warning, for if we do not enjoy ourselves while we are young, all means of doing so, will be denied us hereafter.

I must indeed, look to it, for I find that I am already 33 years old, and am only a junior captain, when I ought to be a general officer at least. Our service is sacrificed to personal interests— old men who are passed their work are put into positions for which they are totally unfitted, from age, and very often from natural stupidity.

I am just going up to Simla from which place I shall most probably have something interesting to tell you.

Love to all,

Your affectionate Henry.

Simla, May 22nd, 1847.

My Dear Mother,

I have leave till the 15th June, and you see that I am at Simla. I was carried in a *palki* to the foot of the hills about forty miles, and then I had horses stationed, and rode the rest of the journey. You recollect the story of *Jack and the Beanstalk?* well here I have realized it. I left Umballa with the thermometer at 107° in the shade, and with a strong wind blowing, and the next morning here I am in a new country. I climbed up the beanstalk, that is the beanstalk of the Himalayas, and am now sitting with good cloth clothes on, contemplating the snowy range of mountains.

Nothing can be more sublimely grand than the scenery around: all that I have hitherto seen dwindles into utter insignificance in the presence of these peaks, the region of eternal snow. The climate is lovely, just like a fine summer's day in England; the thermometer stands at 68° at noon. The snowy range is about 24,000 feet above the sea level, and Simla is only 7,500, and everybody, who can get leave, comes up here to escape the hot weather.

Game of all sorts and kinds is plentiful, but it is necessary to go two or three marches towards the snow in order to find it. The governor-general and all the heads of departments are also here, as well as Lady Sale, a horrible woman. The society is unfortunately *Indian*, so I do not intend to mix much with it. A ball is also coming off to which I am invited, and as I hear some hill chiefs will be there, I think I shall go, as they may be worth seeing. Lord Hardinge gives the ball. Mohun Lall is here too; he wrote a book in English and he has a pension from Government.

The roads are about eight feet broad with a precipice on one side, and no wheeled carriages are used; the ladies gallop along on horseback and accidents are very rare. Yesterday, a sudden storm of hail came on and covered all the hills so that it looks all around like Canada, but the sun then shewed its face, and in one hour all was again summer.

Will you inquire and let me know whether the following books can be procured in London, and if they are expensive?

1. *Poesios Asiaticae Commentarii*, by W. Jones Cadell, Strand, 1774.

2. *Specimen poeseos Persicae*, by Baron Revizky.

3. *Specimens of Arabian Poetry*, by Carlyl.

I still go on with my Persian. I like the language, and the writing is very pretty indeed. Next season I shall try and go up to Chinese Tartary, but it will be difficult, because they do not like to see Europeans in those regions. I have met several niggers, who have a decided Chinese look, and they do not speak any known language. A few marches from here, they have no idea of money, and will not take it; they, on the other hand, all ask for medicine, so I shall lay in a stock, put on a queer dress, and pretend to be a *hakim*; there is nothing like humbug in this world, so I shall bleed, cup, and physic, as many tartars as come to me, which will be a cheap way of travelling.

Ladies, when travelling, frequently use a kind of *palki* which is called a "*janpan*."

Love to all,

Your affectionate Henry.

Umballa, June 17th, 1847.

My Dear Mother,

I have just arrived here from the hills, and a shower of rain has already fallen and cooled the air. I have got a few hill curiosities, but cashmere shawls are very dear, they cost from £70 upwards; a pair. Only fancy, for once I have a credit at my bankers'. I receive £76 a month; I wish they would give as good pay in England. I made the acquaintance with Mohun Lall in the hills; he speaks English very well. I am told he behaved well to the English ladies, on the Afghan retreat; he has just written me a letter in tolerably good English. Lord Hardinge and Gough are in good health; in fact when a person's affairs are prosperous they are always well. I feel convinced that if a person were even at the point of death, and suddenly heard that he had been left a large property he would recover, and live many a long year. Most rich men never die till they have burnt to the socket—do you remember the play of Richlieu?

I still continue my Eastern studies, and Mohun Lall has written to Lucknow to get me a learned man, for the ordinary Moonshees are grossly ignorant and do not serve my purpose. Even, with the little knowledge which I have gained, I can see that our Bible is incorrectly translated, and how could it be otherwise? Even the New Testament is not free from blunders. Our bishops have a favourite text, "*almost thou persuadest me to be a Christian.*"

According to *their* homilies, they would have it that Paul's argument was so convincing that King Agrippa was almost inclined to be converted to Christianity. Now the truth is, the original has not been understood. After Agrippa had heard the marvellous tale of Paul he said, contemptuously:

"very fine! we shall soon see you trying to make me a Christian."

Your affectionate Henry.

My Dear Mother,

The rains have now set in, and, although it is very uncomfortable, I am as well as anybody can be who takes no exercise. The company sent an order for the 3rd Dragoons to return to England but Lord Hardinge has kept us here on his own responsibility; he knows full well the value of European troops if any outbreak of rebellion should take place. At the Battle of Ferozeshah, not one single black regiment behaved well. An officer who is here, seeing the governor general's bodyguard proceed to bolt, came and joined a European regiment, and behaved most gallantly. At Simla, the other day, he said that they were a pack of cowards, which is as notorious as possible.

Lord Hardinge has dismissed him from the bodyguard, and Lord Gough has sent him here to join his own regiment, thus shewing how impolitic it is to speak truths that are displeasing to those in power. Lord Gough only followed the example of the Duke of Wellington, and indeed how could an officer be kept in a regiment which he has publicly charged with cowardice? I believe he is going to publish a book called *Revelations of Ferozeshah*, which he had much better not do; the truth will be known hereafter, in time, it is now too soon to promulgate it.

At present all is quiet at Lahore, but how long it will continue so is another thing. Here am I a captain only, and I am getting quite bald on the top of my head. I have shaved it to see if I can make the hair grow again and I look like an old monk. I also rub in rum and oil, but am afraid it is all up with my *chevelure* for ever. A very large portion of Indian officers are hopelessly in debt, and the natives have suffered great losses by them; but now it is not so easy to get them to lend money.

Many Europeans would borrow as much as £10,000 without any intention of ever paying, from the shopkeepers; millions have been stolen from them in this way. These shopkeepers are frequently very rich, they hoard all they make, and hardly ever spend anything; so that, in fact, the loss of money is no real loss to them. Before we came on the scene, the native princes used to rob these poor devils at a certain season every year, so you see they have always been used to it.

When I was at Simla I saw the governor general's bodyguard, which I have already alluded to, they looked very fine tall fellows, and had scarlet uniforms; and have, since Ferozeshah, obtained the sobriquet of the "scarlet runners."

Your affectionate Henry.

Umballa, July 21st, 1847

My Dear Mother,

I have little news to tell you. All manner of reports go about concerning our coming home, but the truth is, no person knows anything about it; it will entirely depend upon political circumstances, which may change from day to day.

I have heard of the arrival of my lathe. The government have valued it at £100 and they charge me a duty of five *per cent* on it; it will cost me full £20 to get it up from Calcutta.

At Lahore, all things are quiet at present, and now I think there will be no more disturbances; at any rate, before three or four years. We have got a Sikh regiment here, composed of the very same men who fought against us in all the late actions in the Punjab. They hold the *sepahis* in the utmost contempt, especially the native cavalry, and with reason, for they would beat a dozen regiments of them. I have made enquiries as to why the cavalry are inferior to the infantry, and I find that the reason is, that all the low caste men enlist in the cavalry, as the high caste men will not touch a horse, to clean one would make them lose caste.

This caste question appears strange at first, but it really is not so; there is just the same distinction in England and all other countries, only we are not quite so bigoted. Here the highest caste, that is, the nobility, are the Brahmins; and the *mehters*, or men who sweep the streets, the lowest. Now in England, a nobleman would not tolerate the society of a street sweeper or indeed, associate, on equal terms, with the middle classes. The other day I had a conversation with my learned *pundit* on this subject. I told him that I could not see any difference between a Brahmin and a man of a lower caste, and he replied, that he could not see any difference between me and the governor general, except that he held a higher rank in the public service.

"But I eat with the governor general," said I

"Ah! that is a matter of religion with us, he rejoined, and has nothing to do with the question."

Since writing to you my last letter, I have removed another

piece of bone from my leg, but although it will not heal, it gives me no pain, so really it is of no consequence. The more I study languages the more I am of opinion they must have a common origin like all religions. The Hindu theology is identical with that of the Roman, and there is a great mixture of both in Christianity. However different a name may appear, still it may be derived from a common origin.

I recollect seeing a French caricature of a couple dancing the polka with this remark underneath, "This dance is written in the Hungarian language, '*Kutchoulskinka*,' which word is pronounced '*Polka*.'" Now in a book on Hindu mythology many similar cases occur: thus Apollo, Helios, and Bel, are all the same word: Helios, Abelios, Aelios, Apelios, Apellon, Apollon. Cut off the A from Ahelios and you have Helios, from Abelios and you have Belios or Bel. Of course the French caricature is only a piece of fun. The Arabians call 'Plato,' '*Aflatun*.'

I think that this letter will go *via* Calcutta.

Your affectionate Henry.

Umballa, 13th August, 1847.

My dear Mother,

The hot weather has now gone, and the thermometer stands at 85°, and the mornings and evenings are very pleasant: I have heard that my lathe is very near and will soon be here, of which I am very glad as I have nothing to amuse me but my Persian. There is a strange report here that the Duke of Wellington is going to be married. Lord Hardinge goes home next month, I wonder who will be his successor. Johnny D. is not here, I wish I could get him to study the language and pass his examination; he would then be certain of an appointment, it requires no interest, and it would be an addition of 100 *rupees* a month to his pay. I have asked him to come and stay with me for the Umballa Races. He only gets 190 *rupees* a month which is too little.

Umballa, September 2nd, 1847.

My Dear Mother,

I received Franciscans letter. The rains are now nearly over, and in another month the cold weather will set in. I am covered with a kind of nettle rash, which is called here " the prickly heat," and I am told it is a sign of being in good health: I am glad of it, but it is very troublesome, nevertheless.

I met with a story in Persian the other day which I think is worth telling you:

> A man made a bet with another, and it was agreed that the one who gained the wager might cut a *seer* of flesh, about two pounds, from the body of the one who lost. The man who lost, however, refused to pay, and the winner cited him to appear before the *cadi*. The *cadi* recommended the winner to relinquish his claim for the sake of mercy, but he declined the advice, upon which the *cadi* became enraged and said—'Cut off the *seer* of flesh, but if you exceed the weight of an exact *seer*, I shall punish you according to the nature of the offence.' The plaintiff, seeing the impossibility of complying with the conditions, had no remedy, but dropped the prosecution.

Now, evidently, this is the same story as Shakespeare's *Shylock*. It must have been of Arabian origin.

My lathe has arrived to my great delight, it has cost me just £25 for carriage. There is a report that Lord Fitzroy Somerset is to come out here as commander-in-chief, and I think that it would give general satisfaction, but then who is to take his place at home?

The wolves here are queer customers, a few days ago they carried off a man who was sleeping with some twenty others, one having first seized him by the throat, the others caught hold of him to carry him off to the plains, but the body was recovered. I never have seen one, and I never, heard of one being shot.

I have just bought an old tent at a sale, and I intend to send it out and have it pitched about twelve miles from the cantonments, where there is plenty of antelopes and other game. I shall then gallop out in the evening, sleep there, shoot early the next morning, and ride back to dinner.

I wonder that ordinary people do not go mad here in the hot season, for they have no occupation, and to them it is simply six months' imprisonment every year.

I feel convinced that we shall not hold this country permanently, as I do not believe that any Northern nation can make a settlement in the East. We may hold India, indeed, for many years to come, but it will only be by military force. In fact, we cannot mix with the Indian race; half a European and half a nigger is always a degenerate animal. Nature says it shall not be, and there is an end.

Your affectionate Henry.

Umballa, September 21st, 1847.

My Dear Brother,

You seem to think that it would be a bad thing for me if the 3rd were to come home, but you are quite mistaken. I know very well that I could not remain in a cavalry regiment in England, as I am too poor; but I could get a good round sum to exchange into the relieving regiment, and that would be a sheer profit for me. You do not seem to know that Queen's officers are not eligible for Indian appointments. If a man has merit, he can get on in the Indian service up to a certain point; but beyond this all goes by interest and favour. Everything here is very dear. I am forced to have seventeen men and two women servants. Only fancy a captain in the army with nineteen servants! and many who can afford it have a dozen more and upwards. So many servants may appear superfluous to you; but it is a positive necessity; here is a complete list:—

One head man who waits at dinner
Two men to take care of clothes.
Three water-carriers.
One washerman.
Four grooms.
Four grass cutters.
One watchman.
One sweeper.
Two women to grind corn.

These are all the servants that I keep, but other captains who are better off than I am, have in addition:—

One tailor.
Four *punkah coolies.*
Two *coolies* for messages.
One *hookahbadar.*
One assistant ditto.
Two bearers.

You will see that I have not counted my Persian *moonshee* among my servants. I take my lesson every day, and can make myself understood in Persian, which will be of considerable use to me if I travel in the hills.

Mother wants to know what I get to eat here. I get just the same as you get in England, with some few Indian additions; I can assure you that we do not starve! Postage costs something considerable in this country; I have to pay eighteen pence for every letter from Umballa to Bombay. Tell Jack I will send him the seeds that he wants to have. *Adieu*, I am just going to bed.

Your affectionate brother, Henry.

Umballa, 1st October, 1847.

My Dear Mother,

The mornings now are delightful, quite cold and enjoyable. I have little news to, tell you. Lord Hardinge dines with us on the 27th of this month, and goes home immediately afterwards. I hope either Lord Fitzroy Somerset or General Napier will come out as commander-in-chief. You may expect a parcel containing a few seeds, also a shawl, very soon. The several regiments all march and change quarters next month; we remain, however, at Umballa. All my horses are well and fit for service, and we commence our exercises on the 15th of next month. India seems quite quiet, and I see little prospect of seeing any service this cold weather. I met an officer named Wingfield; I wonder whether he is any relation of the family you know? Peter asks me whether I have written to Dr. Outram. Why, what have I got to say? and besides writing humbugging letters is not in my line; however, I will see what I can do.

Your affectionate Henry.

Umballa, 18th October, 1847.

My Dear Mother,

The weather is delightful, and we have commenced riding, much to my satisfaction, as that, an any rate, is something to do. There is so little news, that I have not enough to fill up a letter, so I intend to write bits from time to time, and send it off when there is enough to make up a good sized epistle. My turning lathe is a great source of amusement to me, and that, with my Persian, enables me to kill time with some profit. I have to pay my learned *moonshee* £3 a month, and another officer pays him £7, so that he gets £10 a month; so difficult it is to get anyone in this country who really understands languages.

There seems to be nothing going on in England, but things

look as bad as any one need wish in Europe. I must say I would not give anything to see an Indian campaign, but a European one would be worth seeing. I send by this mail, a small parcel containing a Cashmere shawl and Jack's seeds. I believe that the Himalaya fir grows well in England. My last charger is a very beautiful animal. I gave £70 for him, and have paid for him out of my savings; only fancy, I have actually saved money. Fred's fractured leg is of no consequence, and it will soon be as well as it was before.

Umballa, December 1st. No news, everything goes on just as usual. The weather is quite cold and I have fires. Strange to say we have more sick than in the hot weather.

25th December, 1847. Nothing new. I am afraid Johnny D. is not studying the language. I wish I could persuade him of the immense advantage it would be to him if he could only pass his examination. I always anxiously expect the mail which arrives here every fortnight.

Umballa, January 16th. I go out deer stalking and black partridge shooting once a week. There is nothing to tell you of any importance. I see things are getting very bad in Ireland, and it is possible we may be ordered home if more troops should be required in Europe. Let me know if you got the parcel safe.

Kurnal, February 12th. I have been ordered away from Umballa to get horses for the regiment, and am now at a place about fifty miles from Umballa; I expect to be absent about a fortnight. I march about twelve miles a day, and I shoot as I go along by the side of the road. Kurnal was formerly a great station, but it was abandoned on account of its unhealthiness, and the troops have been shifted to Umballa. The place is now deserted, and all the beautiful buildings are useless and going to decay. I went yesterday to visit the old cantonment; a more melancholy sight could not well be imagined; splendid houses with the roofs all fallen in, left to the wild beasts. I saw two beautiful *sphinxes* over a gateway, which were brought from Italy at an outlay of £1000, and I went into the church which has not been built more than about twelve years, and which will soon be a solitary ruin. *Sic-transit,* &c.

February 16th. I have now got all my horses, sixty-five in number, and I march tomorrow for Umballa. I hope sincerely 'that they will like them at the regiment.

February 23rd. I am now again at Umballa, and have received your letter in which you ask my opinion on the Hambden affair; could you not guess it? I think Lord John Russell was in the right and that Dr. Hambden is a *khur*, which is the word for an ass in Persian. As for the protest of the bishops, it is only what was to be expected; it is no use reasoning with those who have formed their opinions. The only way is, if you have the power, to act, the only thing that bishops understand is "*die That*"
I see that they have admitted a Jew into the House of Commons, this is a great step in advance, and I was glad to see it progress is slow, but advances steadily with a measured tread, and truth and common sense are sure ultimately to prevail. It is impossible to lay down, thus far you shall think—thought will not be controlled. Everyone thinks that his superstition is the only true faith.
I was reading my Sadi the other day and I came on this passage which exactly meets the case in point: "*everyone is born with a natural disposition to Islamism, but it is owing to his parents whether he becomes a Jew, a Christian, or a Fireworshipper.*" Now if Sadi had said '*with a natural disposition to believe in God*' he would have been nearer the mark; but the latter part of the sentence is true, with some rare exceptions.

February 29th. I have applied to go to Simla for six months.

Simla, 3rd May, 1848.

My Dear Mother,
At last I have some news to tell you. There is every probability that we shall have another war with the Sikhs. If you take the map and look down the River Sutledge, south from Lahore, you will see a place marked Bahawalpoor, and near it, if you slant your eye up north, you will see Mooltan, which is a strong fortress. I have no doubt you will see an account in the papers of the affair before you receive this, but things are so misrepresented that I may as well tell you the true state of the case. Mooltan belongs to the Lahore Government, which has at its head a little boy Dhulip Singh, who of course, is nobody. Sir F. Currie is the English resident. Two civil officers; Vans Agnew, and I believe Anderson, went to Mooltan with an escort of five

hundred irregular troops.

On entering the fort they were treacherously set upon and wounded. They were however rescued, and retired to their tents outside the fortress. After the camp was pitched the Mooltanies attacked it, and murdered the two unfortunate officers. Agnew, although wounded, made a desperate resistance, shooting the first man that entered his tent, but both were soon cut to pieces. The Sikhs are flocking from all parts to Mooltan. Orders were at first issued for us to march, immediately, but when the season was taken into consideration, and the enormous sacrifice of life which would accrue if the troops were to march at once, the order was countermanded. It is the opinion of those in authority that we shall have all the fighting to do over again next season.

However this may be, my trip to the hills is knocked on the head. I was just on the point of starting on my journey with Lord Gifford, when Lord Gough stopped my leave, and now we are under orders to march at a moment's notice. Under these circumstances, I am going out to shoot curious hill birds, and shall make myself very comfortable till I am wanted. I forgot to mention that the five hundred men of poor Agnew's escort all behaved like treacherous cowards, and never attempted to defend their officers. It is wonderful the state of ignorance of the people at home. They think that there is a real Indian army. The truth is, there is no real army except the Queen's in India; the black troops are ciphers. I have heard no news from Europe, except the French Revolution. I will write when I learn more.

Your affectionate Henry.

Simla, May 10th, 1848. The adjutant general who seems to have the best information, says that we shall have another campaign next cold season; so much for Lord Hardinge's policy. The desperate folly of men who are esteemed of first-rate capacity is such, that we outsiders do not know what to think. They not only do not take warning but they will not even take example. Bossuet said in one of his sermons before the French king: "*les hommes agissent mais Dieu les mene*" so according to him. Lord Hardinge, Louis Phillippe, Lord John Russell as well as the British Parliament, have all been guided in their ineptitudes by God. In fact it has been entirely a case with them of, "*Quos*

Deus vult perdere prius dementat." Now I think that Bossuet was like most preachers, simply a very eloquent fanatical ass, and what he said was a libel on the Almighty. God will always be found to be on the side of prudent statesmen, talented generals, and heavy battalions. If Bossuet had said "*nullum Numen abest, si sit prudential*" I think, he would have been nearer the mark.

With regard to Lord Hardinge, everyone must admire his noble character; his splendid services in the Peninsula and elsewhere; and his kind and genial disposition. But he was quite unfit to be Governor General of India. He was sent out to India by private interest, and without any consideration for the public good. He was past sixty years of age, and that alone was sufficient to render him ineligible for a post of such responsibility and difficulty. He had received no high education, and he was totally ignorant both of the language, habits, and dispositions of the people whom he was to rule. How then could it be expected that he would make a good ruler? I myself liked him very much, personally, and when I was at Simla, he shewed me much more attention than so insignificant a person as myself had any right to expect. He was a noble soldier, and this was all he was fitted for, as a governor general he was a perfect nonentity.

These natives are the most unaccountable idiots that it possible to imagine. Old Shah Alum was very kindly treated by the English after the affair at Delhi in 1803. They presented him with half a dozen six pounder guns to fire salutes, and keep up a semblance of royal dignity. Although he had no force under his command, the very next morning he attacked the English, and began firing shot out of his six-pounders at the British army, which was encamped outside the city.

A company of infantry of course immediately took possession of the old fool's guns, and there was an end of the matter. Such is the character of these natives, they are, in a measure, like little children, and should be treated as such. The fault we committed was this:—when we had the country we should have annexed it. Lord Hardinge now goes home, and we have all the work to do over again; and just consider the loss of life that must occur! but that is a very small matter in comparison with the loss of money; killing men does no harm, there are too many of them already, but loss of tin is an evil indeed!

My leg heals up again and again, but I know right well that

it is sure to break out again, and will continue to do so till all the dead bone has come away, and such is the case, figuratively speaking, with the wretched bungling of the English Parliament in its treatment of the Irish difficulty. The dead bone of discontent should be removed in some way or other; either tax the absentees two-thirds of their incomes and give the Irish a Parliament on College green; or send an army, establish military law, and treat Ireland as a conquered country: these are the only effectual methods, palliatives will be of no use.

Free trade in religion, is now the order of the day; or rather, I should say, free trade in opinions, for that is the proper expression. Now I am on the subject of politics, I will give you my opinion on things in general, in England, I think that we have arrived at a period when great changes are at hand. All earthly things, and we know nothing of any other, are a question of time; and I say that now it is a question of a comparatively short time, when we shall see a great amalgamation of classes, and the downfall of an hereditary aristocracy, with a government more on republican principles. This is my firm opinion, and I prophecy that some of us will live to see it.

I myself do not object to a monarchy without any power; but when the English Revolution comes, it will be on the grounds of expense. People will say "since we have every freedom, and there is no tyranny, why then should we pay for a monarchy, which is a mere idle pageant? The Church too has gone mad. Only think of their cutting their own throats in the matter of Dr. Hambden? But so it is when men are urged by their pet superstitions, common sense ceases to have any influence.

Although this letter is dated Simla, I am not there. I am now writing at a place called Nagkunda, about five marches from that place. When my trip to Cashmere was knocked on the head, I wandered forth alone, among these magnificent mountains to shoot, and I have just received a most important despatch which will put an effectual stop to my sport.

The troops are ordered to take the field immediately. A wide spread conspiracy has been discovered; whole regiments have deserted, and only fancy! the troops have marched on Lahore; at this season of the year there will be a fearful loss of life. Our regiment luckily for me does not move, we are to remain at Umballa till September. This is the present arrangement, but who can tell what will happen? Only yesterday there was nothing to do or to say.

Simla, May 11th, 1848. Now there is a plethora of news. Of course, when this news reached me, I got on my horse and reached Simla the next day, where I am now waiting events.

The overland mail reached Delhi in thirty-three days and seventeen hours, and splendid news it brought! The horrible tyranny of Austria has at length met with its just retribution. I have not felt so happy for many a long year "*Sic semper Tyrannis.*" Wars must come, but after some good fighting the world will settle down quietly—till the next time.

If anything fresh occurs I will write and let you know immediately. I shall keep this letter open for some time. I have shot some birds for Jack, and have got some very beautiful butterflies.

I will now tell you something curious, which I believe is not known in Europe. Amid the eternal snows of the Himalayas there lives a great fish; it burrows under the snow, and the natives say that it will eat a man: the skin I saw was two feet long, and hard enough to resist any weapon: it is of the same nature as the shark skin which you see sometimes on surgical instrument cases; it has two fins, and very large eyes; Indian officers have never heard of it, but I saw the skin. They are taking it as a present to a hill *rajah.* I have named it Icthiokeion.[3] All the regiments have marched, except the 3rd Light Dragoons. European cavalry are far too precious to be thrown away by sending them to fight with the sun, which at this season is a far more dangerous enemy than the Sikhs.

Near the Source of the Ganges,
16th May, 1848.

My Dear Mother,

You see that I have left all civilization behind me, and am here, quite alone, amidst these magnificent mountains. Just before starting, I had a large portion of bone removed from my old fracture, and can walk tolerably well, I have with me a double gun, and a double and single rifle, as well as a carbine, musket bore; so that I am well armed, and I have fifty followers to carry my baggage and provisions. Everything I want I must carry

---

3. I believe this is all a myth, and that my Icthiokeion does not exist.

with me, as nothing is procurable in these mountains. I did not forget a bag of small shot to shoot curious birds for Jack. My marches were as follows:

May 5th. Left Landour, and marched to Jalki, 8 miles. Found a party of three officers encamped, who were on a shooting excursion: they had seen and fired five shots at a tiger that morning; a very rare occurrence. It must have been a stray beast which had got up one of the ravines. Agreed to go with them and look him up the next day.

May 6th. Got up early and took double gun and rifle: the road led along the brink of a terrible precipice, so that I had some idea of turning back, and should have done so had I not reflected that the officers who were with me might have thought that I was afraid of the tiger. The path of the precipice was only four inches broad and two men were my gun carriers. I myself always walk with a long stick: the dangerous part of the road was only a few dozen yards in extent, but I never felt so uncomfortable; facing a tiger was as nothing to it.

When we came near the spot where they had seen the tiger, I found it was situated on a place which had a slope of about thirty-four degrees down the side of the hill. A Mr. Hopkins of the 53rd had gone down some twenty yards and was poking about with a stick among the brushwood, and he had just said: "it was just about here that we saw him" when, with a roar, out sprang the brute—for there he was sure enough. Hopkins made a rush for a small tree that was near, he had no gun, for that was in the hands of his *shikaree* who was on the road close by me. All the hill-men immediately ran away putting down the guns on the road.

As for me, it was very certain that I should not follow their example, for on level ground I cannot run much, and in these hills, not at all. I called to Hopkins to come to me and take his gun, and stood ready to receive the tiger with my double rifle; but the brute thought better of it and went off to my left. I could see his course by the waving of the long grass, but could not see him to get a shot.

When I got home, I found that the cap of my second barrel was bad, so that had the tiger charged, I should only have had one chance, but that I think would have been enough, as we were at such close quarters that I could not have missed him.

On all these occasions when accidents occur, it is generally through fear preventing the shooter from taking a deliberate aim, for a tiger is very easily killed if he is hit in the right place. I returned home very tired.

Monday, May 17th. Marched to Bara Secunder, five miles; very hilly road; saw a large *langur*, a kind of ape, but could not get a shot.

May 8th. Marched to Dhumnoti, six miles; a beautiful encamping ground with a splendid view of the snowy range.

May 9th. Got up early to try and get a shot at a *kaker* or barking deer; saw two but they were out of range; went on in the evening to Kado Kal.

May 10th. Marched to Kaudia Ghurria, about 8 miles. Shot a large *langur*.

11th. Marched to Johangee; a little rain fell.

12th. To Teree. Made the *rajah* a present of an airgun with which he was delighted, and he sent me a horse in return.

13th. To Godee, four miles. *Rajah* sent me a soldier and a guide.

14th. To Buldana, on the banks of the Ganges; shot two otters.

15th. To Charni. Here is a rope bridge, it is on the same principle as an iron suspension bridge.

16th. To Baretti; here is also a rope bridge. Shot a number of curious birds and one black partridge. This is the place from whence I am dating my letter.

Simla, June 10th, 1848.

My Dear Mother,

I did not write by the last mail as I had no news to tell you, but now we have received orders to hold ourselves in readiness to proceed to Lahore, by forced marches, at a moment's warning. It is totally impossible to form any idea as to what may take place, and there is no means of getting any information, nobody knows anything. I believe, however, that we shall march on the 1st of October, but who can say what may happen before that?

Those who appear to be the best informed say that we shall have all the Punjab battles to fight over again. I have well considered the matter and feel convinced that the Sikhs will offer no serious resistance. We may have a campaign, but it will be a bloodless one.

> (*Note.* The event will shew how wrong I was in my judgement. We should never prophecy unless we know, according to the example of the ancient Hebrews, who always were in the right; inasmuch as their prophecies were always written after the event).

If the present governor had any energy or sense he would immediately annex the Punjab and also Kashmir. I think the handing over of Kashmir to the infernal rule of that Rosewater wretch, (*N.B.* Gulab Singh means, rose water lion) was one of the most profligate acts that have ever been perpetrated in modern times. The hill people are of the very best sort, and Lord Hardinge handed them over to the tender mercies of a savage, whom he knew to be a murderer and a villain. That Lord Hardinge has saved money for his late masters there can be no disputing, and this is all that they care about. Lord Hardinge took no care of the interests of the wretched inhabitants of the country, he merely considered the interests of a set of rascally merchants, and handed over or rather sold the people to the grinding tyranny of a wretched barbarian.

Kashmir was sold for a *crore* of *rupees*, or about one million sterling.

I feel convinced that a day of heavy retribution will be experienced by England, for she deserves it well. I should like to know what the next campaign will cost? The rains have now set in, and nothing can be gloomier that the outlook; I keep quite well.

Simla 11th June. I dislike the wet season so much that I have agreed with a captain to take my place at Simla which will put me first on the list for leave next hot season, when I shall, if all is quiet, go to Kashmir. The 32nd. Regt. was ordered to march from Umballa to Lahore some ten days march, one captain and six men died on the road and one man shot himself. It must have been terrible with the thermometer 130° in the tents. This is my last from the hills.

Umballa, 21st July, 1848. I have very little news to tell you. The general opinion is that the insurrection will be put down without having recourse to the army. When I was at Simla, I heard an official of rank say that we should have no fighting in the Punjab. Here the general opinion is just the contrary; all is in a state of uncertainty. The weather is very hot and the discomfort very great, but I keep quite well. If the rain does not come soon we shall have a famine; it is full twenty days late, and such a thing has not been known for the last twenty years.

Things in Europe seem to progress pretty smartly, as a Yankee might observe, perhaps I shall be at the siege of Paris one day. I see that the lords and bishops are cutting their own throats. "*Quem Deus* etc." Peter will tell you the rest of the quotation. You had better tell Fred that it would be well to send me here any papers that may require my signature. I met with the story of Shylock in the course of my Persian readings, where could Shakespeare have got it?

These Easterns are a very strange people. I met a Mussulman in the hills, apparently dying by the side of the road. He asked for water, but he would not drink out of my flask. Sadi, in his moral tales (?) points out how everything, however vile and impure, may be turned to some good account; even the water in the well of a Christian might be used to wash the dead body of a Jew. Such is the pernicious influence of superstition, even a cup of water becomes impure when it belongs to a person of a different opinion from themselves. What are such men? they are little better than the lower animals.

Your affectionate H. A. O.

Umballa, August 16th, 1848.

My Dear Mother,

I am happy to hear that I have got a little niece. They call little bibs in this country "*butcha*," which word is a corruption of the Sanscrit "*vatsa*" and means calf. We have had a terribly dry season and still want more rain; notwithstanding which, I keep in very good health, but in this country you are quite well today, and are buried the next. Two field officers of the 10th who marched to Mooltan are reported dead. It will be a very pleasant thing to settle Moulraj's little affair at Mooltan; then get a little *batta*, and go next season to Kashmir, and be guided by circumstances whether I extend my travels further into the hills.

What a terrible affair this French Revolution seems to be; however, good will come of it, in my opinion. The cause of the disturbances that are now in action, was explained by Malthus about the time of the last Irish rebellion in 1798; he has never been refuted, never even fairly answered; for the only objection to his views, that were made, pointed to to the state of America and other parts of the world that were sparsely populated. The massacres and wholesale deportation now going on only prove that he was quite right in his views. I do not look to a massacre in England, but a deportation, on a large scale, must soon take place or we shall eat each other up. Nature is inexorable and stands no nonsense.

I am glad you like the miniature of the Queen of Lucknow. There is only one person in India who is capable of executing such a painting. I cannot preserve or stuff birds, it is not in my line, I will try and hire some nigger who can do so; it is a very profitable calling and I have heard of an officer who made 3000 *rupees* in one year by the birds alone that he shot in the hills.

The mornings are now pleasant and I go out, regularly, fox hunting. The niggers, as they are called here, catch the foxes, which are bagged. I then go out with a lot of terrier dogs, and the fox is turned out on the plain: he is obliged to run straight, and it is all the same to him which way he goes. One ran full five miles and nearly beat all the dogs. Some few get clear off, but the generality are killed. The foxes in this country are much smaller than the English fox. I have made up a parcel of two sable jackets; they can be taken to pieces to make any other thing you please, and two shawls for Mother, and several other little things.

Love to you all.

Your affectionate H. A. O.

Umballa, September 7th, 1848.

My Dear Francisca,

I was glad to hear that all is well at home. I will now proceed to give you my news. I think that I told you that I had left Simla, and am now in the plains, and have had about three months of hot weather. It was a very trying time, but I have been in very good health all the time, and, in fact, never was better in my life. The regiment also is in excellent health and condition. There was a cavalry regiment stationed here, in equally good condition, the 14th Light Dragoons—they received the order to march, and are now at Lahore—that is to say the remnant of them. A letter says:—90 men were struck down with apoplexy on the march, 30 died outright, and somewhat less than 300 are in hospital.

For service, the regiment is useless, in fact, had a great battle been fought, they could not have sustained a greater loss. The 32nd Regiment has suffered in the same way; and all this loss of life and misery has been caused by obstinate recklessness of the civilians in power, who acted against the strong advice of Lord Gough. Sir Fred. Currie, having full powers, sends an order for European troops; he is obeyed, and we see the result. *Quicquid delirant reges plectuntur Achivi*: the old old story.

The present intention is to form a large army. We are to march and all I can say is, that if we do so before a month's time, we shall suffer the same as the other two regiments. Those who have got money are comparatively better off, as they can have good tents and good food, and other comforts which the men have not; consequently the officers suffer much less. I do not think, however, that we shall march before the 10th October. I have been put to great expense, having had to buy and keep camels for the last three months. I am amusing myself making a garden, and perhaps somebody else will enjoy the fruits of it, for when we march, I do not think we shall stop short of Peshawur.

9th September. News has arrived that affairs have assumed a more serious aspect, but I still think that there will not be much fighting, but it is impossible to say what may happen, particularly if Goolab Singh joins in the revolt. You ask me about Johnny. I have not seen him, he is staying with Mrs. Ford at Simla. I am sorry to say that I do not think that he will do much good without passing in the languages; he never will be able to get any appointment, and he will not pass an examination, as he will not even try. He is among a terrible set, and if he comes off safe it will be next to a miracle. I have been told that he is not in debt, but who can tell what may happen when he sees all around him bankrupt? The Indian army, as a body, is positively bankrupt; if there is one clear, it is a solitary exception.

There are some 300 ensigns and 1500 subalterns in the Indian Army, and I believe, indeed from published documents I know, that in one bank, (the Agra) last year, there were not half a dozen that did not apply for loans at about 18 *per cent*. How can it be otherwise? A subaltern's pay is 200 *rupees* a month, which is totally inadequate, without exercising the greatest self-denial. Beer is two shillings and sixpence a bottle, and the quantity consumed is fully treble what it would be in England. My wine bill last month was 189 *rupees*. Nearly everybody drinks beer, and four bottles a day is not considered out of the way by many. I do not care for it, but stick to my claret, which agrees with me much better.

I asked an old officer about Johnny, and he told me that he did nothing but smoke and drink beer, and was obstinate when spoken to; I have written to him, but sometimes he does not answer me, and I am afraid that he thinks his mother has asked me to watch his doings. I will try and get him to read, and will give him the necessary books, which are very expensive, but he must first promise me that he will try to pass. When I have seen him, I will write more fully. I myself go on with my Persian, which will be of great use to me if we go on to Peshawur. I have now nothing more to tell you, so I send my love to you all.

Your affectionate Henry.

Camp in the Jungle, near Sobraon,
October 17th, 1848.

We marched from Umballa three weeks ago. All the country, in what is called the Punjab, which word means "five rivers," is in a state of insurrection, and we march against the enemy to-morrow, and expect to come in contact with them in a few days. There is no possibility of coming at the truth among the conflicting reports that are rife at present. So far as I can make out, the articles you have seen in the *Times* are all bosh about a certain Mr. Edwardes and his victories. An incapable, called Sir F. Currie, was sent to Lahore, with full powers. The Lahore Government hatched a conspiracy with the governor of the fortress of Mooltan, whose name is Moulraj, who is now called a rebel. Sir Frederic sent Mr. Edwardes, as a political Agent, to the vicinity, and he, without orders, collected a rabble of niggers, and proceeded to attack Moulraj. Moulraj, a very clever fellow, sent out some of his worst troops, there was a distant discharge of fire arms and some dozen or so may have been killed—these are the victories in question. But it soon transpired that European troops were required, thereby proving that the so-called victories, were all a hoax.

A European force, the 10th and 32nd Regiments, with a siege train, together with a *sepoy* force, supported on the part of our native allies, the Rajah of Bahawulpore and Shere Singh, with some 8000 Sikhs, attacked the fortress, and in an injudicious assault, we lost a number of officers and men, killed and wounded, of which affair, you will see an account in the Indian papers which I have sent you. Some days after this, Shere Singh and his Sikhs deserted to the enemy, and in the place of besieging Mooltan, we have been obliged to retreat; indeed the officer in command could not do otherwise. The whole country has now risen, and we, with our weak force, will have some difficulty in recovering our position. Lord Hardinge has made a pretty mess of it.

In England, the public weal is not the first consideration; personal interest alone carries the day. Lord Hardinge was sent out to India to reward him for past services; he was too old, and he knew nothing of the Eastern character. All Easterns are alike, there is no trusting them, there is only one thing which they understand, and that is what our German neighbours call "*die That.*"

We are now within twenty miles of Ferozepore, so I rode out and saw Johnny Delamain. I had a long talk with him, and, upon the whole, I can report favorably of him; but I saw at once that I could never get him to study to pass his examination. He can speak the language of the country very well; but to pass, he must know three languages, which is beyond his power of application. He is a first-rate go-ahead officer, and we shall have him with us in the field. We have suffered much from the heat, but have only lost two or three men and five horses by deaths. I have just visited the fields of Moodkee and Ferozeshah, and I found among the heaps of bones, the foot of one of my own troop horses; it was where a Sikh battery had been, and was known by the troop number branded on the front of the hoof. I intend to bring it home with me if I ever come.

We are in high spirits at the idea of meeting with the Sikhs, but I cannot think that there will be much honour in British troops against inferior races. Our losses in the former actions were not owing to their merits, but to our own folly. The despatches, as is usual on such occasions, were all made up without any regard to truth. We always took the bull by the horns, and naturally we sometimes got gored. I have learned all about it from our officers, who were present, and I intend to impress upon my men that they are to stay by me, and not gallop off like a disorderly rabble, directly they see the enemy, like they did before. The men were so eager to get at the Sikhs, that they rushed at them without keeping any order, and as I am told, without orders. The correct thing with Sikhs, is to open on them first with a few rounds of artillery, which they cannot stand, and then, when they begin to bolt, charge home in line.

I have an old sub. who has put me up to a few wrinkles you see! I am also fortunate in commanding the right squadron of the regiment, about 160 sabres. The Duke of Wellington found the same fault as I have described, with the 13th Light Dragoons in the Peninsula. I have got an excellent charger that was in all the former actions; he has two bullets now in his body, which could not be extracted; he is a perfect animal and affords me every chance of coming safe off.

More than two thirds of the officers who were killed, lost their lives through unmanageable horses, which ran away with them into the midst of the enemy.

The thermometer has been as high as 106° in our tents; now it is only 96° so I hope that the worst is over, but then we have to look forward to the cold. I send you herewith a newspaper, and will send you others regularly. We have some 6,000 camp followers, and we issued £3,000 today to pay them; all in *rupees*: the weight alone of this sum is 750 lbs., or nearly two camels' load. Our camp is pitched regularly with streets, and it looks very pretty. This is all my news, for the present, so with my love,

    I am

                      Your affectionate Henry.

Army of the Punjab, Camp near Ramnugger,
November 11th, 1848.

My Dear M.

At length we are in the field and I am writing on outpost duty
to the advanced guard. Johnny is with his regiment near us. The
enemy is quite close and we killed the first man yesterday: he
was a spy, and four native cavalry gave chase. He cut down two,
but the third man speared him. I have about 50 men with me,
and am about one mile in advance of the camp, with my horse
ready saddled standing near me while I am writing, to save the
mail: my present duty will last twenty-four hours. We had a
gallop of some six miles after the enemy's cavalry, but we could
never get near them; they will take care of that, and will not
make any stand until we get near their entrenched camp; then
all will be over, after perhaps one battle; that is my opinion.

It is almost inconceivable, the ignorance of the people in England about Indian affairs. Lieutenant Edwardes has actually
been made a major and a C.B. for his "victories." If there had
been any truth in his doings, why are we here at the present
moment? The great heat has passed away and now we have to
contend with the cold. We are halted at this place, and shall not
move until the whole army joins us, which will be in a few
days, we shall then cross the Chinab. We have just heard that
Peshawur has fallen, but whether it is true or not I cannot say.
For political news, you must look to the papers which I herewith send.

Your affectionate Henry.

Ramnugger, 24th November, 1848.

My Dear M.

Two days ago, we advanced and found the Sikh army of some
20,000 men, posted partly on this and partly on the other side
of the river Chinab, their immense encampment covering the
opposite bank. Lord Gough, who has joined the army, at once
determined to clear the Ramnugger side of the river; he himself
came to the front with a troop of cavalry and some horse artillery. The 3rd Light Dragoons were with the advanced guard,
and Lord Gough ordered a squadron of them to clear the Ramnugger side of the river. I was ordered to perform this duty.
The artillery opened on the Sikh camp and I set off with my

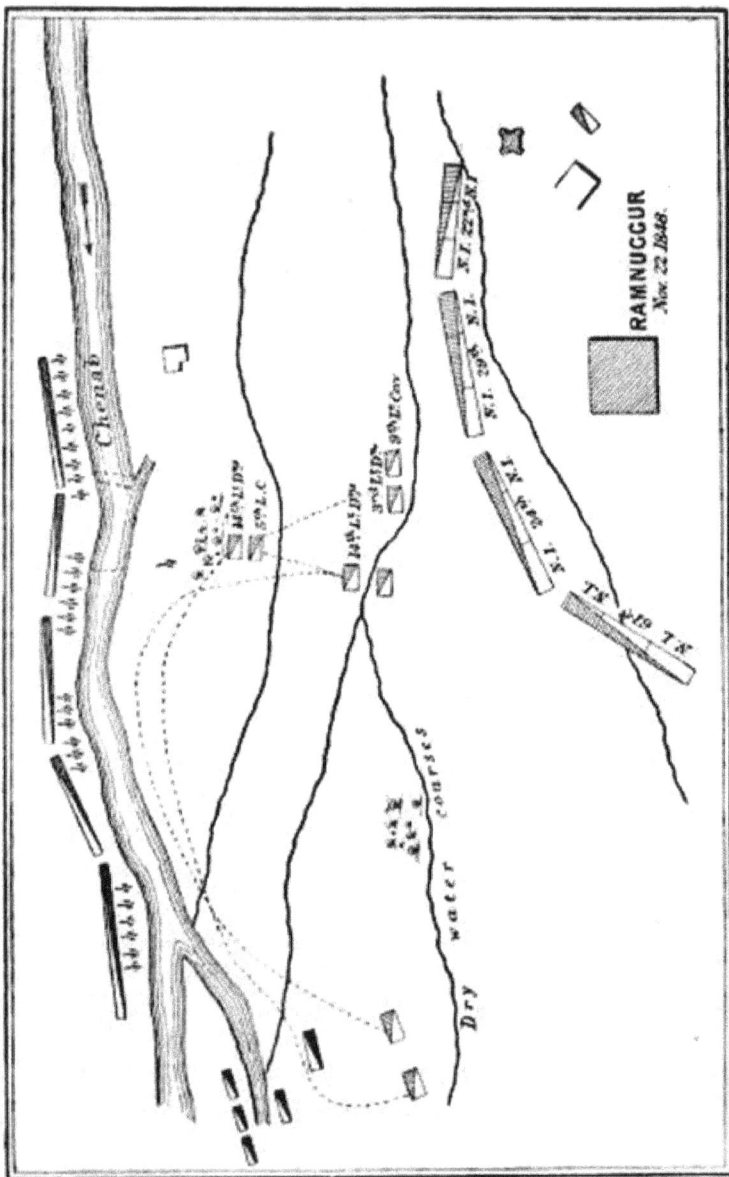

The Combat of Ramnugger

Troops of Horse Artillery accompanied the Cavalry. The remainder of the Artillery was massed in front of the Second Brigade from the right. The position of the abandoned gun is marked in front of the grove.

N.B.—For "2nd" read "2nd Europeans."

squadron, about 130 strong, to cut up the scattered small bodies of men on our side of the river. The moment the stragglers saw me advancing at a gallop to cut them off, they all rushed and threw themselves into the river, where they were quite out of my reach.

I pursued my sweep along the bank about a mile, having only cut up one man, who could not run fast enough, when a Sikh battery on the opposite bank opened on my squadron at point blank range. Hearing the trumpeters sound the recall, I went about, and retired at a gallop, presenting the smallest mark possible to the Sikh battery, that is, I retired with my squadron in line. The Sikh gunners fired so beautifully that every shot came within a few feet of the edge of my line. At last a round shot ploughed through the squadron, passing clean through two horses, wounding one man and knocking the pouch belt off another. Seeing I should come to grief if I continued my line of retreat, I went threes right and soon got out of their range. I then joined my regiment.

We marched at three o'clock in the morning, and our advanced guard, of which my regiment formed the chief part, arrived within sight of the Sikh camp at 8 a.m. and while I was clearing the bank of the river on our side, Lord Gough opened with the battery of horse artillery on the Sikh camp. The Sikhs were taken by surprise but they soon recovered, and replied with an overwhelming fire from the guns on their side of the river; their superior weight of metal soon forcing our guns to retire, with the loss of one, the carriage of which was smashed by a round shot.

The Sikhs now appeared with about 1,500 cavalry on our side of the river, somewhere about the place where I had turned back after my advance, which I have described to you, and my regiment and the 5th Native Cavalry were ordered to charge them.

Having opened on them with our field guns with shot and shell, our brigadier formed one line and advanced to the attack. I commanded the Squadron on the extreme right of the line and felt very astonished that the enemy stood firm, even when they heard the cheer of our men as they spurred their horses for the shock. The reason was very soon apparent, a vast and deep chasm called a *nullah*, completely separated us from them.

My squadron came first on to the brink of the *nullah* and of course we pulled up short; the rest as they came up followed our example. While we stood looking at each other, the Sikhs dismounted, and kneeling by the side of their horses which stood quite quiet, they gave us a volley of carbines. There was a great whistling of bullets, but they all went over our heads, so that they must have expended a great quantity of lead, to no purpose.

Some of our horses, however, were hit, and our brigadier, White, seeing that nothing could be done, ordered us to retire, by squadrons, when the enemy, thinking that we were going to give up the game, actually began to cross over the *nullah*. We went off slowly, in order to let them get well across, then suddenly wheeling about we charged them home and succeeded in cutting off about twenty. The rest escaped by recrossing the *nullah*, which we now perceived was full of infantry; and thus we halted, when the Sikhs opened out on us from the batteries on their side of the river.

We now retired over the same ground that I had done in the morning and were again exposed to the fire of the same guns. We were in open column of troops. As we retired, the Sikh cavalry again crossed the *nullah* and the fire from the Sikh batteries became so hot that we soon broke into a gallop. Just at this moment a round shot struck my charger just behind my left thigh, completely smashing his hindquarters and, at the same time, wounding my subaltern's horse. Of course I came down, and then, indeed, I was in a predicament. I took one of my pistols out of the holster, the other flew out and was lost in the sand.

One man fell out and came to my assistance, but nothing would have saved me, as the Sikh cavalry were very near in pursuit, had I not fortunately seen a horse near me which had its bridle entangled in its fore foot. I cut the reins with my sword and was soon on his back; and, as I gave him the spur, I looked back and amid a cloud of dust could see the Sikh horsemen dismounting to strip my poor horse of his trappings.

I was soon at the head of my squadron again, not much the worse for my fall. In this little affair, we lost fifteen horses and seven men wounded, one man mortally.

My Dear M.

When last I wrote, we had just finished the affair of Ramnugger and were encamped at that place, with the Sikh army occupying the right bank of the Chinab.

Lord Gough now determined to send a force under Sir J. Thackwell to cross the river and take the enemy in flank, while he was to cross over also and attack them *en face*.

On the 1st December 1848, a force of some 6,000 men, with artillery and a pontoon train, under Sir Joseph Thackwell marched, according to orders. He had with him the 3rd Light Dragoons, the 24th and 61st Foot, thirty pieces of artillery and the rest native troops. We marched at 12.30 a.m. and there was said to be a ford about twelve miles up the river. Owing to many delays through bad management, we did not reach the ford till half past 1 p.m. twelve miles in thirteen hours, and the day was very hot. When we arrived at the ford, we found it occupied on the opposite bank by the enemy, and Sir Joseph considered it to be too dangerous to force a passage; so we went on twelve miles further as far as Wuzeerabad.

The ford at Wuzeerabad is over three branches of the river, one of which is deep and dangerous and, as it was sunset when we arrived, Sir Joseph determined to bivouac for the night on a sand-bank, we having been eighteen hours in the saddle. We had plenty to eat and I passed a very comfortable night. The water was very cold, so we waited till 9.30 a.m. of the 2nd, when we waded the ford, having taken off our overalls and drawers, as the water was over our saddles; you cannot imagine what an odd figure the regiment cut! The ford was four feet ten inches deep in places, and we lost a few camp followers and one or two native soldiers by drowning. Except this, we sustained no loss as the opposite bank was clear. We halted and bivouacked, as all our tents had been left behind.

On the morning of the 3rd, we proceeded, when a round shot through our columns first informed us that we were in the presence of the enemy. We saw that the Sikhs had discovered our plan and had broken up their camp and were now advancing to attack our detachment with their whole force. Lord Gough had failed in his attempt to pass over the river.

53

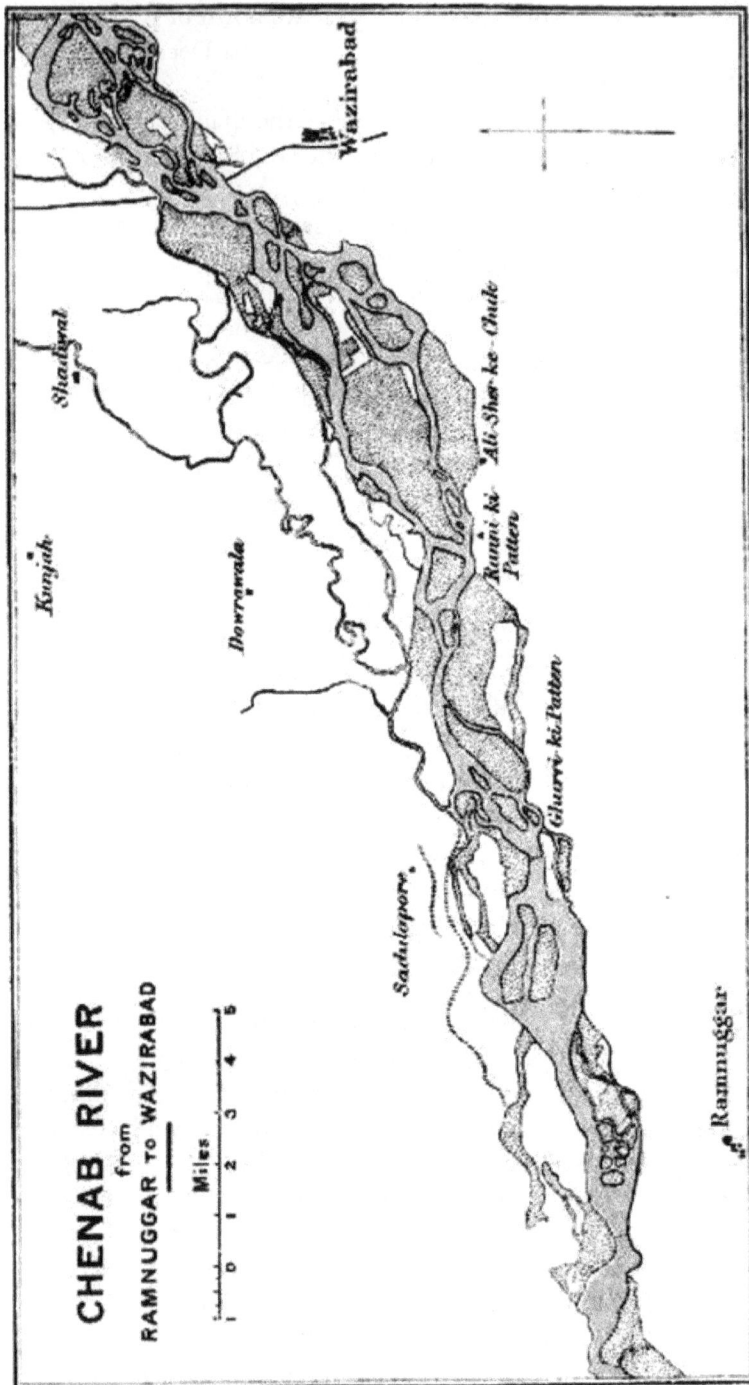

CHENAB RIVER
from
RAMNUGGAR TO WAZIRABAD

Miles

0   1   2   3   4   5

Wazirabad

Shadiwal

Kunjah

Dowrywala

Runni-ki-Patten

Ali-Sher-ke-Chuke

Ghurri-ki-Patten

Sadulapore

Ramnuggar

The enemy, so far as they could be estimated, were about 10,000 good Sikh troops, with a rabble of perhaps double that number, armed with matchlocks. We had orders not to attack alone, so we halted and forming in compact order, slowly retired. Encouraged by seeing our retrograde movement, the enemy now advanced cavalry to outflank us, so two squadrons of the 3rd Light Dragoons were ordered to check them. I was the senior in command so I advanced, leaving one squadron as a support. As I approached their horsemen at a gallop, they let me get within about two hundred yards, when they gave me a volley of carbines and galloped off.

The flank was now clear, but the Sikh batteries opened so severe a fire on us that twelve men were killed at one of our batteries. Sir Joseph Thackwell now faced the enemy and advanced against them with cavalry and artillery; the infantry lying down in close column. When we got within five hundred yards of them, we opened a crushing fire from our whole twenty pieces. At about the twenty-fifth round the Sikh fire began to slacken and they were soon seen to be moving off, A general discharge of shrapnel completed their discomfiture and they were now in full retreat. If we had continued our advance we should have had all their guns, but, much to our surprise, we received orders to retire and halt for the night, so that the Sikhs carried off all their guns across the Jhelum, and we lost a splendid opportunity. Such was the result of what is now called the Battle of Soodalapore. Lord Gough tried to cross the river in order to co-operate with us, but he failed; his pontoons stuck fast in the sand and nobody seemed capable of managing them, so he could not get across. There was a ford but nobody knew where to find it.

In reflecting on our proceedings, it is lamentable to see how the blood and treasure of the nation is sacrificed by the gross ignorance and inefficiency of those in command. In the first place, the Indian Government is in want of money and not one farthing will they give for information. We go on in the dark; nothing is known of the enemy; we surprise them or we are surprised ourselves; we fight and repulse them, and then never follow up our advantage. Our soldiers are brave and that is all that can be said of them. The enemy get every information from our camp, from native writers; that cannot be avoided,

THE ACTION OF SADOOLAPORE.

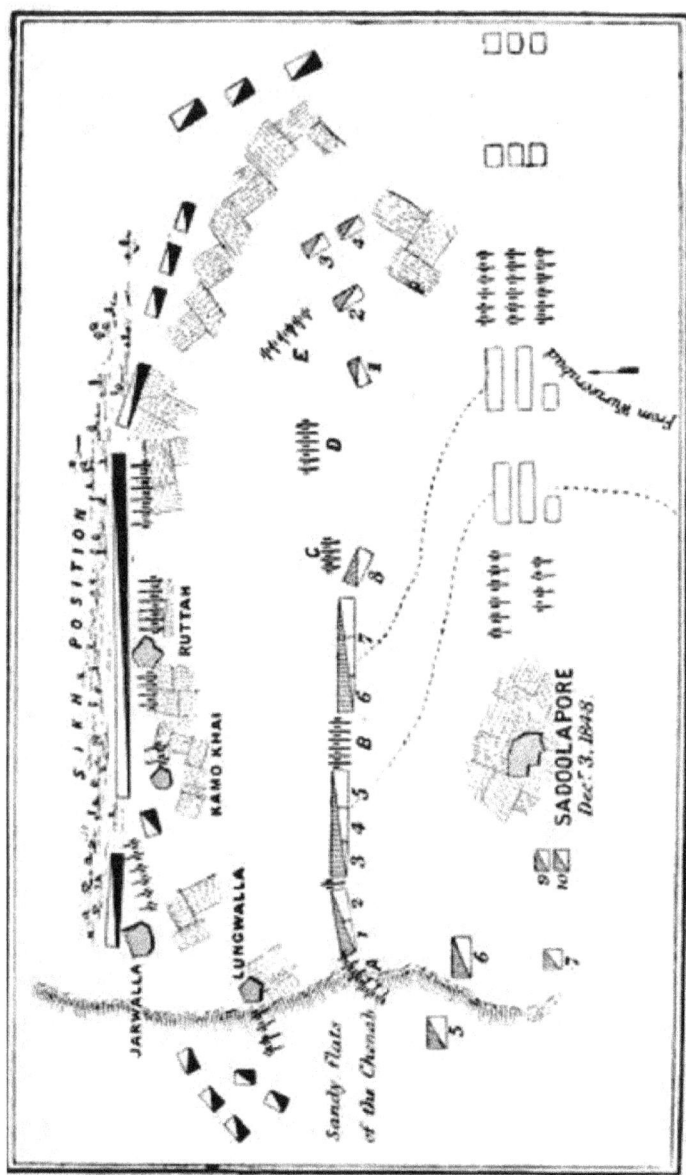

SIKH POSITION
JARWALLA
LUNGWALLA
KAMO KHAI
RUTTAH
SADOOLAPORE
Dec.ʳ 3, 1848.
Sandy Flats
of the Chenab
From Hurrianwallah

ARTILLERY, commanded by
A Warner.*
B Kinleside.*
C Austin.
D Huish.
E Christie.*
* Also at Lungwalla.

CAVALRY.
1. 8th B. L. C.
2, 3, 4, 3rd Light Dragoons.
5. Tait's Horse.
6. 5th B. L. C.
7, 9, 10. Detachments.

INFANTRY.
1. 31st N.I.
2. 56th N.I. } Eckford's Brigade.
3. 46th N.I.
4. 36th N.I. } Hoggan's Brigade.
5. H.M. 61st.
6. H.M. 29th
7. 25th N.I. } Pennicuick's Brigade.
8. Wing of 22nd N.I.

but if a sufficient sum of money were at our disposal, there are many intelligent natives who would obtain for us every information.

The affair of the 22nd was most deplorable. General Cureton, a fine old soldier, and Colonel Havelock, a Peninsula man, were killed; a number of officers wounded and over one hundred men *hors de combat*. In the affair of the 3rd, I was struck by a spent ball on my left arm, which it merely bruised. I am afraid we shall have an unpleasant halt; we ought to advance immediately and drive the enemy over the Jhelum, encamp on the left bank and there await orders. You must not believe a word of the despatches, they are all made up with little regard to truth. They pretend that we have gained a great victory, but that is all nonsense. I do not believe that the Sikhs really lost more than fifty or sixty men, killed and wounded, on the 3rd of December.

Lord Gough, having at last succeeded in passing the river by using the boats of the pontoons to ferry the men over, now joined us a day after the fair, and, instead of at once advancing, he ordered a halt. I happened to be present when he came up, and heard him say to Sir Joseph Thackwell:—"Why, where are your guns?" meaning, where are the Sikh guns that we ought to have taken.

Had I been in a position to reply, I should have retorted:— "Where were you that you did not perform your part in the programme, and support us by crossing the river in time?" It was, however, quite true that we ought to have had all their guns. Sir Colin Campbell urged Sir Joseph to allow him to advance his infantry, but fear of responsibility, as well as his orders not to attack alone, caused him to miss his opportunity. Sir Joseph Thackwell was a very brave old soldier, but he did not understand that celerity in war, on proper occasions, is one of the chief elements of success.

Camp, Army of the Punjab,
14th December, 1848.

My Dear Jack,

We are now twelve miles west of Ramnugger and we have not moved since I last wrote. It is now a fortnight since we crossed the river and here we are doing nothing The enemy have now crossed the Jhelum and are encamped about fifteen miles from us; they are said to have been reinforced from Peshawur, both with men and many guns. There are no roads of any kind in this country. There is a jungle of low brush-wood between us and the enemy, and we blunder along without any information whenever we march. The Sikhs had perfect information of all our movements. They knew that Lord Gough had failed to get over the river, when they broke up their camp and attacked us at Soodalapore. They made every effort to make their men fight well, but the splendid service of our thirty guns was too much for them, and they gave way.

By consulting my last letter you will see the false military position in which we were placed. According to the plan of our operations, we were to cross the river in the direction of Wuzeerabad, but not to engage the enemy until we heard the guns of Lord Gough, who was to pass the river under their fire and attack the Sikhs in front while we attacked their left. The plan was good, only it failed because Lord Gough could not carry out his part of it. The Sikhs, who saw the state of affairs, broke up their camp and attacked our small detachment with their whole force. Of course, had we been opposed by European troops, we should have been annihilated.

I have no idea what we are going to do. Here we remain inactive. Responsibility is what they are all afraid of. Lord Gough, who fears no enemy and no odds, hesitates before responsibility. He does not know what to do therefore he does nothing.

The country is in such a state that letters are constantly lost or they may be opened, therefore I shall sign no more.

Your affectionate brother H.

Camp near Ramnugger,
29th December, 1848.

My Dear Jack,

I have little to tell you this time. We have not moved since I last wrote. I send you the Mofussilite. We have ascertained that the enemy are encamped on the banks of the Jhelum some few miles from us. Nobody knows what we are about; the general opinion is that we are waiting for the fall of Mooltan, but I am not certain that it will happen so soon as they expect. The Bombay troops have arrived, and the siege was to be commenced at Christmas, but in the meantime the season is slipping away and there is the hot weather before us—a much more terrible enemy than the Sikhs. It will take us a month to return to cantonments and March is a very hot month.

I have been laid up for some days by an accident which will keep me idle for some time. I was returning from my morning ride, when I saw a pariah dog stealing away from the vicinity of my tent. Taking up a *chokeydar's* spear which was planted in the sand, I gave chase and, after a long run, succeeded in spearing him. Unfortunately however the spear was sharp at both ends, and it went through the dog into the sand, the butt end going into my side, inflicting a very nasty wound.

I wonder whether they have found out at home about Major Edwardes, C.B. and his victories? In my next I hope to be able to tell you of a great battle. Of course we shall gain the day, although we may sustain considerable loss from their artillery, but they will never come to close quarters with us.

Your affectionate H.

Camp, Army of the Punjab,
January 11th, 1849.

My Dear Jack,

Since we have been halted we have done nothing, but today we marched; tomorrow we shall reach a place called Dinghee, and shall most probably assault the Sikh position on the 13th. But of course many things may happen to prevent this taking place. We have some 16,000 fighting men of which 7,000 are Europeans. The Sikhs number about 40,000 in all, 10,000 alone being regular troops, the remaining 30,000 are rabble. They have about fifty guns, and their position is said to be strong, so possibly the loss on our side may be heavy. No quarter is either asked or given, and in fact, it is war without its amenities. I do not like it myself, it is too much like murder.

I think I told you in my last that I had speared myself by accident. I am sorry to say that the wound is far more serious than I at first thought. I have had an attack of fever which has weakened me much, so that I have to be carried in a *dhooly* with the wounded. Today, however, I am much better, and hope to be able to get on horseback for the fight. I trust that I shall have better luck than on the 22nd *ultimo*. I rode a little black pony in the action of the 3rd, which I intend to use again, as it is far preferable to a regular charger. It is an Arab that I bought at Bombay, its name is Sheitan and it will rush at anything.

News has just arrived from Mooltan. It is said that a shell has exploded in the enemy's great powder magazine, containing some 300,000 lbs. of powder, and nearly all the garrison are blown to atoms, which, if true, will necessitate the immediate surrender of the place. I shall leave this letter open and continue it at Dinghee tomorrow.

Camp Dinghee, 12th January, 1849. We marched this morning, and you may have some idea of our rate of progression when I tell you that we only reached Dinghee at 2 p.m.; ten miles in seven hours. This was occasioned by our marching in battle order as, although we know that we are near the enemy, we do not know exactly their whereabouts. Our heavy guns were drawn by bullocks consequently making very slow progress, and we were forced to make long halts. I am still carried in a *dhooly* as the wound in my side is not healed.

Everybody says we shall fight tomorrow, but the enemy may cross the Jhelum and elude us; the natives say that they will do so, and I think it is probable, but I hope I may be wrong most sincerely, for if so, we can do nothing as the river is not fordable, and we have no means of crossing; and were that possible, the ground on the other side is rocky and bad for cavalry, so that *our* arm would be utterly useless.

I shall now seal this letter, for if we march tomorrow I may have no opportunity of sending it, but I will of course write again tomorrow. When you are excited, tired and wounded, it is very difficult to write at all, but I hope I shall be able to give you a good account of coming events in a very short time.

Love to all,

Your affectionate Henry.

Field of Battle on the Jhelum,[4]
14th January, 1849.

My Dear J.

I have opened my last letter and now send this, so that you will get the two together under the same enclosure. Yesterday we fought a great battle, and it has pleased God that I have come safe out of the fire. The slaughter has been fearful and I am

---

4. Chillianwalla.

very exhausted with fatigue, so can say no more at present than that we advanced on the enemy's position yesterday and attacked, but am sorry to say that, after a dreadful struggle, which lasted the whole day, we retired from our ground at 7 p.m. We marched at 7 a.m. The 3rd Light Dragoons have, comparatively speaking, lost only a few, some thirty-five or forty. The Sikhs fought as they have never fought before, and met us fairly. It gives me great pain to say that we have fought a drawn battle. You must not believe a word of the despatches.

You know that I have been ill, but of course so long as I could sit in my saddle, I could not let my squadron be commanded by anyone but myself. Last night, between five and six, I went out with my Squadron with orders to try and save some of the wounded, when the first man I fell in with was poor Johnny Delamain, who had his left arm shattered by a Zumburruck ball. He was very faint, having been wandering about in the jungle for four hours after he was wounded. A *sepoy* of his regiment was with him: I sent him with a sergeant and two dragoons to the field hospital, where his arm was amputated. I have since heard that he is doing well, and intend to look after him and see that he wants nothing. While I was speaking to him, the enemy opened a fire of round shot on us and I was obliged to look after my squadron.

When I have got over my fatigue I will give you a detailed account of the fight. The enemy are in great force quite close to us, and it has been raining in torrents since 7 o'clock.

I am now writing at 2 p.m. of the 14th, the day after the battle and have been out again trying to save some of the wounded and a dreadful sight I have seen, but, another time I will tell you all. Some of our troops (European) behaved shamefully, and we have had four or five guns taken. I am disgusted. We have taken some eight or nine of the Sikh guns and spiked perhaps twenty, but the enemy had the last shot and have carried off all their spiked guns, but I have no doubt that the victory will be claimed by our side. Possibly we may fight again tomorrow. I am so indignant and disgusted that I can say no more now, but will write particulars hereafter.

Your affectionate H.

Camp, Chillianwalla,
January 15th, 1849.

My Dear M.

I continue my letters and will write every two or three days, so
that you will probably get several letters by the same post.

We have now begun to recover a little from the effects of the
late desperate action. Our loss has been fearful, much more than
I supposed when I wrote yesterday. I cannot tell you our total
loss as I only know that of the regiments that were near me. In
the 3rd we have lost 24 men killed, and 15 men and two officers wounded, together with very many horses. The 24th Regiment of the line have lost the awful number of 250 killed and
about 300 wounded: they only mustered this morning 480 on
parade out of 1100 that went into action. Nearly all the officers
have been killed.

The 3rd (my regiment) were sent out today in order to try and
save some of the wounded. We found 13 officers lying dead
within a space of 20 yards, they were all horribly mutilated.
They were officers of the 24th foot. All the officers of Johnny's
Native Regiment (56th) are either killed or wounded, except
three. The 61st Regiment has lost about 200, men and the 29th
an equal number.

Such a bloody battle, on our side, has never been fought before.
We have lost, on a rough estimate, full double, and some say
treble the amount of our loss at the great Battle of Sabraon, and
the proportion of officers is quadruple.

It can serve no good purpose to go into details as to the horrible things that I have seen, and it is better to draw a veil over
them. A war, where no quarter is given and the dead mutilated,
is a thing so degrading to human nature and shows so clearly
the terrible fact that the boasted reason of man is used to render
him more bestial than the lower animals, that it makes us blush
for our species—

Er nennt's Vernunt, nur braucht's allein,
Nur thierischer als jedes Thier zu seyn.

Today I made an attempt to find Johnny, but I failed to do so.
I have however received a letter from his doctor saying that he
is going on well.

We are as uncomfortable as you can well imagine. Ever since the action, a deluge of rain and wind has swept over us. What we are going to do nobody knows: The truth is the native troops are not worth anything: they will not fight, and the Europeans are terribly cut up and outnumbered.

It is all nonsense for people in England to point to the history of British India and talk about what the *sepoys* have done before, like that old optimist Sir J. W. Hogg. All that is said of them under Clive and Wellington may be quite true, but who did they conquer?—geese—faint hearted cowards—wretched Hindus.

But the Sikhs are regular trained infantry, clothed in better uniforms than ours, regular numbered regiments, all armed and drilled in European fashion, with English words of command, and trained to fight from childhood: added to which they are very brave, and I think that they load and fire quicker than our men. They had ten regiments, and we had only four that would fight. Our native infantry stand and fire away all their ammunition in the air and then say they have no more; and as for the bayonet, they never can be made to move. When they are ordered to charge they stand still and silently disobey; and yet their officers say that they are fine fellows. The native cavalry are just as bad.

It was a very lucky thing for Johnny that I found him, otherwise he would most likely have passed the night in the jungle. I am sadly afraid that he did pass it without cover, but perhaps this was so much the better for his wound and prevented inflammation. His arm was fearfully shattered and I at once saw that there was no hope of saving it.

I am sorry to say that I have lost my first charger. I had it in the rear of our regiment in case my other horse might be killed, and when the disorder took place, in consequence of the rush to the rear of the cavalry on our right, as I have described to you, it broke away from the *syce* in whose charge it was and nothing has been heard of it since; It was worth £160, but I do not despair of getting it back. The man probably got frightened and ran away. I, however, should think myself lucky in coming safe out of this terrible affair and must put up with my loss. I shall see Johnny tomorrow and will then write again,

Your affectionate Henry.

Camp Chillianwalla,
17th January, 1849.

My Dear Jack,

Another night has passed away and a beautiful day has shone out on this field of blood. Yesterday we sent out to bury the dead, which took the whole day. The enemy are encamped about two miles off and have just fired a salute of twenty-one guns. Well may they rejoice!

Yesterday I found Johnny Delamain, with difficulty, and I am happy to say, in good spirits, his wound notwithstanding. His arm is amputated close to the shoulder. He gave me an account of what happened to him after he left me. He had received his wound about two o'clock and had wandered about, under fire, until I found him. Soon after he left me with the two dragoons whom I had sent with him, his strength failed and he could walk no more, so one of the men dismounted and lifted him on to his horse, and thus they found their way to the field hospital His arm was then amputated and, as he was so low, they did not give him chloroform. After the operation, he was put into a *dhooly* and left to shift for himself. These *dhoolies* are not to be had during action, as the bearers are of course afraid to come under fire, and after the action they are too few, on account of the rascally stinginess of the Indian Government.

All is uncertainty, we may be attacked at any time. We have got twelve of the Sikh guns and they have got four of ours. Johnny has passed an uncomfortable night in his *dhooly*. A wounded Irish soldier and a wounded Sikh crept into him for warmth, and laid on him all night, however, he has not suffered in health from it. I have just sent to his tent, for he is now under cover, and he says that he is all right. His regiment, the 56th Native Infantry, got under the fire of the Sikh batteries, and were almost swept away by grape-shot—about 380 I believe were killed; at any rate they have only 150 men left.

You will see the official return of the killed and wounded almost as soon as you receive this. Our greatest loss is the 24th Regiment (Europeans), 250 killed including 13 officers, and 267 wounded including 10 officers, out of 1,030 that went into action. The 3rd Light Dragoons have lost 43 killed and wounded, including two officers, and this loss was all in the left wing of the regiment.

I send my love to you all, and will continue to write as circumstances arise.

Your affectionate H.

Camp Chillianwalla,
January 1849.

My Dear Jack,

We have not moved since I last wrote. We have thrown up fieldworks to protect our camp and we are, I believe, to remain here till Mooltan falls. I will now give you a more detailed account of this memorable battle.

We advanced from Dinghee at 7 a.m. of the 13th January, with the intention of halting and pitching our camp about four or five miles from the Sikh position at Moonge. We halted on our arrival there, but before the order was given to pitch tents the enemy came out fairly to meet us, and a heavy cannonade on our right showed that we were attacked; and which indeed gave us the first notice that any enemy at all was near. There was a jungle in front of us so that we saw nothing, and as we never send out cavalry to explore, we stumbled upon the Sikh army, which were within short range of our guns. On our right was some native cavalry, the 29th Regiment of the line, some native infantry, the 14th Light Dragoons, and one wing of the 9th Lancers; on the left the 66th Native Infantry (Johnny's regiment), the 24th Regiment of the line, one wing of the 3rd Light Dragoons, and some native cavalry and infantry. The right wing of the 3rd Light Dragoons and the left wing of the 9th Lancers, were near the centre of our line. Most of the guns were in the intervals, but some were in the rear and unfortunately were not brought into action.

The battle commenced at 12.30. p.m., and became general about 2 p.m. The Sikhs had about sixty guns, all brought well into action; while we, by some unaccountable mismanagement, only replied from forty, although we had seventy at our disposal.

At about 2.30. p.m. the 24th Regiment were ordered to take the enemy's guns at the point of the bayonet. Unfortunately they did not advance dose enough before they charged, the consequence being that they came up blown and being met

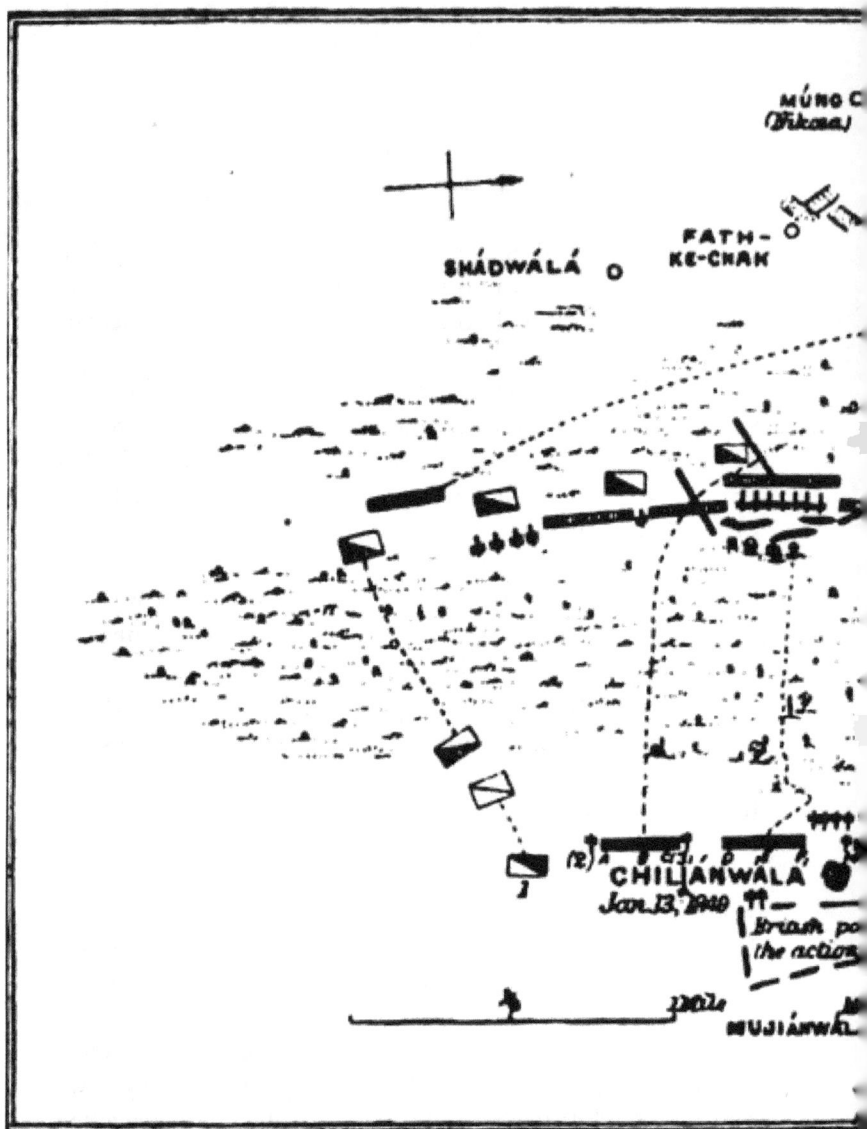

SHÁDWÁLÁ O

MÚNG C
(Fikosa)

FATH-
KE-CHAK

CHILIÁNWÁLA
Jan. 13, 1849

MUJIÁNWÁ

CAVALRY.
1. White's Brigade (3rd Lt. Drags.,
5th and 8th Light Cavalry).
2. Pope's Brigade (14th Dragoons,
squadron of 9th Lancers, &c.)
ARTILLERY.
1. Heavy guns.
2, 3, 4 5, 6, 7, 8. Field Bat. & H.A.

Jhelam (Hydaspes)

KÓT

LAKHÁWÁLÁ

LALAHÁRÍ

Sands

RASÚL

(6)

(7)

B. Penny's Reserves

A 36th N.I.		G 30th N.I.	
B H.M. 61st	} Hoggan's Brigade.	H H.M. 24th	} Mountain's Brigade.
C 46th N.I.		I 56th N.I.	
D 45th N.I.		K 31st N.I.	
E H.M. 24th	} Pennicuick's Brigade	L 2nd Europeans	} Godby's Brigade.
F 25th N.I.		M 70th N.I.	

with a general discharge of grape and musketry, were repulsed with the loss of half their number and nearly all their officers. They rallied, however, charged again and this time succeeded in spiking all the guns of the battery opposed to them, but finally were again driven back to their original ground.

Our fire here on the left was so well sustained that the enemy's guns were all silenced and the Sikh Cavalry coming to their front was immediately charged most gallantly by the wing of the 3rd Light Dragoons led by Captain Unett, but being unsupported by the native cavalry, were forced to retire after having dispersed the Sikh Cavalry. They sustained a loss of 22 killed and 16 wounded.

On our right, a battery of our guns under the eye of Lord Gough advanced, supported by the 14th Light Dragoons and two squadrons of the 9th Lancers, together with a native cavalry regiment. These regiments appear to have got in front of their own battery while advancing, instead of keeping clear of the artillery, thus preventing it from firing. But however it was, most unaccountably, the whole of that body of cavalry became panic stricken as soon as they saw the Sikhs advancing. They all went about and galloped to the rear, deserting our battery of guns, and the Sikh horsemen charging home cut up our unfortunate gunners and took six guns. They retired again as quickly as they had advanced, being unsupported, and the 29th Regiment coming rapidly to the front, charged and retook two of our guns as well as the opposing Sikh battery, which they spiked.

The rest of the battle was an artillery one and, as darkness spread its veil over this bloody scene, nearly all the Sikh guns were spiked, carried off, or deserted.

Some evil genius advised Lord Gough to retire to the place where we first intended to pitch our tents. As we retired, the Sikhs saluted us with a few parting shots and in the night they carried off all their guns, including those which we had spiked, except twelve, which we retain. The Sikhs have got four of our guns and several standards, and the 24th have lost their Queen's Colours. Had we bivouacked on the ground we fought on, we might have taken fifty guns and the enemy would have been totally defeated. So satisfied were the Sikhs that they fired a royal salute of twenty-one guns that very night.

It has been a horrible affair and what will come of it, God only knows. They are not able to do anything at Mooltan and it will be very unpleasant if we are to wait here till it falls, as it would take the troops there a fortnight, or indeed three weeks, to get to us. How we are to attack the enemy again it is difficult to see, after what has occurred. We have only four greatly weakened regiments of infantry and our cavalry must have lost their prestige in the eyes of the Sikhs. As for the native troops, they may be looked on as men of straw.

The reason why the 26th Native Infantry lost so heavily was that they got into the fire which nearly annihilated the 24th Regiment. The whole thing has been most disastrous, and all through wretched generalship and the panic of our cavalry on the right of our line.

In my next, I will try and give you some further particulars. It is now pouring with rain and we are all very uncomfortable; but of course everything is for the best. Love to you all,

Your affectionate H.

Camp Chillianwalla,
February 6th, 1849.

My Dear M.,

We are still at the same spot and have thrown up some entrenchments, while the enemy are encamped about three miles off. We have been so badly used that we cannot attack again till we get double our present numbers, in fact, never was a British army in more uncomfortable circumstances.

Mooltan, however, having fallen (surrendered) the troops that were besieging it are now marching to our assistance and as they commenced their march on the 27th January, we expect them to reach us about the 20th of this month when, doubtless, we shall again attack the Sikh position.

In the meantime if the Sikhs should venture to attack us, they will be beaten, for our artillery is much superior, and we have cut down the jungle for a mile round our position. We lead a very uncomfortable life here.

The cavalry are out from 8 till 6 p.m. protecting the camels and camp followers. At capturing camels and light cavalry duties, the Sikhs beat us hollow; for every camel we take they get fifty of ours. Johnny Delamain has got quite well again and will be sent to the Hills shortly. He has got one year's pay and a pen-

69

sion of £75 a year for the loss of his arm: with this, and a staff appointment, he will be able to do very well.

Since I have been on the campaign I have learnt to like him better than I thought I should have done at first and he is too good to throw away in the Indian service. If I had any influence, things should be greatly altered in this villainous land. Well may Charley Napier exclaim against the rascally government, and yet how people in England try to get a Cadetship for their sons!

Only fancy, during the action on the 13th. I lost my first charger, worth 160 guineas, send I am not able to recover a farthing for its loss. When I made application to be paid for my other charger which was killed at Ramnugger, I was made to sign a certificate, on honour, that I was mounted on its back at the time it was killed. I intend to apply to the governor general to try and get the value of my first charger which I also lost.

I told you before that the despatches are made up with a view to deceive the public, but by comparing my truthful accounts with them, you may make a just estimate of their value.

Your affectionate H.

20 February, 1849.

My Dear M.,

I write as usual and direct my letters to Jack for fear of their being opened, and my name being seen on the cover. I can only tell you that which is strictly necessary, and you must look at the plans in order to understand our position. We moved from our entrenched camp near Chillianwalla on the 14th, and now occupy a position at about eight miles due south of Guzerat.

On the 12th, just two days before we broke up our camp, I was sent out in command of two squadrons—about 200 men—to watch the enemy's movements. The Sikhs had detached a large force to Dinghee. They turned out two regiments of infantry and a cloud of cavalry and began to advance towards our camp. I immediately sent information to our head-quarters and prepared to retire.

They came on boldly, driving in my vedettes; and knowing that the general commanding would support me, I retired slowly. Their cavalry, however, came on so fast that I broke into a trot,—and seeing this, their cavalry, a cloud of irregular horsemen in no regular formation, came on at a gallop. When they were within about 100 yards of me I halted, and fronting them delivered a volley of carbines, upon which they immediately shewed their backs. I then opened out in skirmishing order and they retreated.

As I resumed my retreat they again advanced, and I again met them with the same tactics. They approached within a mile and a half of our camp, and I skirmished with them till darkness came on. The whole of our force stood to their arms and Lord Gough witnessed the affair from the top of a village, but as he wished to avoid a general action he did not leave his entrenchments.

As darkness set in the enemy retired, not liking to approach too near our entrenchments and so come within range of our guns. Lord Gough was very much pleased with the result.

On the 14th., in the morning, we saw that the whole Sikh camp had disappeared, had vanished into thin air, and nobody knew where they had gone. Everybody said that they had crossed the Jhelum; but it was nothing of the sort. They had broken up their camp and occupied Guzerat in the rear of our position! I am so lost in wonder that I can hardly trust my senses. Shere Singh, their general, intercepted and took all our mail bags with the overland letters, but in the most gentlemanly manner he sent them into our camp, with his compliments to Lord Gough, by one of the 3rd Light Dragoons who had strayed too far from our lines and had been made prisoner.

Part of the army under General Whish joined us to today, and the whole will join tomorrow, when we shall attack, and the unfortunate Sikhs will be defeated with terrible slaughter, in all human probability.

We are now within five miles of the Sikh camp, and with this letter you will probably get another if I am not knocked over by a Sikh cannon ball. I am in the saddle nearly all day so can only write a little. This plan will give a general idea of the situation.

Your affectionate H.

21st February 7 a.m.

I am going to mount my horse. The enemy have stood at Guzerat. The whole of the Bombay force have arrived and joined us. We attack immediately, and if I escape I will finish this, if I do not, you will get it as it is.

Your affectionate H.

Camp Guzerat,
22nd February.

My Dear M.,

We met and totally defeated the Sikh army yesterday. I escaped unhurt as did every man in my regiment. I will write you an account of the battle, but I am unable to do so now from fatigue. We have got about fifty guns and their whole camp.

Adieu, H.

Army of the Punjab, Camp Guzerat,
28th February, 1849.

My Dear M.,

I write the latest safe day for the mail.

THE BATTLE OF GUZERAT

On the 21st February, 1849, at 7 a.m. we struck our camp and formed up for the purpose of attacking the Sikhs. The affair was very simple. The field of battle was a vast plain of boundless extent, Salisbury plain ten thousand times magnified, but much flatter: such ground for cavalry and artillery was never seen.

We advanced to within a thousand yards of the enemy and opened a crushing fire from 100 guns which we kept up till 4 p.m., when their whole force broke without our ever having come hand to hand with them. They fled and left us all their camp, baggage, and guns, about 60 in number: it was a total rout and very extraordinary would it have been had it been otherwise.

We have not lost more than 400 killed and wounded. My regiment pursued till total darkness set in, and none were spared: few made any resistance, and they were slaughtered by hundreds. There is not one Sikh this side the Jhelum. The Afghan horse had joined the Sikhs previous to the battle. They would not be afraid to meet us hand to hand but they cannot stand an artillery fire, round shot make a very disagreeable whistling, and I must say that I am not very partial to them myself.

Nobody knows now what our next move will be, but the general idea is that the Punjab will be annexed and, in fact, I cannot see how it can be otherwise. General Gilbert, with a strong division, must have crossed the Jhelum by this time, and they say that he is to go to Peshawur, but time will shew. Johnny, I think I told you, has left the army and gone to the hills: he is quite well.

Your affectionate H.

Note—I estimated our loss at about 400. The day after the battle it was found to be in killed and wounded nearer 1000. The further pursuit of the enemy was entrusted to Sir Walter Gilbert, and on the 14th March Shere Singh with 16,000 men laid down their arms and surrendered near Rawal Pindee and hostilities ceased on the 21st by the occupation of Peshawur. The 3rd Light Dragoons remained at headquarters, and upon the army breaking up they were ordered to Umballa. They reached Lahore on the 28th.

Lahore, 28th March, 1849.

My Dear M.,

First I give you the political news in the following extract from governor generals orders:

> . . . . the British subjects who were prisoners in the enemy's hands have all returned in safety. One hundred and fifty-eight pieces of artillery have fallen into our hands during the Campaign.

29th March. Today I went to the Durbar of the little Maharajah Dhuleep Singh and saw him sign away his kingdom, so it is now ours. I afterwards went and had in my hand the celebrated Kohi-Noor, it looks like a bit of glass as big as a small egg, but it is not brilliant like our diamonds in England. I also visited Moolraj and had a long talk with him. He is a little ugly man and they say he is to be hanged.

The heat is now 94° in my tent which makes me so lazy that I can scarcely write. They say that we are to get a year's "*batta,*" and a star or cross or something of the kind.

Your affectionate H.

Wuzeerabad, 14th March, 1849.

My Dear Francisca,

I received your letter on the 13th January. Only fancy, on the

10th of next March, I shall be 36 years old. Since I last wrote Shere Singh, his father, and the rest of his officers, have surrendered themselves prisoners, and the whole Sikh army have laid down their arms, so that the war is at an end.

I do not think that we shall annex the Punjab immediately, but at any rate we shall hold possession of it. We left the field where the battle was fought yesterday, for we were horribly annoyed by the stench of the dead. The Sikh dead lie unburied, a prey to dogs and vultures, which do not do their work quick enough.

We have got some 85 or 90 guns, and have recovered those that we lost so disgracefully. I wish the fact could be blotted from the page of history—but all perfumes of Arabia, etc.

You say that Peter does not like the newspaper that I sent him, but it is the best we can produce out here, no doubt it is very scurrilous at times. With regard to what it says of Lieut.—or, I beg his pardon. Major Edwardes, it is much too violent, really, he is an officer of great merit and talent, and in the woeful absence of those qualities in this country perhaps he may merit some reward. Knowing what we do here, however, he certainly did not deserve the honours which he got; but in England they jumped at a conclusion and all the papers took up his case; and afterwards, when the truth came out, the whole affair was forgotten.

They say that we shall get prize money, at any rate we shall get '*batta*,' which will just suit me as I want to come to England for two years. The heat is just commencing and we are anxiously looking out for the order to march for Umballa, I suspect that this letter is the last that will contain any news. Indian news henceforward will be blank.

Your affectionate brother Henry.

Umballa, 28th April, 1849.

My Dear J.

You see that I have got back safe to Umballa and very glad I am, for depend upon it, whatever they may say, nobody likes campaigning in India. I have already told you of the loss of my first charger. When the Sikhs laid down their arms, I took an opportunity of going to look for him in the Sikh camp, I saw Shere Sing and spoke to him in Persian. He told me to go and look about for him and then he alluded to other subjects and, seeing me puzzled, for my Persian would not serve me except for very simple matters, he remarked that he thought my knowledge of Persian was '*bisear kum*' that is, very limited, which in fact was the truth. I went, and followed his advice but I found no charger.

One of my sergeants, however, as we passed through Lahore went to look at the captured guns, and while he was there, an officer came for the same purpose when, to the sergeant's astonishment, he saw that he was mounted on my first charger that I lost at Chillianwalla. Not having his wits about him he went up to the officer, and, like a fool, said "I beg your pardon, Sir, but that horse you are on belongs to my captain." No sooner had he spoken than the officer set spurs to the horse and galloped off, and then my horse was indeed lost forever.

This needs explanation to you in England. The sergeant said that he took the officer for a field officer in the company's service, but he knew, from his dress, that he was not belonging to our service. The sergeant ought to have watched him home and then have given information to me. This horse stealing on a campaign is not uncommon, I know myself of three other cases. When detected, they say that they bought the horses, which may have a grain of truth in it, but they bought them for a mere song, knowing them to have been stolen.

I have got six months leave of absence and intend to go off to the Himalayas and explore towards the source of the Jumna and Ganges and shoot wild animals. If I get '*batta*' most probably I shall come home next season. Who do you think I met this morning? Mrs. D——'s sister, who ran away with a man named W——? What a fool she was, she will repent of it in less than a year when she finds into what a position she has put herself, and reflects on what she has lost.

Johnny Delamain is very well at Simla. By the bye, I have got a decoration of some sort, so am what the French call '*decoré:*' but I am too old now, and too philosophic to attach any value to it. After what I have seen and learnt, no medal, cross or star, will have any charm for me—all is humbug, a peacock's feather to please children. I will get you some curious birds and other small animals. I march first to Gungotree and shall see all the beauties of these glorious hills and shoot wild sheep and bears and all manner of things. Only fancy! at the foot of the hills are herds of wild elephants and no end of tigers. I am off immediately.

While I was at Lahore I went and discoursed with Shere Sing, Shutter Sing, and Moulraj: and I will tell you hereafter what we talked about

My love to you all.

Your affectionate Henry.

Camp near the source of the Jumna,
May 25th, 1849.

My Dear F.

Here I am amidst these magnificent mountains writing in my little tent I am not quite cut off from civilization for I received my letter from you yesterday telling me of the death of my Aunt Campbell. It was what I expected and a most happy thing for her that she died free from pain after having lived far beyond the general average of even those who die of old age. I see also that James is coming to India; of course he gets his commission for nothing. I do not think that he will ever get a medal for service in India and I hope that I shall not get another. I say with Max. Piccolomini:

Den blutgen Lorbeer geb Ich hin mit Freuden,
Fürs erste Veilchen das der März uns bringt,
Das duftige Pfand der neuverjüngte Erde.

Since I last wrote I have travelled on, shooting by the way. I have not yet seen any tigers, but today I have dined off one of those beautiful pheasants which abound in these parts, the same that Jack has got in the glass case at home. I can buy them from the natives for nine-pence the brace. These mountains, with their peaks covered with eternal snow, are indeed sublime. If Mont Blanc so inspired, what would not these hills have done?

Mont Blanc appears—still snowy and serene,
Its subject mountains, their unearthly forms,
Pile round it, ice and rock, broad vales between,
Of frozen floods, unfathomable deeps,
Blue as the overhanging heaven, that spread
And winds among the accumulated steeps
A desert peopled by storm alone.
. . . . how hideously

Its shapes are heaped around! rude, bare, and high,
Ghastly and seared and riven,—is this the scene
Where the old Earthquake-Demon taught her young
Ruin? were these their toys, or did a sea
Of fire envelop once these silent snows?
None can reply: all seems eternal now.

And such is the scene upon which I am now looking. I think it is a question whether these mountains were the result of fire.

26th May, 1849. Last night I left my hut and climbed up a very high mountain to try and get a shot at some *Theer* and wild goats. At six o'clock I met with a great many within shot, but I was so exhausted with my pull up these steep ascents that I missed everything. There are numbers of beautiful pheasants and I intend to try and bring some home alive. All my *shikaries* ascribe my bad sport to my not having propitiated the Dive of the Hills.

Yesterday my head man told me that it would be necessary to assemble the whole village and offer up prayers to the demon of the mountains. I was not in a good humour and accordingly told him that he was an ass and that there no god but one. He went away muttering that hill-men had gods of their own; and the same man, when he saw me miss a large goat at about twenty yards distance from me, was in a terrible state, and actually offered to go all the way back to call out the villagers to offer up prayer. I told him the reason why I had missed, but it brought no conviction to him, as he had seen me break a bottle at a hundred yards; so now all men think that I have incurred the displeasure of the Dive of the mountain, and that I shall have no sport.

This morning, after having slept at the top of the hill, I again went out, but I had so frightened the goats the night before that they had gone into places inaccessible to me. I tried to round one point, but found the walking much too dangerous; in fact to have proceeded with my shoes on, would have been certain destruction, so I gave my rifles to my *shikaries* who wear no shoes, and who are capable of passing the most frightful abysses without danger to themselves. They have since returned unsuccessful, all owing, as they tell me, to the anger of the demon of the mountains.'

Jumnotrie, 30th May, 1849. I have just returned from a most interesting expedition. Yesterday I ascended to the hot springs and have brought away a bottle of the water. They burst out of the rock quite close to the snow, and have the power of petrifaction or rather I should say incrustation, which I believe is common in all hot springs.

I met two officers who had been up the great glacier some 1,500 feet higher than the springs. They said that the ascent was not so dangerous as the descent: I knew, however, that if I could get up, the coming down would be all right. I therefore got a piece of rope about 100 yards long and having made knots in it I commenced my ascent; and well it was for me that I did so, as I could not have ascended at all without it. As it was, I ascended and descended safely. The descent would have been very dangerous without the rope. My hill-men held it at the top and had they let go it would have been an awkward affair for me. The glacier is very wonderful and it is a beautiful sight to see the streams issuing from the eternal snow to feed the rivers below. I told you before that these hill-fellows are not men but monkeys. Such places as they pass with a heavy load on their heads or shoulders, I never could have believed had I not seen it. A monkey carried my tent on his back over a place where I felt the most intense horror. I would sooner face a battery, any day, than a giddy precipice. I wish I could draw better but this will give some idea of it.

1st June. In the night some wild animal carried off all my fresh meat as well as my beautiful pheasants: luckily they were skinned so I have not lost the most valuable part of them. I have only been three miles to day to a most , beautiful hot spring. It is gloomy and looks like rain.

3rd June. I got a fine *Theer* and two hen-pheasants on this day's march. Now my postman is going off so I send you all my love.

Your affectionate Henry

(The rains now set in suddenly, and I had a dreary uninteresting march back to Mussourie which I reached in about a fortnight).

Mussourie, 28th June, 1849.

My Dear A.

Your letter reached me just after I had been driven in by the rains. I was very glad to hear that you were all so well, and I shall be also glad if we have nothing more to do with the Sikhs, because it is a most savage and brutal warfare, and more resembles murder than anything else.

It is all very well for people sitting at ease at home to talk about our not making prisoners, but you must be on the spot to judge, and those who expect the amenities of European warfare out here, are asses with whom it is lost time to argue. If a soldier writes home and tells some disagreeable truth, it is immediately denied, on authority, and this lying denial is repeated if any indiscreet Member of Parliament should ask a question in the House; and there the matter ends. This is what is called the "*mensonge officieux*" or as the Church would call it, a pious fraud, lying being a righteous necessity, according to Eusebius. . . .

As for the late Sikh war, we are well out of it, but how would it have been had we had European troops to deal with? I do not wish to be a prophet of evil, but I cannot conceal my fears that when we measure ourselves against a European force, unless we have better and younger men to command, it will be a sad thing for England.

I have very little news to tell you. The rains have set in, and I am confined to the house and find it rather dull. Within a few miles of my house there are tigers and wild elephants. A young lady was coming up to the hills in a *palanquin*, when a large wild elephant appeared on the road, and the bearers of course dropped her and ran away. The elephant came up and took her out of the *palki*, and after having looked at her he put her back again and went away without doing her any injury—a very civil animal *n'est ce pas?*

It is a very remarkable circumstance that these wild elephants are hardly ever shot. In Ceylon, numbers of elephants, are continually shot, but here, somehow, the bullets will not kill them. I believe the reason is, that here they shoot down from *houdajs*, while the hunter should be on foot, so that the bullet may have an upward direction in order to reach the brain. These animals are very destructive, particularly those which have run wild after having been in a tame state.

There is a government reward of £100 advertised for anyone who can shoot one which has run wild here at the present time. Last season a captain in the 9th Lancers went out with four double guns in his *houdaj*. He soon fell in with the brute and discharged four barrels into its head, without effect. The elephant charged him and upset his elephant, broke his guns to pieces and he himself had only just time to seek refuge behind a large tree where he hid himself. The wild elephant looked about for him for some time and then went away leaving a cub behind about as large as a small donkey. The cub followed the officer home and seemed quite to like it.

Johnny Delamain is still at Simla, and I believe quite well I had a letter from Charles yesterday. He is at Bombay and has been shooting bison.

Remember me kindly to Dr. and Mrs. Outram. Colonel Outram is coming out to Bombay. General Napier is at Simla, and I have no doubt that he will give a great deal of trouble. I do not think that I shall be able to come to England yet, but I look forward to it with much pleasure. I have now been away three years, which seems a long time. I shall not be able to write to Francisca by this mail, but you can shew her this letter which will be all the same.

Your affectionate nephew, Henry.

Landour, 14th July, 1849.

My Dear Brother,

I have just received your letter and am delighted that you are all so well at home. The rains have now set in, so that there is no going out of the house for the next two months. To idlers, this is now the most terrible time, nothing to do and very few books.

The state of recklessness of some, induced by ennui, would astonish you in Europe. Officers come up here, lose large sums at cards and then quietly decamp without paying, and this is now so common that very little is thought of it. Two men, neither having a farthing, will play a game at billiards for 100 gold *mohrs* a game. A gold *mohr* is about thirty-two shillings. The gambling transactions in this land of corruption are simply disgraceful, but how to put a stop to them, that is the question.

Sir Chas Napier has issued an order prohibiting all leave of absence, so I think that there will be very little chance of my coming home till the Regiment comes. People say that after three years the desire of returning to England is at its strongest, but that after seven or eight, the desire becomes weak and then ceases entirely. I certainly now have a very great longing for home, but nevertheless I manage to amuse myself pretty well. I am translating a Persian work which I have some intention of publishing, but, at any rate, it is something to employ my time. It is said that we are to have no '*batta*' for the late campaign. I can believe anything of this rascally government as Charley Napier justly called it. In all their transactions, the mean and sordid spirit of its origin, as Sheridan justly remarked, appears.—*vide* trial of Warren Hastings.

A few days ago, a large snake, nine feet ten inches long, took up its abode in my house: it coiled about three feet of its tail round one of my *gurrahs* or waterpots, and then reared its head six feet high. One of my men shot it and I have got its skin. The servants of course said that it was of a very poisonous nature, but I have examined one of its teeth and feel convinced that it is merely a boa-constrictor and not of a poisonous nature at all.

Last night a very pretty little dog ran under the wheel of my carriage and was unfortunately killed. You do not tell me if you have got the butterflies which I sent home.

You mention that you hope I may get an appointment specially: but I do not see how that can be, unless they offer me the Bishopric of Calcutta. Seriously, I am not eligible for any appointment, not being in the Company's Service. The only appointment open for Queen's officers is that of *aide-de-camp*; and besides, all appointments are generally given through interest. Major Edwardes got his appointment by attacking the government; to shut his mouth they gave him an appointment, and directly he got it his attacks ceased. I myself do not know him, but I asked about him and find that he is a clever pushing character who attacked the government in a series of letters signed "*Brahmini Bull*." Now that he has got what he wanted, the government may do what it pleases so far as he is concerned. Such is the way of the world!

The state of Europe seems tranquil for the moment, but how long will it last now that knowledge is more widely spread? People now-a-days are beginning to see things more in their proper light, and they will not allow all the good things to go to an aristocracy much longer. Who get all the pickings? All the best of the Church livings are given away by favour, generally to the idle and worthless. Who get all the best appointments in the navy? Why the friends of those in power, without any regard to personal merit. In the army, certainly, it is better through the purchase system; but then that system is fundamentally wrong and unsound; and even there, the few things to be given away, such as staff appointments, always go, by interest, to the friends of those in power. Then look at the great, the enormous wealth of England, and then turn to the wretchedness and misery of the masses.

I see no hope except in a long war, which would thin the population. Emigration would fail; because the people would not go voluntarily, and there is no law to compel them. When I was at Rivière du Loup, in Canada, a poor Irish emigrant girl said to an officer of the 68th Light Infantry, "I have plenty to eat, and meat every day, but I would rather starve in Ireland than live in plenty out here." She was evidently suffering from a true disease, called "nostalgia" I now long for England, although I am much better off here as to pay. Depend upon it that war is the best remedy. Without wars a nation soon becomes cowardly, and when that is the case it falls before the arms of savages, even as Rome did.

I heartily wish the Hungarians success, that Emperor of Russia is a bully and I hope he will get a lesson I have seen the Hungarian troops; their Light Cavalry is excellent.

What language do you suppose that Abraham spoke? I have been learning Hebrew and Arabic and I say he did not speak Hebrew, for when he lived there was no Hebrew to speak; and, again, what language was spoken before the flood?[5]

As to the great population of England, only look to Genesis 47. Here we see that only 70 individuals of the Jews came into Egypt and they increased in 430 years when they left, to 600,000 men, besides children. I wonder where the women were? Besides, they must have had at least 1,000,000 children. I believe in England the population doubles itself every 60 years; and, to carry out emigration effectually, fully 200,000 should

---

5. It is now forty years since I wrote the above absurdity, (as at time of first publication). I was then unacquainted with German Biblical criticism: I now know that such a person as Abraham never existed, and that there was never any general deluge, and that the whole so-called Mosaic account is a mere legend, and has no claim to be considered as historical. *Vide* appendix (1).

emigrate annually. But this they will not do, so they must be killed somehow, either by war, pestilence, or famine, and this will certainly take place—nature stands no nonsense.

July 1st 1849. My Dear F. You tell me I shall be tired of home in a week, perhaps so, but then the love of change is inherent in the human breast. My idea of happiness is comprised in the following quotation, the excellence of which I hope you will admire, for there can be no doubt of its truth:—

> *Toute la science du bonheur est renfermée dans un seul mot et ce mot est*—occupation. *Tout depend de savoir remplir le vide de la vie* (to kill time). *On ne pent vivre qu'avec les illusions, et dès qu'on a un peu vécu, les illusions, s'envolent* (mine have all flown away long ago) *Il n'y a de bon qu'en, occupation dont on soit toujours sûr, et qui nous mène jusqu'au bout en nous empêchant de nous ronger nous-mêmes.*
>
> *Il faut savoir aimer sa destine, il ne dépend pas de nous de la changer, mais il dépend de nous, de nous attacher à une occupation habituelle, qui se répéte chaque jour, ayant un but determiné. Les occupations sérieuses sont celles qui répandent le plus de calme, les occupations frivoles et de pur amusement, distrait momentanement, mais ne désennuient pas: au lieu de remplir le vide qu'on sent en soi, elles ouvrent toujours un nouveau.*

This is very good. Kill time you must, and this is so well known that there is a proverb among the Easterns answering to the "*toujours perdrix*" of the French. And this is chiefly the reason why I now wish to come home, for I am very well off here and have got more money than I want. I am in very good health and my leg[6] has healed up and got quite well.

The order is out and we are to get '*batta*' after all. The rascally government would willingly have cheated us out of it, but they were afraid, the army would have petitioned, and you know that "*Preces armatae*" are always successful. I shall be quite rich. You need not be afraid of my giving you a sister that you would not like. Whatever I may have said, you may rest assured that I shall never marry for money. I have seen that which I never should have believed if I had not seen. Everybody is disgusted at the honours given for this campaign. The only two men who held any command and who behaved nobly got noth-

---

6. I broke my leg in Canada some years before.

ing—Markham of the 32nd and Franks of the 10th Foot They were both disagreeable men, but in action they were splendid. Honours have been given to men who never saw a shot fired because they had interest at the Horse Guards; and also to men who misbehaved before the enemy.

The Duke of Wellington is either a superannuated old fool, or worse. I cannot tell you all now, but I foresee great misfortunes in store for the British Army, if ever they are employed on the Continent against Europeans.

I do not see what chance Peter or Jack have of getting any good Church preferment, they have not got the bad qualities necessary, and they are not the style of men to get on in the Church. I heard the story of a good man to whom it was told that the Bishop of London had said that he was an excellent minister, and who replied, "I wish he had said that I was a worthless one, a second or third-rate one, then I might have expected a good living."

The expensive rate of living in this country would astonish you in England. I am very moderate personally, yet my wine bill comes to £240 a year out of £900, which is my income. I only wish I had as much out of the army I would not be long before retiring. I have got a medal and three clasps, but I am quite disgusted and do not feel it as any honour, seeing that they are given indiscriminately to all alike—to those who fought and to those who ran.

The mail is now going off so I have only time to say that I will write again soon.

Your affectionate brother, Henry.

Landour, August 24th, 1849.

My Dear Francisca,

I was very glad to hear that John has a prospect of adding to his income, but if it can be amicably arranged a little loss is better than a law-suit: The Bishop of Oxford I think had better marry you, I think that you would just suit him.

There is no chance whatever of my coming home at present Charlie Napier, our new commander-in-chief, will give no leave at all. He plays many eccentric tricks but I like him notwithstanding. He is not such a liar and hypocrite as other men who get a little temporary power. I certainly cannot pride myself much on my morality; sorry I am to say so, but I have not arrived at the stage of your friend the duke, who can get up and make a statement in the House which he himself knows to be false. You drink the duke's health, I never do; he has constantly been unjust through life; and as, in my opinion, everything is contained in that little word 'Justice,' he who is without it, all other crimes may pass for virtues in him.

We have constant rain now, which makes life very miserable. One hour's ride in the evening and the rest constant imprisonment in the house, under pain of death—for death it is to go out.

This is a terribly rheumatic place, but strange to say I never suffer at all, and never was better in my life than I feel, now. I buy books at sales and try to amuse myself, but times come when it is very irksome.

I have met and visited Mrs. D—'s sister, who ran away with W—. She is living quite alone, close to me. W—is a worthless fellow; a lieutenant, with nothing but his pay. She has about £200 a year, which is nothing out here. This man W. came up here to the hills with her; went and gambled and lost £200 in a week, and of course could not pay a farthing. He has been ordered to join his regiment at Lahore, and she is left destitute. Her two sisters (the wretches), have cut her. That Mrs. D—who sold her, ought to be shut up in a prison for life, if she had her deserts:—"*satis odiosis.*"

I will now give you the history of Sug, this word is merely the Persian for dog. About eighteen months ago I had a little pup given to me. She was the colour of a fox and a first-rate fox hunter. She ran down and killed 25 foxes at Umballa when only ten months old. I never met with a dog like her and would give £20 to see her back; but that cannot be as she has met with a terrible death. She was a terrier about an inch taller than Una, and much stouter. She went through the late campaign with me, slept on my bed and always followed my horse in action, she was the only one wounded in my troop at Chillianwalla. She went with me to Jumnotri, and used to come and wake me every morning, to have her nose pinched: I could almost cry when I think of her.

About a week ago, I was returning home from a ride in a carriage, I got out at the foot of the hill to walk up, and as my black horse, which I rode during the campaign, was in the carriage, Sug stayed behind as she was so much attached to the horse. I had hardly got out of sight when a most horrible wild beast, a cross between a wolf, a panther and a tiger, called here a "*lakra-bagher*" sprung into the road, and poor Sug instead of saving herself actually flew at it. It took up my poor Sug like a cat takes up a mouse and disappeared with her into the thick jungle by the side of the road—one scream of agony and she was gone. Alas! poor Sug. I must erect a memorial to her in Aunt North's garden and have already made a sketch of it, the inscription is all in Persian and is of my own selection—

"ALAS POOR SUG!"
The last sleeping place of everyone is but two handfuls of earth!

I am glad M. keeps so well.

Your affectionate brother, Henry.

The Hills, 20th September, 1849.

My Dear Francisca,

I have got very little news to tell you, having been confined to the house on account of the rains. There is a strong report that our regiment is coming home, but I hope not as I am in the break and should be sure to be put on half-pay by reduction. I have been most unlucky, not a single step went in the regiment during the whole of the last campaign. I have been 17 years in the service and have spent £5000 but the prospect before me is very bad.

You do not mention whether you received the things that I sent you. I see that the 12th Lancers are under orders for India so that probably I shall arrive in England about next June.

I think that it was a very cool proceeding of the governor- general to appropriate our prize money. Lord Dalhousie, in personal appearance, is very much like a respectable waiter. At a ball given by him up here the other day, an officer of the 14th Light Dragoons having drank too much champagne became exceedingly annoyed at the very coarse nature of the provisions on the buffet, which most probably were supplied by contract. Taking a plate of very dry sandwiches in his hand, he went up to Lord Dalhousie and, taking him for one of the waiters, gave him a dig in the ribs to draw his attention and holding out the plate he said, "Here, Sir, do you call this a proper dish to place before a gentleman?" He was placed under arrest and sent to join his regiment at Lahore; but has since been released, as the whole affair would have looked too ridiculous in print.

Yes, I do sometimes look at the English papers and it appears to me that men are not quite so great fools as formerly. As soon as the people get a little more enlightenment we may expect great changes.

My love to you all,

Your affectionate Henry.

Umballa, 1st October, 1849.

My Dear Francisca,

I am now at what I may call my home in India, and have no doubt shall be very comfortable till the hot winds come, in about six months. Certainly this climate is very beautiful for about six months in each year.

I wish you to give £5 to Louisa Pinner, the wife of my late Gram man G. Pinner; she will call for it.

I laughed heartily at the picture of Moulraj in the *Illustrated News*; of course it is not a bit like him. He is a little ugly decrepit old beast, a cowardly crying rascal, whom I would have turned adrift as we used to say at sea, and bid him do his worst. When I visited him he would not say much, but kept muttering about the "Will of God," fate &c. He was sitting with a small *hookah* and one attendant to fan him: and was very dirty and not a soldier at all. He had nothing to do, personally, with the defence of Mooltan. He coined gold during the siege: gold *rupees*, I send you one of them. Our men got into his mint and made short work of its contents. You will find the gold coin under the seal of this letter: of course it is a swindle and not worth a *rupee*.

You ask me concerning my interview with Shere Singh. He was sitting in his tent, and afterwards, his father Chutter Singh and his younger brother came in. I commenced by asking him, in Persian, if he had my horse which I lost at Chillianwalla, in his camp. He advised me to go and look about I broke down in my Persian and he smiled and said that he thought my knowledge of Persian was "*bisear kum*" that is to say, very small, so I then spoke to him in Hindustani. He was highly amused at my holding my glass in my eye. I lent it to him and he tried, without success, to keep it in his eye; while an old man who was present said that there was '*Jaduee*' in it, that is to say, magic. The very same thing occurred when I was with Goolab Singh in Cashmere, and his son made the same remark.

All these Easterns believe in magic. We then talked of the late battles, and I was loud in my praises of the gallantry of the Sikhs. He said that all was written in the Book of Fate. I told him that such might be quite true, but that if he had taken the trouble to read what was written therein he would not have come to grief. He replied that it was not given to mortals to read therein. "There you are mistaken" I said, "any wise man can read pretty distinctly in the Book of Fate, provided he uses the intellect that nature has given him."

Pointing to my horse, I asked him which would win a race, say of five miles, a man mounted on the horse against one on foot? Of course, the man on the horse would win, they all, at once exclaimed, but they could not see the application. So I explained: "You are of a race intellectually inferior to Europeans; you cannot even make an iron shell; your guns are inferior, and you cannot fire them quickly enough, and your army is incapable of discipline. How then could you suppose that you would succeed in a struggle where all the disadvantages are on your side?" They were all silent, but Shere Singh said "you have spoken the truth."

But one thing I added for their comfort. "Notwithstanding all that I have said of Feringhi superiority, the rule of the English in India will not be permanent, that is plainly written in the Book of Fate. In this world nothing is lasting, and there is no more hope for nations than there is for individuals." Such was the general tenor of my interview. And now while I think of it I want Peter to go Cox's to see Mr. Powell and ask him if the regiment is really coming home. Love to all.

Your affectionate brother, Henry.

P.S. I herewith send you as I promised, an Eastern tale which I composed at a *dak* Bungalow, on a rainy day, (*vide* appendix (2). I should tell you that the names are Sanscrit—*Satyama* means Truth; *Pramada*, Error; *Kusalam*, is the Fortunate.

"SATYAMA OR PRAMADA?"
(TRUTH OR ERROR)

Many years ago, in the beautiful vale of Kashmir, lived an old king who had an only son whose name was Kusalam When the young man had arrived at a suitable age, his father wished that he should marry, so he looked about and soon found a neighbouring prince who had two lovely daughters, the eldest was called Satyama, and the youngest Pramada. The two sisters, although they were considered by some to be equally beautiful, were so totally unlike both in features and disposition, that no person would have taken them for such near relations. Satyama was a blonde, exceedingly clever and fond of study, while Pramada was a brunette with black eyes and long lashes, who gave her mind entirely to amusement and dress, and, while her sister was occupied with her books, employed her time either with her lute or in painting her eyes, so that she remained profoundly ignorant, being scarcely able even to read or write.

The father of the young prince, thinking that his son would be happier if his inclination were consulted in the matter, desired him to make a visit to the court of the father of the two princesses, when he would have an opportunity of making his choice. Accordingly Kusalam set out, and in a few days arrived at the court of the father of his intended bride.

The two sisters had been informed of the honour which was in store for one of them; they equally received the intelligence with joy, but acted in a totally different spirit, Satyama putting on her ordinary white robe and dressing her hair in a simple braid, while her sister spent the whole morning in preparing for the great event. She painted her eyes with kohl, stained her fingers with henna, and hung Kadamba flowers in her ears instead of earrings; her whole body was redolent of sandal oil and other fragrant perfumes, so that when she went out the bees all followed her, captivated by the sweet scent which they mistook for flowers, and one bee, taking her rosy mouth for a water lily, actually kissed her lips, while another alighted to her great annoyance on one of her beautiful arms, thinking it was a tendril.

As you may suppose Kusalam was not long under these circumstances in making up his mind. On being presented to Satyama, as being the eldest, she met him with a cold smile, and gave him a long discourse in the Sanscrit tongue signifying, that those alone are blessed, who remain continually dwelling in the mountain caves, and contemplating the Supreme Being with an abundant effusion of tears, which are ardently drunk up by the birds which sit on their knees without any fear. When however he was presented to Pramada she received him with the most amorous glances from her lovely eyes, and in the prettiest *patois* bade him welcome to her father's court, and stringing her *vina* she sang a plaintive air the burden of which was:

Now in the spring time,
The complaint of the nightingale,
Borne on the mountain breeze.
Excites the mind to love.

Satyama was indignant at her sister's want of modesty, but Pramada took no notice of her ill-humour and continued to sing and amuse Kusalam till the time of evening separation.

The next morning on paying a visit to Satyama he found her in company with a crowd of pundits occupied in a discussion concerning spiritual existences The young prince listened attentively to all that they had to say, particularly to Satyama who acquainted him that the state religion of his father was a popular superstition, and that Rama, Siva and Vishnu, were merely ideal beings who had no real existence; that the much venerated incarnation of the Supreme Being in the form of the son of Nanda, the shepherd Krishna, was a more silly superstition than any of the rest, and in short, that no human being knew anything whatever of the gods, or any other spiritual existences whatever. True, a great cause existed which was nature, but what it was, one, or more, was beyond our grasp; and this, she concluded, was the sum of all human knowledge.

Kusalam who had been brought up at his father's desire entirely by the priests of Krishna, was profoundly shocked, for he regarded Krishna with feelings of the greatest reverence as an incarnation of the Supreme Being. He however said nothing, but making a low obeisance went to pay his respects to Pramada who received him in a lovely bower in one of the palace gardens.

On his approach, her handmaidens significantly smiling, retired in great haste, leaving the young prince alone with Pramada, who put forth all her blandishments and attractions in order to ensnare the heart of the already fascinated Kusalam.

The young prince felt exceedingly timid in the presence of the young beauty, which she was not slow to perceive, so she determined to give him every encouragement in her power. It was the season of "Orishma," or hot season, and Pramada, dad only with a very light silk dress, gave Kusalam several opportunities of viewing her beautiful neck and arms, under pretence of tuning her lute, and as she was well acquainted with most of the love songs then in vogue, after several side-long glances at him, she sang as follows:

At the sound merely of his name.
An involuntary tremor seizes all my limbs;
But when his enchanting face comes to my view,
A cold perspiration inundates my body.
Ah! when he shall come, that master of my life—
When his arms are thrown around my neck—
When he presses me to his heart.
Then, alas! I feel that all my boasted firmness
Would vanish like smoke in a moment.

"It is a little piece from *Amaru*" said Pramada, watching the effect that her song had on the young prince, and seeing that he was enchanted with the amorous ditty she handed him the *vina* and begged him for a song in return. Kusalam played well, and his natural timidity being somewhat overcome by the encouragement that he had received from the young beauty, he eagerly seized the instrument and after striking a few chords fell into the following:—

Resting under the shade of the trees in the grove
Behold my love came holding her robe over her bosom.
Thus as it were impeding the rays of the moon.
Her head was crowned with a garland of flowers,
And her smiling mouth resembled a water lily,
Her lovely body was scented with crocus and sandal,
And her eyes glanced tenderly like those of a young gazelle.
Ah! of such, I said, are composed the Beauties of Paradise.

Pramada was loud in her praises of the young prince's performance, and now his timidity being completely vanquished, they sat singing and talking till the close of evening.

The next morning, Kusalam proposed in form to the old king

for his youngest daughter, according to court etiquette, and it was arranged that Pramada should be sent to Kashmir where the marriage was to take place. Satyama was not surprised when she heard of the success of Pramada; she had seen enough of Kusalam to despise him heartily, she had no affection whatever for her sister and was very glad to get rid of her, all she said on the occasion was a quotation from a learned poet.

Better to live in the wild mountains among beasts.
Than in intimacy with fools, even in the abodes of Indra.

As soon as the old king had given his consent, Kusalam re-turned to Kashmir, where in a short time Pramada arrived and the marriage was celebrated with great rejoicings.

Kusalam found Pramada all that his fondest imagination had ever pictured, he was supremely blessed and lived with her in the greatest happiness for six years, during which time she had borne him two sons and as many daughters who were as beau-tiful as the moon.

One day, Pramada having lost her temper struck a slave girl who was painting her eyes and dressing her for a great *fête* in honour of Krishna, at which the celebrated Gita Govinda was to be sang and danced to. The slave girl determined to be revenged, and watching the return of Kusalam from hunting, acquainted him that his adored Pramada was false to him, and had a lover in a young musician who was one of the principal singers at the *fête* of Krishna.

Kusalam was thunderstruck, nothing but ocular demonstration could properly induce him to believe in the infidelity of his beautiful Pramada, he therefore determined to attend the *fête* in disguise and satisfy himself of the truth or falsehood of the girl's story. Led by his informer at night, the prince approached a beautiful moonlit bower from which the tinkling sounds of a *vina* issued; with caution Kusalam advanced, and soon the well known accents of his beautiful Pramada became quite distinct as she sang a voluptuous air from the Gita Govinda to her en-raptured lover who was at her feet. Just as she was singing—
"Thy half shut eyes timidly gazing captivate my heart,"

—the prince entered the alcove and drawing his sabre he at once sacrificed her lover to his jealous rage.

Regardless of the cries of his wretched Pramada, the prince

called in a guard of eunuchs, and she was borne to the *harem* prison to await the sentence of her injured lord. Wounded in his most tender point, Kusalam's thoughts turned to the rejected sister Satyama. "Ah!" said he to himself, "had I not been a fool I should have made a wiser choice, Satyama would never have thus deceived me, I was led away by the soft and mendacious glances of the artful Pramada, and like a vile swine rejected the pearl that was at my command—but it may not yet be too late;" thus reflecting he hastened to the court of his wife's father, and entreated him to allow him to marry Satyama.

The old king was greatly shocked at Pramada's misconduct, she was his favourite daughter and he loved her far more than the perfect and well conducted Satyama. His consent was given, though with much reluctance, to the divorce of the prince from his first wife, and to a new marriage with his remaining child Satyama was very beautiful, and gazing on her sweet face Kusalam thought that he might still be happy, he accordingly carried her to one of his most beautiful palaces, where his children resided. Fair as the day, he presented these lovely pledges of his former marriage to his new wife hoping that in her they would find a second mother; but Satyama, looking coldly around her at the magnificent rooms and then at the children, quietly remarked from the sage, *Bhartrihari.*

Lofty palaces, beautiful children, countless riches and a faithful wife, together with youth and health, may he considered benefits by the ignorant man, thinking that he can enjoy these forever in the prison of this world; the wise man, knowing their instability, learns to despise them all.

Poor Kusalam remembered how different had been his reception by the frail Pramada. and how much more joyous his feelings on the day of his first wedding. Things did not improve, Satyama's mind being cast in a different mould from that of her husband, she could never fall in with his ideas, and the result was much unhappiness. One day, which happened to be that of the celebration of the festival of the god Krishna, Kusalam was preparing to go in state to the grand temple and wished Satyama to accompany him. This she positively refused to do, and horrified her husband by giving it as her opinion that the whole story of Krishna was a mere myth, without any substantial truth in it.

A dispute ensued; Kusalam said that those who denied the divine Hara, the glorious victor of so many demons, could never attain the blessed abode of the Ganas. Satyama could not contain herself, and on her telling her husband that fire might be conquered by water, the heat of the sun by an umbrella, a furious elephant by a sharp goad, an ox or an ass by a stick, various diseases by medicines, but for a fool there was no remedy, Kusalam in a fury pronounced her sentence of divorce, and she was sent back to her father. When Pramada heard of her sister's disgrace she caused letters to be written to Kusalam in which she begged his forgiveness, protesting that she never had deceived him, but that she was merely taking a singing lesson when he had surprised her. Kusalam admitted her excuse and reinstated her in her former position, for, said he, she is a woman, and in this world it is a woman that I want, and not an angel.

"Thus your Majesty sees," said the sage, "that in this world our happiness greatly consists in illusions. Do away with these, the cold truth remains indeed, but with our illusions our happiness also vanishes forever."

★★★★★★

[The 3rd Dragoons were now ordered to England and I find that I was there in December 1850. I obtained my majority in that regiment in 1854, and not being able to remain any longer in England as I was too poor, I exchanged into the 9th Lancers, and arrived at Umballa in 1855. I had married during my stay in England, and I went out to India with my wife by the Cape route.]

Leaves From My Journal

May 4th, 1857. Left Umballa by *dak* with Mittie. We had two *dhoolies* only, our servants having already preceded us with orders to await us at Bhimber. Pecksy, our tame bird, got out of its cage when we were about a mile from Umballa, and we found it hiding in a corner of the *dhooly*. Arrived at the *dak* bungalow at Khana-ke-serai about 9 a.m. the next morning. The night was very cool and pleasant Four *dak* stages, equal to about forty miles.

Passed the day in the very small *dak* bungalow. We put up *tatties* and had a *punkah*, so the heat was not very oppressive. Mittie was bitten by a wasp and she thought at first that she had been stung. Made claret-cup for dinner, which consisted of one fowl killed for the occasion; as, however, we had an English tongue, we were not badly off. Started at 7 p.m. and arrived at Loodiana at 2 am. on the 6th. Three stages, about 30 miles.

May 6th. Loodiana, in the *dak* bungalow. Thermometer 86° at noon. Poor Mittie very unwell; we feel the want of servants very much. Dined at 5, and started again on our journey at 7 p.m. Arrived at Jullunder at 4. 30. *Palki* bearers took us, without orders, to the hotel, a miserable little house. I ordered the bearers to take us to the *dak* bungalow; 32 miles; made good in all 102 miles.

May 7th. Jullunder. Mittie much better; I am in great hopes that her health will be completely restored. A gardener brought us some fine strawberries for sale; bought a pound for ninepence, very dear but very good. Read some excellent articles in the *Westminster Review*. "*Wahrheits liebe zeigt sich darin, dass man uberall das Gute zu finden und zu schätzen weiss*," as Goethe justly remarked. I had some books with me, and among others some poems of Victor Hugo. As a rule I do not much admire French poetry, but these verses to his daughter, or rather, on his daughter, I think worth transcribing—

Elle avait prit ce pli dans son age enfantin
De venir dans ma chambre un peu chacque matin
Je l'attendais ainsi qu'un rayon qu'on espère
Elle entrait et disait, "bon jour mon petit père.
Prenait mon plume, ouvrait mes livres, s'asseyait
Sur mon lit, dérangait mes papiers, et riait.
Puis soudain s'en allait comme un oiseau qui passe.
Mon oeuvre interrompue, et tout en ecrivant,
Parmi mes manuscrits je rencontrait souvent
Quelque arabasque folle, et qu'elle avait tracée,
Et mainte page blanche entre ses mains froissée
Où, je ne sais comment, venait mes plus doux vers.

Noon. Thermometer 86°. From this time the heat gradually increases two or three degrees, until 4 o'clock, when it is at its maximum. Started at 5 p.m. it being nearly 50 miles to the next halting place. Thermometer in the *dhooley* 98°. Night got cool at 9 o'clock. Arrived at Umritsur at 8 30. a.m., 59 miles.

May 8th. Umritsur. A fine new staging bungalow here. Mittie rather fatigued with her long journey, but evidently improved, upon the whole, in her health. Pecksy very tired with her journey, has gone to sleep. Here I must say a word concerning that vicious bird's qualities. She carries letters and finger rings, and feeds whoever she is told, with cardamom seeds and other minute things; flies at command and picks a wafer off the forehead of anyone, and draws water. But none of these feats will she exhibit unless she is hungry, and is shown the seed which is to be her reward.

She bites furiously and throws away her letter indignantly as soon as she has eaten her fill. She is constantly let loose, but always flies back to the hand. She looks, and is I believe, what is called a bastard canary. I am told that these birds build pendulous nests. She cost 12 *rupees*. She has a string around her body in order to tie her up. In short, she is very much like many human beings in her general character and disposition. Started by *dak* at 5 30. and arrived at Lahore in about nine hours;—32 miles; made good in all 195 miles.

May 9th. Lahore. This is the second time I have been at Lahore. The first time was just after the Battle of Guzerat. At Mean Mere, about 4 miles distant, is the cantonment where our camp was then pitched on a barren waste, now a flourishing cantonment. I regret to say that I was unable to take Mittie to the Shalimar Gardens but the great heat forbade the idea. She bears the journey well. Thermometer 86° at noon; a very cool comfortable day.

Found a lot of books at the bungalow sent there by the American mission: took up a *Life of Newton*, expecting to read something about "*the* Newton:" instead of which I found it was the life of some ignorant fanatic of the same name, much to my disgust. Turned over some leaves of the *Dairyman's Daughter*, weak fanatical nonsense, if it had been the rat catcher's daughter it would probably have been better worth reading.

The only book worth looking at among the whole was *The Pilgrims Progress*. The humbug of these missionaries is very sickening: Only fancy a man of ordinary common sense coming to the *dak* bungalow and having to choose between *Allein's Alarm* and *Baxter's Call* and a dozen others of the same stamp. How disgusting! If these gentlemen would send some really good books of a moral and interesting nature to these bungalows, some good might be done: but these fanatical effusions are not read: as a proof of which they all looked quite new, and had evidently not been used at all.

Left Lahore at 6 p.m. and after a beautifully cool night's journey, arrived at Goojeranwala (40 miles); made good in all 236 miles.

May 10. Goojeranwala. I well recollect being in this place during the last Sikh War, it was the residence of a *guru* or Sikh priest. All Runjeet Singh's family are buried here. I am now writing in the garden attached to his tomb: his ashes were placed under a raised slab after cremation, with his ten wives, who were burnt alive at his funeral. The centre one is over the ashes of Runjeet, the other ten are to his wives and family. Things are not now so prosperous as they were. The poor priest who watched over the tomb, and who got fifteen *rupees* a month has now only four: he came begging to me, I gave him a *rupee* and said:—

هرکرا خوابگاه اخر بدو مشتی خاکست .
کو چه حاجت که بر افلاک کشی ایوانرا

97

My thoughts wandered home, and I imagined a time might come when some traveller in our fallen country might meet with some poor bishop watching over the ruins of St. Paul's and begging of the barbarian stranger, while looking at the tomb of Queen Victoria. Certainly whoever conquers England will not keep up the pay of bishops.

Left Goojeranwala at 6 p.m. and passing through Wuzeerabad, arrived at Guzerat at 4.30 a.m. on the 11th.

The word "*Abad*" at the end of the names of places, means "the populated" from a Persian word "*abaden*" to populate; thus Wuzeerabad means "the populated by the *wuzeer*, or prime minister." The native name of Delhi is Shah Jehanabad.

May 11th. Guzerat. The *dak* bungalow here is an old public office appropriated by the new government, and by that turned into a staging house. It is not fit for European occupation, but it is only for a few hours that we stay here. Started at 9 a.m. for Bhimber where we arrived at 3.30 p.m. on the 12th. Thermometer 87° noon. Bearers killed a snake on the road.

May 12th. Bhimber. Found all my things ready here, so we only took a cup of coffee and started on our journey as soon as we could get our *coolies*.

A very bad road indeed, or rather I should say, no road at all. Had to walk a great part of the way, all up hill. The first range of hills is about one thousand feet in altitude. When we got to the top of the "Ada Tak," we got a splendid view of the Kashmir Punjal, and could plainly see the Pir Punjal Pass, which will take us six more marches to reach. Arrived at an old *serai* at 3 o'clock, having been nearly nine hours on the road. Mittie had a very beautiful hill pony called Crab, or she would have had to walk too, and as it was she had to dismount frequently.

4 p.m. Thermometer in the *serai* 94° Took out Pecksy to make her carry a letter, she was in a most vicious humour and flew out of the window after having pecked at me two or three times because I would not open my hand and give her some seed. I do not think she will come back again. Gave my six-barrelled pistol to a grass-cutter to carry. Out of curiosity he pulled the trigger just behind Mittie, fortunately no mischief was done. Dismounted and gave the fellow a good thrashing with my stick, I intend to cut him half a month's wages as well. Colonel Yule joined us at dinner and we had a very pleasant evening. Pecksy never came back. Several of our boxes left behind, the *coolies* having ran away. Mittie very tired, but I think improved in health. I have prepared a dandy for her tomorrow.

May 13th. Noshera or Newtown. Most probably built by one of the Delhi monarchs, is a very interesting place. Our encampment is in the very same garden that Shah Jehan used for the same purpose. A beautiful well constructed for him, with inscriptions in Persian, and a date, which I copied. These splendid wells or *baolies*, are to be found all over India. Noshera is celebrated for its fishing. Went out to try my luck, but the fish were very shy, and would take neither fly nor minnow, in the evening however I caught two *mahseer*, the largest weighed two pounds. Bathed, and found the water delicious. Mittie with a bad pain in her back, she played backgammon with Lt.-Col. Yule, He marched on in the morning, leaving us halted here. Slept in our tent. Thermometer 87°.

May 15th. Got up at 5 a.m. An abominable road, so that riding was quite out of the question, except occasionally for a few hundred yards. Poor Mittie had to go nearly all the way in her *dandy*. A very uninteresting country, low hills covered with Scotch firs; had trouble about *coolies*. *Kotwals* in Kashmir not celebrated for telling the truth. Arrived after about ten hours (counting halts) at Chungus Serai. The *serai* having fallen in, we took to our tents and just as we were coming to the end of our journey, we were overtaken by a storm. My pony fell down as I was crossing a stream, no harm done except wet feet; dismounted and waded across. Found our tents pitched on a green bank. Went out to fish but caught nothing. Bathed in the river, most cool and delicious.

May 16th. Marched at 5 am., and having gone five *coss*, breakfasted under a tree, after which, pursued journey to Rajsori, a large town with an old *serai*; very long and fatiguing march and the road infamous. Found Lt Col. Yule at the *serai*. Went out to fish but caught nothing, although I saw a great many fish; bathed in the river, water rather cooler, this is the last time that I shall be able to bathe as the snow water will be too cold at the next halting place.

May 17th. Started at 6 a.m., a rather long march but much better road and not hilly; rode a great part of the way; at a small village halfway we halted for breakfast and Mittie made a sketch. Arrived at Thana at 3 p.m., none of our baggage turned up, all the *coolies* supplied by the *rajah* ran away, after having put down our luggage on the road, our servants however managed to seize, with the aid of a *sepahi*, a number of villagers and we got all our things in very late. Col.Yule dined with us, Mittie very unwell. Sent to the *kotwal* and got a contrivance made up like this plate, which cost two *rupees*. I believe it is the same kind of thing that the native ladies use.

May 18th. Halted at Thana. Cut all my wine boxes in half, they being too heavy. Found the old wells mentioned by Vigne as having some sculptures; they are of Hindu construction. The sculptured figures have been mutilated, most probably by the Sikhs. Here many of the inhabitants came to us for medicine; their dirt, sickness, and general wretchedness is most deplorable. There is here also a fine old *serai* of Akbar, now in ruins, he must have had a very large retinue.

May 19th. Marched at 5 a. m., to ascend the Ruttun Pir on the road to Barumgulla. Mittie's throne answers very well, pony of great use occasionally. The Ruttun Pir is situated at the summit of a mountain range where an old *fakir* of great sanctity lies buried. The view is magnificent; halted and took breakfast; had to walk the whole of the descent, which is very precipitous, to Barumgulla. Thermometer 80° at 2 p.m. Mittie is much more at her ease in her new conveyance, but she is still very unwell. The sun is very hot, but our tent is a double one and a capital protection from the heat.

May 20th, 1857. Marched at 5 p.m. and crossed about thirty wooden bridges over mountain torrents; they are only temporary affairs as they are swept away by every flood after rain. Our ponies passed over them without any fear. The Sogdollager, however, did not like them at first, but he soon got used to them. I walked half this march and was carried in my dandy the last part Arrived at Poshiana, just under the Pir Punjal pass, which we are to ascend tomorrow. Saw much snow on this march in the clefts of the rocks and in the valleys; ate some of it, which put me in mind of England. A gentleman who was one march ahead of us, lost his horse at the first bridge we came to, it fell off the bridge and was drowned.

Thursday, May 21st. Marched at 5 a.m. and ascended the Pir Punjal, a most fatiguing ascent. I got a *dandy* for myself, and Mittie was carried all the way in her machine. We passed over several glaciers, some of them of immense size. We got no view from the top as the atmosphere was too thick. Reached our camping ground at Alliabad at 11.30. Met here a Mr. Harrington, an officer of the artillery, who informed me that there was great disaffection and even mutiny among the native regiments; that the colonel of the 15th Native Infantry had been murdered; and that all officers, without families, had been ordered to join their regiments immediately. Rain set in at 2.20 p.m. and it became very cold. Thermometer 56° in my tent. The enormous loads that the coolies carry over these fearful ascents appears almost a miracle.

Friday, May 22nd. Marched at 5 a.m. Descending to the valley, the most beautiful scenery I ever saw, all the clefts of the rocks filled with snow. My pony was a great help to me occasionally, but I was very tired upon reaching Hurripore: about 12 miles. Here is an old ruined *serai* of Akbar's. Pitched tent by a stream; beautiful country.

Saturday, May 23rd. Marched at 5 a.m. Met three officers of the 8th Regiment, going to join their regiment; they told me that, they had received an order so to do. If I should be ordered to rejoin my regiment, I am sure I do not know what I can do. Mittie quite knocked up with her journey and very ill indeed; directly we reach Kashmir must send for medical advice. I find it is only two marches to Islamabad and that I can get a boat there for Mittie. At 2.30 p.m. the *kotwall* brought me a notice, in English, signed by an officer of the name of Fleming, senior officer in Kashmir, ordering all officers (under instructions from the chief commissioner) to join their regiments. Determined not to go back by the road I came, as Mittie could not live through another 20 days' march such as we have passed.

Sunday, May 24th. Marched towards Islamabad, about 20 miles, breakfasting at Hohunpoora. Mittie suffering from fatigue. Met Captain Sanctuary;[1] who told me most astounding news of a general mutiny among the native troops. Halted and took boats for Kashmir, this being the shortest way of getting out of the country; a great disappointment for me, as I had intended to go to Islamabad and photograph Martund. What I am to do with Mittie, I really do not know. This row in India will come to nothing; there are no greater alarmists than the English. A few may be murdered, but as for a general insurrection, in my opinion, that is out of the question.

The great fault of the English is that they lose sight of the fact that the natives are *Easterns* and not Europeans. If they were to take as a model the great Akbar and rule accordingly, it would be well, for be it recollected than an *Eastern* does not change with the times; such as

---

1. He was killed shortly after.

he was in the time of Akbar, so is he now, his nature cannot be eradicated.

عاقبت گرگ زاده گرگ شود

گرچه با آدمی بزرگ شود

A regiment mutinied—what was done? It was disbanded. Now, what would Akbar have done under similar circumstances? Far more humane than the English, he would have blown away the ringleaders from the mouths of his cannon; a few scoundrels would have perished and the whole disturbance would have been suppressed. Now we shall have to massacre whole hecatombs of *sepahis* before we re-establish our rule. Verily, if God has given courage and honesty to our rulers, he has most certainly denied them sense and wisdom. Again, consider the country I am now travelling in, what would it be under English rule?

A governor general said that Goolab Singh was a veritable tyrant. Why he is the very man they want, and my firm opinion is that the inhabitants are much happier under his rule than they would be under that of the English. There are no highly paid Commissioners to absorb the fruits of a province here. Brutes the people are, and brutes they will remain, like the lower animals, to be ruled only with a stick. Nothing will they do for love and money, all they understand is *compulsion*. If it be tyranny to take coolies by force, then it is tyranny to plough with oxen, to ride horses, or to steal the milk of cows. Halted about nine miles from Islamabad.

May 25th. Floating down the river to Kashmir; most lovely weather; reached the city of Kashmir at 7 p.m.; slept in the boat. Met Captain and Mrs. Synge of the 52nd Regiment; he was on his way to Islamabad.

May 26th. Got into a house in the garden called "Hurree Singh," no glass in the windows. Goolab Singh sent me a present of two sheep and a quantity of provisions, also a few copies of the Lahore Chronicle, by which I learnt that all the reports that I had heard were true. A shocking massacre has taken place at Delhi, and a general mutinous spirit rules throughout among the native troops. Nothing will come of it, it is simply an *emeute*; there will be no revolution, Found no letters at Kashmir. Mittie still very unwell. Met Captain Thomas and his wife here; he having hurt his foot cannot proceed to join his regiment.

May 27th. Received a letter from Grant; all officers to join the regiment; answered it to Colonel Grant. Mittie seems rather better this morning. Went in a boat through the city. Goolab Singh sent me a loaf of bread, I am glad he did not expect me to eat it.

May 28th. Went out with Mittie in a boat, she seems better today; got three photographs of the city. In the evening went, by appointment, and met Goolab Singh on the river, he was in his State barge. Our interview lasted about an hour; he said that he would take charge of Mittie if I went to join my regiment. Saw the Lahore extra; quite a panic at Simla; much more fear than danger; however, affairs do look rather queer; determined to get to Umballa as soon as possible. Received a letter as senior officer at Kashmir. It was a notification that sick officers might remain m Kashmir at their option. The defection of the Goorkha regiments is the most serious news that I have heard as yet. Will the Pateala *rajah* remain true? I think he will. The disarming the Peshawur regiments looks fishy. I wish I was with my regiment.

May 29th. Went out in a boat and took photographs on the river; most delightful weather. Mittie keeps improving.

May 30th. Went out with Mittie and Dr. Smith on the lake as far as the celebrated Shalimar Gardens. Visited the Isle of Chunars: there is a picture of this island in Vigne, and I made a sketch of it as it appears now. There was a building on it, which Goolab Singh destroyed for the sake of the stone. The island is gradually becoming overgrown with small shrubs, but the two noble trees remain. I measured the largest *chunar* and found it to be 30 feet in girth. Copied an old inscription on a bridge on my way home.

Sunday 31st. Went to a review of the troops in Kashmir; the young *maharajah* was present, Goolab Singh had gone on a journey. For a native army it is the best I have seen, there were about 5000 men, of all arms, present The young *maharajah* was very civil indeed; he is a very handsome young man of about 26 years old, and his little son, a pretty boy of six, was also there. He behaved to me with the greatest dignity, as most native boys do, on similar occasions. At the *serai*, I met two Frenchmen, after the review: they belong to some Paris house, and are here for the shawl trade. They told me that a good Kashmir shawl cost £100 and that it would sell in Paris for about £140. Mittie much better, thank God.

Monday June 1st 1857. Went and photographed an old temple, a very remarkable ruin, about three miles from the city. In the evening went to the shawl merchant and inspected his shawls of which I was no judge; they seemed to me to be very dear.

June 2nd. Went out for a row with Mittie on the river. Tried fishing with a fly but none of these fishes seem to rise, I do not think that they ever find flies here.

June 3rd. An officer sent me the *Lahore Extra*, by which I see that the 9th Lancers are at Paneeput. Sent a letter immediately to Goolab Singh, requesting permission to go through the Jummoo pass. Heard of poor Anson's death; his Indian career has been short indeed

June 4th. The *maharajah* sent an excuse, in order to avoid granting permission to go through the pass by the valley of Jummoo. Sent to him and requested an interview. Weather inclined to be stormy. Rode through part of the town which was so wretched and filthy that I was glad to get out of it again.

June 5th. To add to my difficulties, the rains seem now to have set in. How I shall ever get through these mountain passes with Mittie, during the rains, I really cannot see. Vigne's book says that the rains do not cease in these hills until the middle of July. Goolab Singh met me on the river in his state barge. He was with his son the future King of Kashmir. After a long talk, he allowed me to leave the valley by the Jummoo Pass.

June 6th. Still raining. At 12.30 p.m. the rain ceased, and as the sun came out I sent to the *maharajah* for a *"perwanah"* or written permission, to go through the pass. In the evening rain came on again; no marching possible.

Sunday 7th. Took a few photographs which, owing to the rainy state of the atmosphere, came out badly. Saw a *Lahore Extra*,—the plains in a very disturbed state. Massacre of Europeans reported at Hissa and Hansi Went to the *maharajah's* parade. He was very civil to me and seated me between himself and the prince, his son. Goolab seemed very fond of his little grandson. I took notice that the boy had charms suspended from his neck, when the *maharajah* remarked that he once had a charm which rendered him bulletproof. A *fakir*, or holy-man, sat on the body of a man killed in battle, and pulling out his teeth he said certain prayers over some peas, while he filed the dead man's teeth. Any one possessing one of these peas was bullet-proof. The *maharajah* assured me that he had himself proved the fact in his own person, and that he had seen a bullet strike him and fall dead on the ground without doing him any injury. The young prince observing a kind of incredulous smile on my countenance perhaps, said "Father, it is of no use speaking of these things to Europeans, who are all unbelievers!" I have got my "*perwanah*" and intend to start tomorrow.

June 8th. Rain! rain! rain! still obliged to halt; no moving in this weather. The little grandson of the *maharajah* came to my bungalow to see Dr. Smith, who happened to be with me The little fellow came upstairs, and I gave him an English knife with which he appeared highly delighted. Went out in the boat for fresh air. Thermometer 58° which is the ordinary temperature during the rains.

Tuesday, 9th June. Went out to the shawl merchant and inspected his shawls; cloudy and rainy day; start tomorrow if fine.

June 10th. Still raining. Mittie unwell, could not go out at all to day. No news; have a suspicion that our letters have been detained.

June 11th. This morning the sun broke through the clouds and, as the Punjals were quite visible, I ordered our baggage into the boats and set out for Islamabad, at 11.16 a.m. Received a letter from Johnny Delamain; I think they must have stormed Delhi before this. Saw a snake in the water, five feet long, killed it, but it was not of a poisonous nature. A beautiful day; slept in the boat.

June 12th. Floating down the river; a most lovely day, I hope it may continue. At five o'clock, the rascally boatmen said that they could not get nearer to Islamabad as there was no water. I felt convinced that they lied, but they kept poling about in the *nullahs* for full three hours, although they knew the proper channel very well; gave up in despair at about seven o'clock and sent the *sepahi* for *coolies* who came the next morning. I slept in the boat and started on foot on the road to Islamabad. I had not got a mile when I discovered the right channel Complained to the *kotwal*, who ordered all the boatmen to prison; never did fellows better deserve it. I had been very kind to them, so of course they thought I was a muff; and perhaps they were right

Oignez vilain il vous poindra
Poignez vilain il vous oindra.

What a vile thing uneducated human nature is, or is capable of being made.

Saturday, 13th June. Took up our residence in a very fine new summer house, also, for a wonder, very clean. It was built by Goolab Singh for the English *sahibs*; wonderful fishponds with tame fish in them. Sulphur spring within a hundred yards; bathed in it and felt much refreshed after my dip. Mittie very ill in the morning, but now she has got into a comfortable quarter she feels better.

Sunday, 14th. This being Sunday, Mittie worked the whole morning, and only found out that it was Sunday at five o'clock; Went out and photographed Martund Temple, of all buildings the most mysterious, can get no information about it. The natives say that it was built by the "Pandus," who were the "Pandus"? When people talk about these mythical personages, I always put them into the category of the "humbugs." It is an amusement here to throw a piece of bread into the sacred tank and see the fish scramble for it. These fish have been protected for some hundred years, and yet there are none above one pound and a half in weight. The *pundit* told me that a *sug-i-ab*, (otter) came and carried off the larger ones.

June 15th. Sky became overcast, I feel very much afraid that it is coming on to rain. I sincerely hope that our journey will not be put off tomorrow. Went out and visited a house where part of a shawl is being made; now, I do not wonder that a good shawl costs £100. The *baradurree* or summer house, where I am now writing in, has been built lately by Goolab Singh for the English *sahibs*; it is defaced with charcoal scribblings in Sanscrit, Persian and English. Among other inscriptions some traveller has written from Moore's poem:—

Oh! who has not heard of the vale of Cashmere?
With its roses, the brightest the earth ever gave,
Its temples, its grottoes, and fountains as dear
As the love lighted eyes that hang over the wave.

Which has been parodied by some prosaic snob, as follows—

Oh! who has not owned half a nose in Cashmere?
But has felt a conviction deep, solemn and grave,
That the people's objection to wash is as clear
As the very great horror they have of a shave.

This last effusion seems to have disturbed the equanimity of some not very literate. Scotchman, who has added his reply thus—

Fool! if you were placed in their position yoursel (sic).

You, Mr. Critic, would have had just as great a horror to shave,
Perhaps then another your hist'ry (sic) could so tell.
And above your cenotaph write your' (sic) as great knave.

That these people live in a great state of filth is quite true, but the
English in London were quite as bad some two hundred years ago, if
we are to believe some of our chroniclers. We have become civilized,
indeed, in Europe, but at what cost? Some German writer said that
civilization means *"verkränkelung"* and *"verschlechterung,"* and it certainly has been at the expense of our physical powers, and deterioration
of our bodies, and moreover has fostered vices as well, which would
shock even these dirty people. Let any person who feels inclined to be
satirical like one of the writers of the above doggerel verses, let him
only read "Macaulay."

I will be bound to say that this place is not a bit more offensive
than was St. James' Square in London some 200 years ago. Again, Lord
Dalhousie says that Goolab Singh is a veritable tyrant. Perhaps he may
be so in a certain way, but his tyranny is but a fleabite to the tyranny,
the horrible tyranny, which would accrue from the sudden introduc-
tion of our boasted civilization into this country with its simple inhabitants. Only let us fancy such a notice as the following, which is
very common in England—

NOTICE

No person is permitted to bathe between the hours of 8 a.m.
and 9 p.m. by order of the police.

"Plus les moeurs sont corrompues, plus les manières sont sévères" observed a very clever Frenchman. And this prohibition, in a land as
yet uncorrupted by our civilization, would be far more irksome than
many a tyrannical act of the native ruler. We are apt to become very
virtuous all of a sudden in Europe, and especially in England, directly
we have discarded some odious custom, and to be very horror-struck
at what appears odious to us in other nations. In my lifetime I have
known of, and might possibly have witnessed the horrible spectacle
of a young girl stripped to the waist and flogged publicly through one
of our large towns in the presence of the mayor, with a noble lord
looking on, and taking it as a matter of course; indeed that same noble
lord has entered the circumstance in his journal which I believe has
been published. He remarks after having stated the fact, that she was
contumacious and "damned the mayor's eyes." I feel confident that

such an abomination was never perpetrated by the "veritable tyrant" of Lord Dalhousie.

Went and bathed in the sulphur spring; how I wish I could carry it away with me. Bought a magnificent pair of horns of the *Bara Singha*, the gigantic stag of the Himalayas. *Bara singha* means twelve horns. I shall try and bring them home with me.

June 16th, 1857. Marched to Shahabad, about 12 miles. A light shower of rain on the road which lay through rice fields. Asked one of my *coolies* how old he was and he replied, forty; but the poor old fellow must have been at least sixty five. He was nearly beyond a load, but he carried a good weight notwithstanding, and was not far behind the rest

June 17th. Marched at 5 a.m. and halted at Vernag, a sacred spring. I had heard and read of this place before, but as everybody here is ignorant, and as the spirit of lying is very strong, a traveller must be cautious in accepting all the information that is tendered him. Fortunately, I found an old slab of marble which gave me all the information that I required. This splendid spring must have existed for thousands of years; coeval with the formation of the Himalayas. Shah Jehan constructed the octagonal basin into which it flows. Of course the natives and the priests told me that it was bottomless, but I, being naturally of an unbelieving disposition, tied a pistol bullet to a piece of twine and found it to be just sixty feet deep. The inscription, which was beautifully cut on a slab of black marble, had been thrown down and was broken into three pieces.

After having breakfasted, ascended the Bunnihal Punjal, and arrived at Dehigol—a very fatiguing march of ten hours. Here nearly all the villagers came to me for medicine. I gave them a lot of jalap and hope it agreed with them. Although the headman or *kardar* told me that he could give me any amount of *coolies*, I observed that I had the same number the next day.

Thursday 18th. A very fatiguing march of fourteen miles, up and down hill the whole way. I walked twelve miles as the *coolies* let me fall twice when I tried the dandy, besides which the cloth of the dandy being rotten, split right across. Very tired indeed on arriving at our halting place, Ballunder. Here twenty eight of our *coolies* put down their loads and ran away, without waiting to be paid. The *maharajah's* "*perwanah*" seems useless, the *sepahi* could not get me a single one, so I am forced to halt while he goes to the next station to try and get a

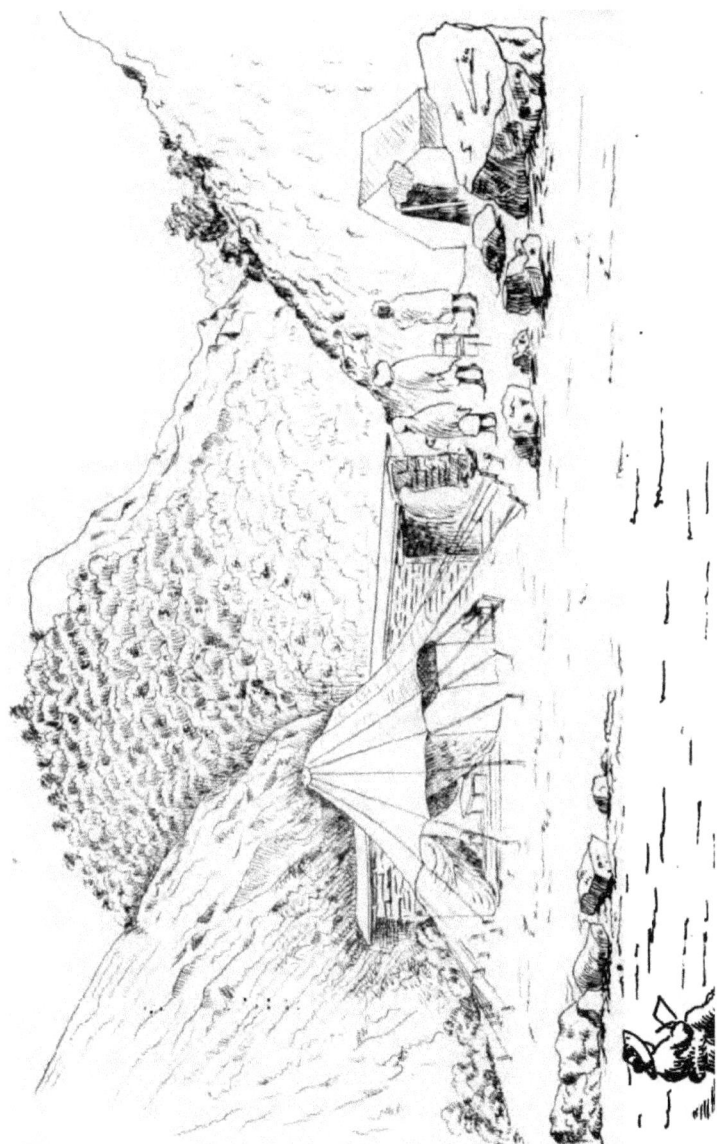

BALLUNDER

fresh lot. I begin to have doubts whether I shall be able to move on; these mountain roads are terrible, and destroy all pleasure.

7.30 p.m. Our remaining twelve *coolies* bolted.

June 19th. Halted at Ballunder under a shady walnut tree. Thermometer in tent 90° at 11 a.m. Sent the *sepahi* on twenty miles ahead to Nasumon to try and get forty *coolies*. Wrote a letter in such Persian as I could command to the *kardar* at Dehigol, informing him that my people were without provisions, I hope he will understand it. Sent the letter by a party of *sepahis* who were marching to Sirinugger.

June 20th. A forced halt. Can neither get *coolies* nor supplies. I heartily wish I was well out of this accursed country; the people are like wild beasts. My *shikari* returned, he had been to Nasumon; the *sepahi* has not turned up; no *coolies*; my *shikari* brought a fowl and some rice.

Sunday 21st. The third day of our imprisonment—no news, no *coolies*. These wretches will neither give nor sell anything; milk is in abundance but not a drop will they part with. I hope Goolab Singh will grind them well, "*optat ephippium bos piger.*" They are only fit for the treatment of beasts of burden, not one amiable quality have they got.

What is uneducated man? a beast. And what, indeed. are many educated men who boast of reason? Well, said Goethe—

Er nennt's Vernunft, nur braucht's allein
Nur thierisher als jedes Thier zu seyn.

And Lord Byron has written with regard to men—

Who knows thee well will quit thee with disgust,
Degraded mass of animated dust.

A troop of fifty or a hundred monkeys have just come down the hillside to feed on a wild apricot tree. How much happier they are than men. With what ease they climb up the steep mountain's side and how miserably hard to get our weary limbs up a rising ground. I really wish I was—not a monkey, for that I am partly already—but an eagle! what delight to soar over these stupendous mountains without any effort, and to be able to seek any temperature, and never to know a pain or an ache!

God has certainly been more bountiful to these. What advantage is it to be able to conceive a higher state of happiness, without the power of attaining it? A future state—What know we of a future state? Alas! all is conjecture and doubt, all thought on the subject unprofitable and useless. Well! I must bear the burden, a wretched *coolie*, in a most wretched world.

Sepahi has just come in, he says he cannot get a single *coolie*.

Monday, 22nd June, 1857. A poor post office boy, to whom I had given some medicine, offered to get me some *coolies*, and at 10.30 a.m. he actually brought me a gang. Started immediately, intending to make the march partly today and the remainder the next morning. There is an insufficient number of *coolies*; was obliged to leave most of our baggage behind. A short but most fatiguing march to a small village. Had to walk nearly the whole way. Dined, and feeling very ill went to bed; had an attack of fever, took the proper remedies and felt better in the morning.

Tuesday 23rd. Got up and prepared to march, but all of a sudden my *coolies* put down their loads and climbed up the hillside, where they sat down at about the height of five hundred feet and grinned at my people just like so many monkeys. These unaccountable varieties of the Simiamidae, after half a march bolted, and left me helpless, never even asking for any pay for their services. When shall I ever get out of these difficulties?

Went and saw a sick man whom the women were howling over, thinking that he was dying. He appeared to be suffering from a fit of cholera; gave him five grains of calomel and a grain of morphia; it appears to have done him good, for the howling has now ceased. Operated on a girl for what appeared to me a new disease; it is the third case that I have been asked to look at. The two first cases were *coolies*, and the disease was situated on the back of the hand. The girl was about fourteen, and she had it on the shoulder blade. The disease looked like the blister of a scald, the blister being full of a watery fluid. On clearing off the skin of the blister with a knife, it is found to adhere in the centre. It appears to be of a malignant nature, for on cutting into it the knife grates. It could not be extirpated except by a very long operation, and would be very painful. I merely made one cut into it to ascertain its nature, and of course did no good.

Wednesday, 24th. A few *coolies* came, so I started, leaving eleven loads on the ground. Although I constantly left a large portion of my effects behind without any guard none of the villagers ever stole

111

anything, and when I sent back to recover it, it was always untouched in the spot where it was left. This was not from any horror of theft on the part of the natives, but from fear of consequences. All uphill, a very stiff ascent, which I felt severely after the long downhill march to the river side. "Nasumon," or as it is now called "Rain." Here the *ayah* I left behind with, the baggage joined us. One of my servants was bleeding having been stoned by these villains.

25th. Half our baggage being still behind, we were obliged to halt and send back for it. Heat dreadfully oppressive, Ther. 92°. There is a large *baradurree* here, built for the use of the *maharajah* when he visits Jummoo. A *sepahi* brought me a letter from Colonel Grant, dated June 6th. Alipore (near Delhi). The troops were then preparing to take Delhi. I am like a hunter stuck in a bog, seeing the hounds going gallantly. However, there is no help, I can only crawl along.

Friday 26th. Marched at 4 a.m. Rain came on at 5 and continued till 2 o'clock. Spent the day in crossing the Chenab by a swing bridge, a most tedious affair, and to some it would be a source of great terror, but Mittie did not seem to mind it at all, and I, having been a sailor, thought nothing of it; and after all, there is positively no danger. The drawing on the opposite page will explain. Found a *baradurree* on the opposite side of the river at Govindpore; wet, muggy, and miserable; the river is about two hundred yards wide at this point, and it took a quarter of an hour to pull one load over.

Saturday 27th. Marched with the same coolies at 5 a.m. A steep and dangerous road; saw two wild goats; passed by a village called Muta-pani close to which was a very remarkable sculptured Well, and a curious "*deotar*" or Hindu temple, also sculptured with a male and female idol; the faces of both figures were smeared with ghee. The whole structure was built of hill fir or "*deodar*." Arrived at Butot and pitched the tent on a beautiful, cool spot covered with verdure and in the vicinity of some very fine cedars.

Monday 29th. Our baggage not having arrived, halted in the hopes that it would come up, but was disappointed. An old Hindu monument having been displaced from its position and thrown down, probably by the Musselmans in their bigoted zeal in the time of Akbar, I determined to replace it; and after two hours work I at length succeeded,' much to the delight of my Hindu followers. I rigged a *derrick* with two of my *palki* poles, and some thirty men clapping on, it slowly rose to

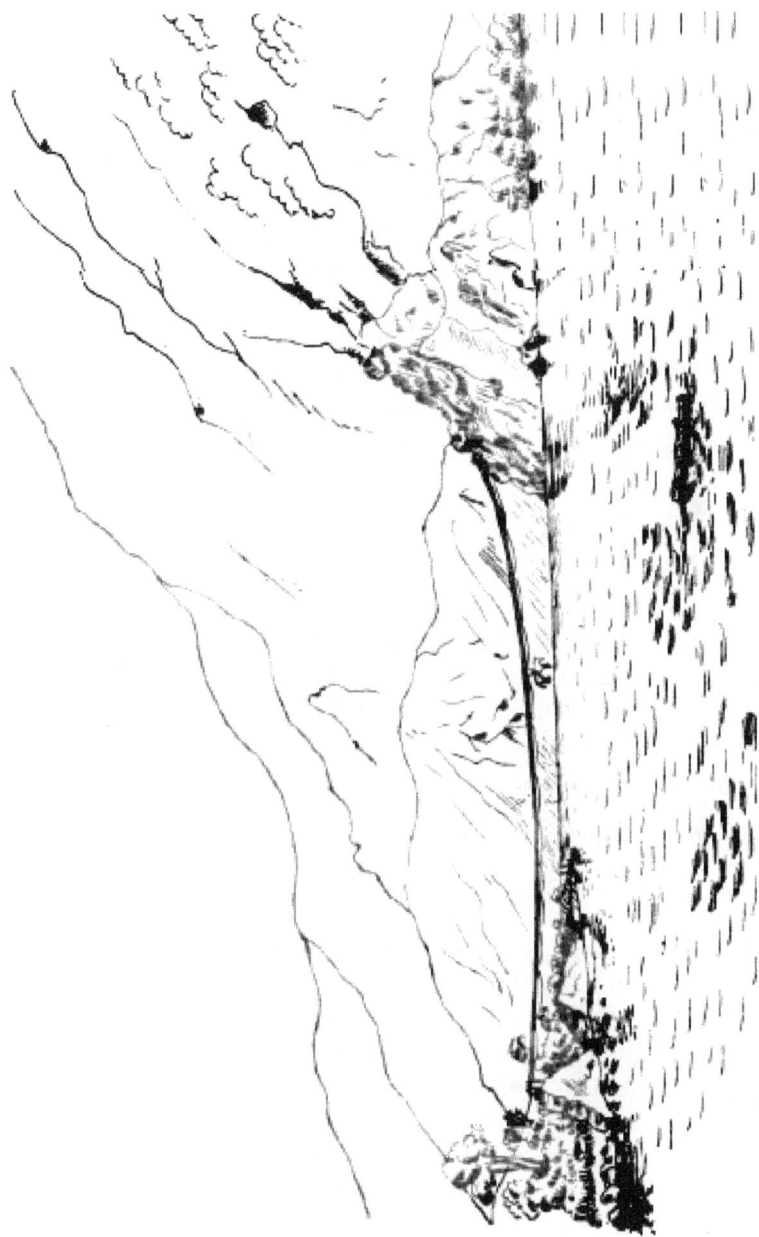

MY WIFE'S HORSE BEING PULLED OVER THE RIVER BY A WIRE BRIDGE.

its original basement. It appears to be of great antiquity, and there is the sculptured figure of some divinity on the second division.

Performed a very successful operation on a boy; he came to me for advice. He had a kind of tumour on his face which disfigured him greatly; he said that he had had it for fourteen years, and he was otherwise very good-looking. I thought that it was a wen, but he was so very pressing that I stuck a large abscess lancet into it, when an immense quantity of indurated pus escaped, and the tumour of course collapsed. The boy was intensely delighted, but I do not feel sure that the sac will not again fill up. A woman now came for advice. She had lost the two first joints of her fingers on both hands: the disease seemed to be eating them away. I told her that it was caused by her dirt, and advised soap and water. My baggage not having come up the next morning I got *coolies* and made a short march of eight miles to Chinini The first two miles were up-hill; from the highest point I got a view of the plains. Chinini a considerable town.

30th June. At Chinini obtained a *dhooly* from the *kardar*, who lent it to me as far as Ramnugger. Left my *mehter* to bring on my baggage which was left behind at Govindpore.

Wednesday, 1st July, 1857. Marched at half past 5 a.m. A long and fatiguing march in the sun. Arrived at Buttee, a very nice halting place near a sculptured Well; no town or village near; had much trouble about coolies. The *makuddam* or *jemadar*, a most intense scoundrel. Got a sheep; stores running short; all claret expended

2nd July. Marched at 5.30, and descended into the plains. A short march to Odempore, where we encamped under a fine *peepul* tree.

Friday, 3rd July. Here I may say ends my hill journal, as I am now in the plains. We marched at 4.30 and made the longest march in the midst of a burning sun, thirteen hours. Passed the fort of Jhaghan and town of the same name, in which were a troop of tame monkeys, and which the Sogdollager chased with great eagerness. From Odempore to Jhaghan the road is level, after which there is a succession of ascents and descents to Ramnugger, where we arrived at 5.30 p.m. Ramnugger is a considerable place with a fine fort built by Incheyt Singh. There is also a magnificent palace built by the same *rajah*; he just saw it completed, and went into his splendid hall of mirrors for one day only, as he was then called away to Delhi where he was killed. Took up our quarters in a most splendid *baradurree*. The climate of Ramnugger is very hot and disagreeable.

4th July. Halted at Rumnugger; much rain fell. Sent the *wuzeer* a present of a pound of gunpowder. He called on me for advice, saying that one of his legs was cold and without feeling; examined him and gave him some compound iodine ointment to rub it with. Tried to explain to him the electric telegraph. When I had done he said that he understood it perfectly—the letter was tied to the wire and then blown along by lightning. Rain cleared off.

5th July. Marched at 3 a.m. An ascent of about three miles and then downhill. Rain at times and one thunderstorm. Thirteen hours on the road and all our things behind. At 8 p.m. a few *coolies* and my small tent came up; pitched it just as rain came on and wetted everything, (nothing to eat since breakfast). *Khidmutgar* and eatables came in at 11, dined at midnight. Was very angry with my servants, but it is of no use, niggers will not march in the rain. Discharged the *sepahi* as he did more harm than good.

6th July. Marched again notwithstanding the fatigue of the previous day, another long march, but no hills, and arrived at Mahinpore at 3 p.m., encamped by a Hindu temple. Trees covered with flying foxes. Shot a few to get specimens; sent for a *chamar* to skin one but he spoilt them all. Passed a comfortable night.

7th July. Marched at 5 a.m. for Basuli, about ten miles, a short march, arrived at noon. This is the last march in Goolab Singh's dominions. Got some buffalo skins and went with Mittie floating on the river, These skins are inflated and a charpoy, or bedstead, is placed on a couple of them, and away you go paddled by natives.

8th July. Marched at 3 a.m. Had to cross the river in a boat; furious thunder storm came on, and we all got wet through, and the poor Sogdollager was swept away by the force of the stream. He landed about half a mile down the river, unfortunately on the wrong side; sent over a nigger who brought him over on a skin. Halted at noon at a small bungalow, half way between Basuti and Noorpoor. Here *coolies* refused to go further, so I was obliged to send for a fresh lot Reached Noorpoor at 10 p.m. In the night a furious storm broke over us, and the rain penetrating the roof of our tent, wetted us through.

9th July. Got up at 4 a.m. and called on Captain Douglas and Major Wilkie. Learnt that Delhi still held out, and also that my wife's brother,

INFLATED   SKIN.

MITTIE ON THE RIVER ON A CHARPOI
LAID ON INFLATED SKINS.

poor Johnny Delamain, had been killed—very sad news indeed. Laid a *dak* and sent Mittie off to Dharumsala, to the Arnold's—she left me at 5 o'clock. Dined with Major Wilkie, who is here recruiting Sikhs and Punjabis If all our officers were of his stamp, we should hear of no revolts; he understands the native character, and his men love him. Laid my *dak* for Jullunder.

10th July. Started by *dak* in a *dhooly* lent me by Major Wilkie; very bad bearers indeed, did not reach Jullunder till 2 p.m. the next day.

11th July. At Jullunder, Found that I could not get the mail cart to Umballa till 8 o'clock the next morning. Was received and hospitably entertained by Brigade Major Holmes. Heard news that the *sepahis* at Jhelum and Sealcote had mutinied, and killed and wounded some of their officers. Very lucky thing for me and my wife that we did not go back by Sealcote as we had at first intended.

12th July. Started by mail cart and arrived at Umballa at 4 p.m.; furious rain during the journey, which consequently was cold. Saw the fort at Phillor; it was being repaired, and guns were to be mounted.

13th July. Waiting for the cart which starts at 4 p.m. At 4.30 p.m. started, the road was very bad, and when I got to Kurnal I was so knocked up that I got out of the cart and went into the *dak* bungalow, after I had learnt that all was quiet in camp before Delhi.

14th July. At Kurnal. The post master is to send a cart at 9 this evening to take me and another officer on to Delhi A telegraphic message has just arrived; nothing stirring in Camp. Agra mutineers are said to be marching on Delhi. Went to the churchyard and visited the graves of General Anson and Brigadier Hallifax. Sketched the two graves.

15th July. Left Kurnal at 9 p.m. of the 14th and arrived at Allipore at 8 o'clock the next morning.

Delhi

16th July. Got up behind a camel *sowar* and arrived safe in camp at 10 a.m., where I found all quiet. Colonel Grant being brigadier, the command of the 9th Lancers devolved on me. Had a visit from William Ford, whose life was preserved in a wonderful manner, when beset on all sides by the mutineers. Found out the man who had buried poor Johnny Delamain, who was killed while gallantly leading his men, when General Barnard attacked the position of the mutineers

GENERAL ANSON'S GRAVE

BRIGADIER HALLIFAX'S GRAVE

before Delhi

17th July. Went out and disinterred the body of poor Johnny, who had been buried in a shallow hole on the spot where he fell. Placed the remains in a cart and took them to the churchyard; hunted up the chaplain, and the service for the dead was performed at 10.30 by the light of my lamp, and the grave closed on as gallant a fellow as ever fell in battle. God rest him. Hot, dull, and disagreeable day: nothing stirring in camp.

18th July. Alarm sounded in the morning at about 9 a.m. The enemy attacked as usual by the Subza-Mundi. Batteries firing all day. Cavalry saddled up ready to turn out. This will come to nothing today. Jones, of the engineers, severely wounded by shell.

19th July. Field-officer of the day. Went a night expedition with the picket to try and recover some carts: reached the spot where they had been, but found that the enemy had removed all the serviceable ones.

20th July. Enemy attacked; beaten back as usual; cavalry turned out but not employed. Thermometer 100° in tents. Two officers killed.

21st July. Men ordered to get their breakfasts early, as a grand attack is threatened; all turned out to be a false alarm.

22nd July. Camp quiet. Rain fell.

23rd July. July. Enemy attacked from the Kashmir Gate, were repulsed and driven back into the city in a few hours; about twenty men killed and wounded; four officers.

24th July. Rain; camp quiet. Captain French joined the regiment.

25th July. Heavy rain all day; nothing stirring.

26th July. Field-officer of the day. Rained till 1.30, when it cleared up. Enemy employed repairing batteries injured by our fire.

27th July. Rain! rain! rain! Nothing stirring.

28th July. Received news that relief is marching up under Sir Patrick Grant from Cawnpore, where he had defeated the Oude rebels.

29th July. July. Nothing stirring.

30th July. Rain, rain, all dreary. Occupied in conjugating the verb 'Je m'ennuie'.

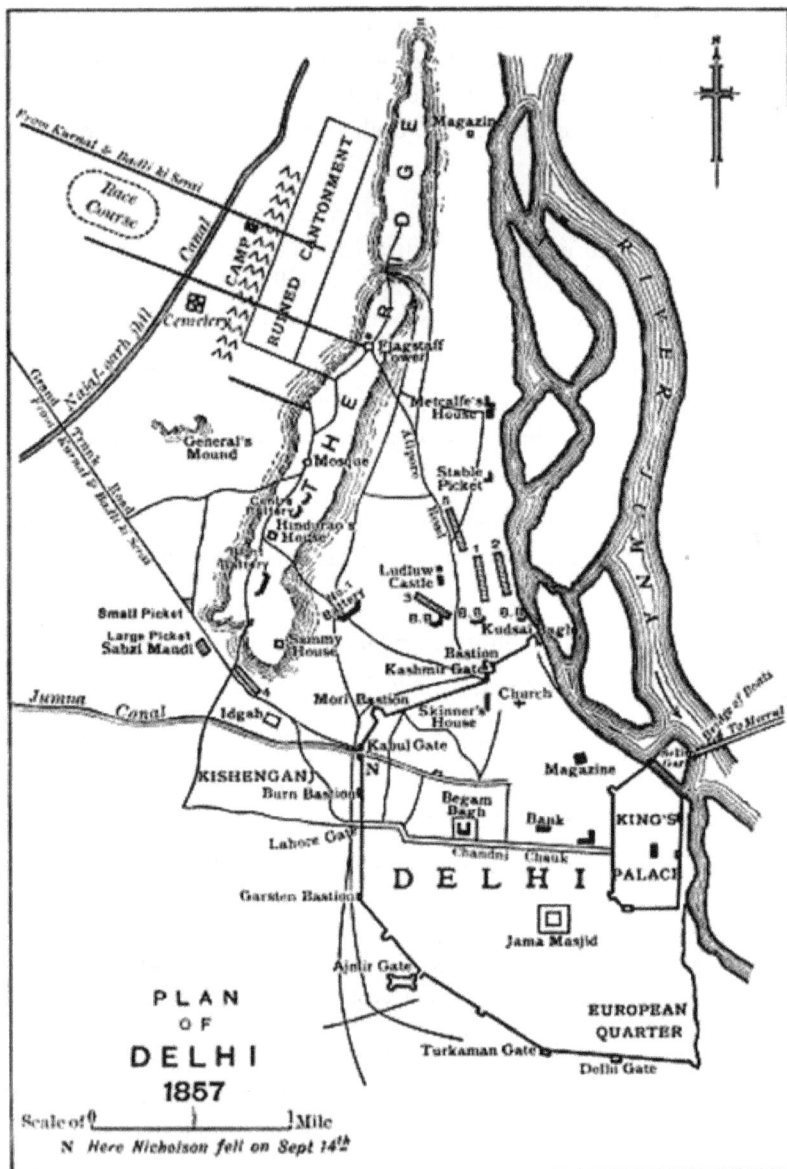

PLAN
OF
DELHI
1857

Scale of 0 _____ 1 Mile

N Here Nicholson fell on Sept 14th

31st July. Alarm sounded. At 11 the camp turned out, but nothing came of it. Furious and continued rain. Sent a squadron out to Alipore to convoy stores.

1st August, 1857. Field officer of the day; constant rain; this is the *"Musselman Eed."* Enemy fired a grand salute. Convoy arrived safe in camp. Enemy attacked our right and advanced posts; heavy firing all night; enemy beaten back with great loss by 10 the next morning. Lost Travers of the irregulars, and about twenty killed and wounded.

2nd. Camp quiet.

3rd. Rain, camp quiet.

4th. Received a letter in camp from Havelock, he is settling them off at Lucknow, before he marches on Delhi. News arrived in camp that Sir H. Lawrence had been killed.

5th. Nothing extraordinary, desultory firing.

6th. Enemy employed in establishing a battery outside the city; firing as usual.

7th. Enemy established a battery outside the walls. They fired rockets and made very good practice, far better than ours. Native *cossids* say that Sir H. Lawrence is alive. Moveable Column with 52nd Regiment expected in camp by the 11th or 12th, in all 1,200 Europeans. With this reinforcement we ought to be soon in the city—*nous verrons.*

8th. Fine weather. The enemy continue to tease the pickets with musketry and round shot.

9th. Cloudy but fine; nothing new. Ordered at 4 p.m. to shift our camp to the rear, in order to make room for the column about to arrive.

From the 9th to the 18th. Column arrived; this gives us an increase of force of some 1,200 Europeans, and some good native regiments. Everything dull and inactive, very few shots exchanged between the city and our batteries. *Je m'enmuie, Je m'ennuie.* On the 17th notification received that I had been appointed to the 2nd Dragoon Guards. Gave up the command of the 9th Lancers and, as my new regiment has not yet arrived in India, I am a gentleman at large. I cannot be attached to the 9th Lancers because it is now under the command of a junior officer. Went to General Wilson and explained my position to him, when he kindly offered to place me on his staff, and attached me to the 9th Lancers in order that I might receive pay.

19th. Fine weather with slight rain at times; nothing new.

20th. Cloudy, muggy, and unhealthy weather; nothing new.

21st. Received news that the 10th Light Cavalry had mutinied and had cut up some of our gunners. Has madness seized and got possession of our authorities? What! leave them their horses and arms after what has happened? verily, madness has indeed taken possession of our authorities.

22nd to the 26th. A fine breeze sprung up; unhealthy weather; sick increasing. 3,000 men went out under Nicholson to seize some guns about eighteen miles from camp. The enemy bolted after a few rounds, leaving thirteen guns which Nicholson brought in.

26th to 31st. Enemy sent in a proposition to surrender the city if their lives were guaranteed—very like a whale. No news. *Je m'ennuie.*

1st September. Field officer of the day, I hope for the last time. Shell came into stables and knocked over nine men and one horse—8 inch shrapnel.

4th. Heavy Artillery arrived in camp. When shall we make use of it?

5th to 12th September. Employed making batteries and getting guns into position. Opened fire on the city, which at once silenced the opposing batteries. Nothing now remains but the assault.

Here is a sketch of Johnny Delamain's tomb next to that of General Barnard.

13th September. There will be no assault today, batteries still continue their fire.

14th. Storming of Delhi. City assaulted; several of the gates occupied; continued fighting in the streets until the 20th, when the enemy finally evacuated the city.

21st. Blew open the gates of the palace and took possession of Selim Gurh, and occupied the Jumma Musjeed.

22nd. Took the king prisoner; he was in the tomb of Humayon.

23rd. Took the three *sdhahzadehs,* or king's sons, prisoners. Hodson shot them all, immediately, without any ceremony.

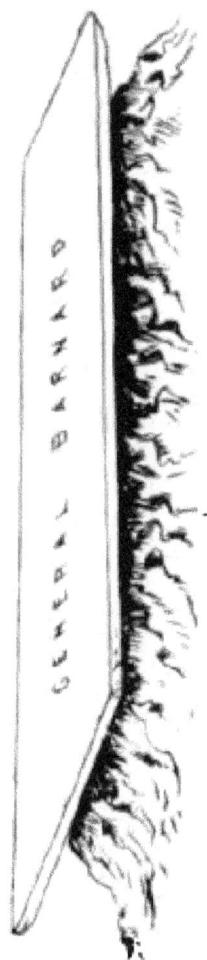

GENERAL BARNARD

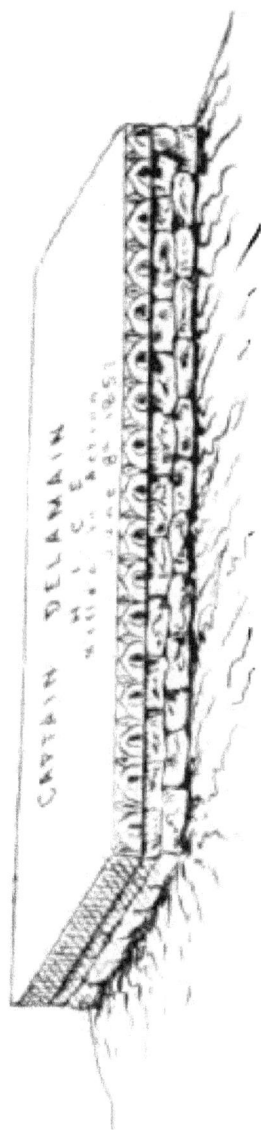

CAPTAIN DELAMAIN
H. I. C. RAILWAY
MILE 149 8 1851

Pursuing column formed, Lt. Col. Greathead in command, Major Ouvry having the command of the cavalry.

Here ends my journal of the Siege of Delhi.

Letters Continued

Camp before Delhi,
July 16th, 1857.

My Dear Jack,

Of course you will have heard the desperate news from India. All your letters to me have been cut off coming upcountry by the rebels, so that I know nothing of what has occurred at home since the date of your last letter of April 16th.

You will see a great deal about our besieging Delhi, but the truth is this, we are encamped under the walls of Delhi, 4,900 Europeans and about 2,000 Sikhs, Goorkhas, and other irregulars, holding ourselves on the defensive. The army has fought twenty three times; 15,000 *sepahis*, mutineers of the Bengal army are in the town and fort; they make frequent sallies in force and we have 1,000 wounded in camp. We have not had much fighting in the 9th Lancers. Colonel Tule has been killed.

Poor Johnny Delamain is gone from us, he was killed. This is his sad history. He came into our camp as a volunteer and was appointed to the 75th Regiment. When General Barnard advanced from Umballa to attack the mutineers, they made a desperate stand at a small fort about three miles from Delhi, and when the 75th advanced, Johnny, who as usual was in front, was shot dead, having been pierced by two balls. Alas! my poor brother Johnny.[1] It seems only the other day that I picked him up on the bloody field of Chilianwala with his arm cut off by a grapeshot. His body was hastily thrown into a grave where he fell, together with that of a bandsman. I will endeavour to find the spot and disinter the body and give it Christian burial.

These fellows fight better for themselves than they did for us.

---

1. He was my wife's brother.

We are familiar with all kinds of horrors, hanging and killing; quarter is neither given nor received. I now command the 9th Lancers, Colonel Grant being Brigadier. Death has cut off all our superior officers; Anson, Mowat, Barnard, all sunk under disease occasioned by hardship and heat. I, myself, am only forty four and feel that I am not what I was in the last Sikh war. No man over fifty has any right to serve in the field in India. Mark my words. Sir Patrick Grant will not do. Anson was of no use; Barnard *ditto*; Bead is good but is now done up; Wilson is good, he has been put over the heads of three or four others who are good for nothing. Chamberlain, a very young officer, is very good and has been appointed General, but alas! the day before yesterday he was struck by a musket ball, and we are deprived of his services. There is a moveable column to keep the Punjab in order. The heat is fearful and our privations are great. We have Crimean officers here and they say that it was nothing to this. I will write when anything occurs of importance, if I am not knocked over, and if I am you will see it in the *Gazette*.

Pandemonium before Delhi,
July 20th, 1857.

My Dear Jack,

He who ever gets well out of this hell will be a wonderfully strong constitutioned man. We are still under the walls of Delhi; we have had twenty-four affairs and each time lost from sixty to two hundred men. The 60th Rifles up to this time have lost 40 *per cent*, of their strength.

As to these *sepahis* forcing our camp that is all nonsense, our men are like lions and these cowardly murderers of women and children although they are 15,000 strong and we under 4,000, no more dare come near us than a hare dare approach a hound

All native towns where there are garrisons have a cantonment which is generally situated about three miles from the city. Delhi is a large city fortified by a wall and ditch. The glacis is very high so that to batter with effect it would be necessary to blow up part of the glacis in order to breach the wall at their foot.

We have only a second class siege train, but we have a twenty-four pounder which was taken from the enemy at the time poor Johnny fell. There is however no shot to fit it, except what

126

we pick up after they have been fired at us from the city. The enemy, on the contrary, are well provided both with guns and ammunition. They have our whole arsenal at their disposal which is full of every kind of missile, and they fire very well.

Yesterday, I was field officer of the day, and the ten-inch shells rained about the bomb-proof tower in which I was stationed day and night. I was visiting my posts in the evening when a shell fell and burst close to the head of my horse which was held outside by a groom while I was talking to the officer inside the bomb-proof. The *sais* dropped the bridle and ran away and the horse galloped along the ridge in front of the camp, running the gauntlet of the whole fire from the walls. No one was hurt although the shell burst at the right time.

July 21st. We were attacked again yesterday evening, losing two officers and a few men.

The flies are a perfect pest. All things considered I am in very fair health, and not low spirited, although the prospect of two months of this work and weather, is anything but pleasant.

Headquarters, King's palace, Delhi,
September 24th, 1857.

My Dear Jack,

I have very little time, so shall only give you important particulars. We established fascine batteries within two hundred yards of the walls of Delhi, and by what the French call a *"feu d'enfer,"* we silenced the enemy's fire by destroying their guns.

On the 14th September, at daybreak, the signal for the assault was given, and three of the bastions were taken at once. The gates were blown open by powder bags and all the defenders in the vicinity, bayoneted.

From the 14th to the 20th, the mutineers showed the most determined resistance; the street fighting was very severe as we merely held what we had got, pointing heavy guns down the streets and bombarding the city day and night. We dismounted a large party of the 9th Lancers and put them to work the great guns and mortars. The enemy held out till the 20th, when *sepahis*, inhabitants and nearly all living things in the place, fled into the open country, abandoning the sick and wounded. We occupied the palace in which I am now writing and in which were found some wounded, who were bayoneted or shot.

127

I have had the cholera, but am now much better. During these operations we lost 1,130 men, killed and wounded, that is from the time of the assault to the 20th. When the city was abandoned all the bastions were then occupied and the city was plundered. All non-combatants, women and children, who came into headquarters were sent outside the walls unharmed, but the poor wretches will in all probability die of starvation.

On the 22nd, the old king was brought in a prisoner; he was not shot on account of his great age.

On the 23rd, the *shahzadehs* or royal princes were taken, and immediately shot by an officer named Hodson. All the wounded were also killed, such a beastly sight I wish never to see again.

The notification of my appointment to the 2nd Dragoon Guards having been cancelled, not having arrived at headquarters here, I could not assume my position in the 9th Lancers, so the general put me on his staff as *aide-de-camp*, and he has now conferred on me a most splendid command.

Agra, 13th October, 1857.

I think I told you that I was put into the 2nd Dragoon Guards which was the relieving regiment of the 9th Lancers, who had served their time in India and were coming home.

When the mutiny broke out, I was in command of the 9th Lancers before Delhi, when the news of my having been appointed to the 2nd Dragoon Guards arrived, so I was obliged to give up the command to the next senior officer Captain Drysdale, who had the honour to command the 9th at the assault.

I had now no status in the camp, and had nothing to do but go away and join Mittie in the hills. However, I represented the case to General Wilson and he very kindly placed me on his staff as extra A.D.C. attaching me to the 9th in order that I might draw pay. During the assault and afterwards, I went on several messages from the general, passing through the breach, I kept him informed of what was going on in the city. When the place was evacuated by the mutineers, I took up my quarters in the old king's palace and placed my bed exactly under the celebrated inscription;

If there is a paradise on earth it is this, it is this!

Ah, my dear Jack, there is no hope for nations any more than for individuals. I thought of this and felt sad. I remembered the

Roman general's quotation on a similar occasion.

Εσσεται ἧμαρ ὅτ' αν ποτ' ὀλώλῃ Ιλιος ἱρὴ
Καὶ Πρίαμος καὶ λαος εὑμμελίο Πρίαμοιοι.

On the 23rd September, a pursuing column was formed and, to the great surprise of many, there appeared in orders Major and Brevet Lieutenant Colonel Greathead will take command of the force, and Major Ouvry, 2nd Dragoon Guards, will command the cavalry.

On the 24th, we formed our camp outside the Delhi gate.

25th. Marched to Ghazee Ud Deen Nugger; about ten miles. The meaning of the name of this town is "the Enthusiast for the Faith's Town."

26th. The bridge over the Jumna having been broken down, we could not get our baggage over so were obliged to halt.

27th. Marched ten miles to Dadur, burnt and utterly destroyed the town, a very large one.

28th. The infantry will have very little to do. I always went ahead with the cavalry and horse artillery, both of which were under my command. This day, we were to march on Bolundshur "the Tall City." The civilian of the district has his spies out, and he being in camp of course I consulted with him as to the roads and whether the city was occupied or not. He said that there was no enemy near. We marched at 2 o'clock a.m., and on my advance guard reaching the vicinity, it was found to be occupied by a brigade of mutineers with six guns. They were said to be commanded by the Welud Ahad a name meaning "the next in succession to the throne" and the Nana Sahib, the Cawnpore miscreant I ordered up two six pounders on the road across which the enemy had thrown a breastwork, and in which he had placed his guns.

I soon perceived that they had nine-pounders, so I advanced a battery to take their gun in the flank on both sides, which opened a splendid fire. Colonel Greathead now came up and assumed the command. He had previously sent me on 100 infantry, with which I occupied an empty house. After firing for about two hours, the enemy retired, carrying off five guns and I was ordered to pursue. Colonel Greathead is a most gentlemanly and excellent commander, he always gives me full liberty to use my arm, the cavalry. He has not a particle of jealousy about him, and knows that if we were to wait for the infantry nothing could be done.

On this occasion coming up to the town, I determined not to wait for the infantry, but forming the 9th Lancers into threes, I ordered them to charge through the main street. I went through with them myself, we passed through a shower of musketry from both sides of the houses. We met with no loss till we got to the other side of the city. There the enemy made a stand for a moment, but the head of the column charging, the rebels took to flight. In this affair, I sustained a loss of four officers, about ten men killed and wounded, and twenty horses. Drysdale's horse being shot, he fell and broke his collar bone; Blair very severely wounded, was obliged to have his shoulder joint excised; Sarel severely wounded, shot through the arm and has had his finger amputated; Thonger shot through the arm.

The Irregular Horse behaved nobly, and no doubt we shall get credit. The fault committed was our keeping up the fire too long. The infantry should have advanced on the flank of the guns, we had no business to charge into the town, but I knew that unless we did so, they would have held the town against us.

The enemy's cavalry were cut up splendidly by the irregulars, who outstrip the lancers in a swift pursuit. They killed at least 200. This was entirely a cavalry and artillery affair.

I think I told you in my last letter, which I am afraid has been destroyed at Mooltan, of the deplorable state I was in just before the siege. I had no horses, no money could procure a horse, so I was obliged to ride troopers, vicious, cowardly brutes, which would not leave the ranks, and are dreadful to ride. I had just had the cholera, which left me with shattered nerves and a feeble body. All around gloomy, the cholera carrying off the men in numbers, the 61st alone lost 200, so that I was nearly giving in. However, I got about a little, but could not eat anything when the siege of Delhi took place.

I cannot now think how I could have been so active, the excitement gave me strength; but it was not till after the affair of Bolundshur that I knew what it was to eat with any appetite. I took the advice of our surgeon who said, appetite or not, *eat,* this I did and am now improving daily. The hot weather is over except in the middle of the day up till five o'clock.

Now I will go on with my adventures with the cavalry brigade. After Bolundshur we halted for four days, a terrible error, as we might have intercepted another body of the enemy with seventeen guns. We halted till the 3rd of October.

On the 2nd, Home, our engineer, who had got the Victoria Cross for putting the powder bag on the Kashmere Gate of Delhi, blew himself up with the fort of Malaghur, which might have safely been left to be settled with afterwards.

October 4th. Marched with the cavalry to Somnah, fifteen miles. A native gave us information that there was an English young lady who had been carried off by a *sowar*, in a village some miles off. I immediately sent three corps of Light Cavalry; they marched so as to reach the village by daybreak. The head man was then ordered to produce the lady or be hung, he went back into the village and returned with the young lady in a *dhooly*, a kind of native sedan chair. She turned out to be a half-caste girl of about eighteen years of age. She said in English that she had been taken by a man named Khuda Buksch, "The gift of God," she stated that he had married her, that she liked him and did not wish to come away, so they left her there and returned after having shot about twelve men, whom they recognized as having belonged to Fisher's Horse, which regiment had murdered their officers

October 5th. Marched to Alighur which was held by some 500 *ghazees* "fanatics." They had about twelve kinds of guns, made chiefly from the bottoms of telegraph posts. These posts are hollow at the bottom and will take a six-pound shot. They bore touchholes in these posts and mount them on wooden carriages. These posts have furnished many a village with a species of artillery. The wire is cut up for langridge, and with such weapons these poor wretches endeavour to resist us—a well appointed force supplied with regular artillery. We halted till Greathead came up with the infantry. The plan of attack this time was more shipshape, the infantry were to march through the main street and the cavalry were to envelop the town on both sides.

We silenced their fire by a couple of discharges and I went

round the place on one side with the 9th Lancers and the 1st Irregulars, and the rest of the cavalry enveloped the other. The infantry advanced into the main street when the wretches took to flight and we caught them *en flagrant délit*; and destroyed them without mercy, full 400 bit the dust. We burst all their guns and a small force was left in the town.

I should have told you that my cavalry brigade consists of—(1) 9th Lancers; (2) Hall's Horse; (3) Probyn's; (4) Younghusband's; (5) Watson's; Harvey's Horse; in all six corps. They are not very strong, but it looks well on paper, six Regiments, 900 sabres in all. Our infantry is only 500 strong, with two Sikh corps

October 6th. We went on ahead with the cavalry, as usual, with the intention of looking up Ackbar Abad. There was a civilian with us a Mr. Campbell.[2] This town had a fort in it, the stronghold of two brothers named Mungal, and Mehan Singh. Mr. Campbell said I might have a chance of finding them at home, but these fellows are so cunning that I doubted it much. When we got within three miles of the place, I instructed the Irregular Horse to gallop on ahead and if possible to surround the town; or rather village.

As luck would have it, the gentlemen were at home, but they heard the sound of the horses' feet and had time to get out into the open, there they were overtaken with about 100 followers and cut to pieces, Mehan Singh died fighting; his brother who had done us immense harm during the rebellion, begged for that mercy which he had never shown. He had cut off all our *daks* and had murdered every soul he could. He was a complete giant in stature, and his death has struck terror throughout the district. The chief commissioner at Agra sent me 2,000 *rupees* for his head, which of course the Irregular Horse got, as it was they who did the work. The fort and town were destroyed, there were also nine guns taken, one being a nine pounder; they were all burst We met with no loss.

October 7th. The column marched to Byaghur Fort on a cross road to Agra, where we halted.

October 8th. Most pressing letters were this day received from Agra, saying that the place was threatened by a large force of Gwalior mutineers, and begging us to hasten to their succour.

2. Afterwards Sir George Campbell.

October 8th and 9th. That is on the night of the 8th, and the morning of the 9th, I took the cavalry and artillery a forced march of thirty four miles, as far as Kundowlee, where I received a message from the chief commissioner, requesting me to hurry on or it might be too late. This letter was followed by two officers who had ridden out from the fort. They urged me to push on, as otherwise the town of Agra would be plundered and the fort shelled, which was full of women and children; all the ladies, the nuns and school girls, as well as all the Europeans of the cantonments were there. I thought to myself what I should do. I could not reach Agra before dark; there is a bridge of boats to cross, and the horses are tired. I felt uncertain; there was a mail cart in camp, so I ordered it up.

The next senior officer in camp was a major of artillery, I instructed him to march on five miles towards Agra and there bivouac and await orders. I then went on alone to the fort and drove on the roads around it, examined natives and officers, but there was not the slightest appearance of any enemy. I accordingly told the chief commissioner that I could not come to Agra that night but that I would be with him in the morning. The intelligence department informed me that a few horsemen, with two guns, were within ten miles of the fort on the Gwalior road. I then returned to my force and pitched tents, giving out orders to march at 4 the next morning.

As I was marching off at that hour, Greathead came up with the infantry. His Sikhs marched well, but he only got up his Europeans by putting them in carts, on elephants and gun limbers, they being in a totally unfit condition to make forced marches. Greathead deserves great credit for the expedition with which he brought up the infantry, under the circumstances.

THE BATTLE OF AGRA.

At about 8 a.m. on the 10th October, 1857, Greathead's force advanced over the bridge and, sweeping round the fort, we encamped on the open plain beyond the cantonments. We pitched our camp, as you see by this plan of the field of battle.

In front of our position was a fine plain, bounded by very high cultivation, six or seven feet high.

The people in the fort were delighted to see us, and most of the officers, myself among the number, went to the fort, a mile and a half distant, to breakfast.

And now I have a wonderful story to tell. Our camp was pitched by about 9 a.m. and we all thought that the enemy had no force across the river, which is ten miles off, so that while we were at breakfast a consultation was held, and it was agreed that Cotton should take the command of an expedition to go and meet the enemy's force near Dholpore. There was a printing press in the fort, and the order for the expedition was printing when all at once a furious fire of artillery told us that through the shameful negligence of the Agra people we had fallen into a complete trap. The Gwalior or Dholpore force were actually in position as we were pitching our tents. Their camp was within three miles of the fort and the Agra people knew nothing about it. Of course it was nobody's fault; they had trusted to native reports and this was the result; but more about this hereafter. I had sent away my horse intending to stay sometime in the fort. Cotton and I rushed out of the fort and neither of us had horses—"*A horse, a horse, my kingdom for a horse.*"

There happened to be a buggy standing near, and without asking to whom it belonged we both jumped in and drove furiously towards the camp of the 9th Lancers. The scene of terror and confusion through which we passed is simply indescribable. All the camp followers were in full flight to take shelter in the fort, there was a regular panic, and at one moment I thought all was lost, but I was soon reassured when I saw the 9th Lancers mounted and formed with the precision of a parade. We pulled up at the rear guard where we found a wounded officer, and my servant holding my horse all ready.

N.B. I had that very morning beaten this man or rather boy. He behaved nobly and I gave him twenty *rupees* afterwards.

The rear-guard were mounted, and I dismounted one of them to mount Cotton who took the command. I galloped to the head of the lancers who were on the left of the position. Our guns as you see on the plan, and a Sikh regiment, had thrown itself into square. At this moment the enemy's cavalry advanced in force, they had reached a disabled gun and cut up the drivers, when I gave the word to charge, and we swept down on them like an avalanche. They evidently did not know that we were there, for as they turned to save themselves they cried "*Delhi Bhala-Wallahs*" that is to say "The Delhi Lancers," the enemy were not aware of the arrival of Greathead's column. We did not cut up very many as they were too quick for us.

A young officer, Watson, did all that was proper on the right flank; he was supported after a time by a Sikh regiment and the European Infantry; he then charged the left of the enemy's position and took two heavy guns, after cutting up a number of the rebels. The 3rd European regiment then marched out of the fort commanded by Colonel Riddell. Colonel Cotton now ordered a general advance of our whole force, the enemy slowly retiring, till we, passing through the high cultivation, came on their camp which they did not stop to defend. Cotton then saw that we had it all our own way and ordered a general pursuit by the whole cavalry followed by the Horse Artillery. The enemy were now a disorganized mass, and we cut up great numbers, and only ceased the pursuit on the banks of the Kharee River, about ten miles and a half distant from the fort. We took all their guns and an immense quantity of plunder.

Such is a short account of the Agra affair, which has been dignified by the name of a battle. I went on ahead with the cavalry and artillery at 11 o'clock p.m. of the 8th and arrived at Agra, forty-two miles. We then fought and pursued the enemy ten miles, as far as the Kharee Nuddy and returned to Agra afterwards; we only halted half an hour, sixty-two miles in forty-six hours, a very great thing in this country.

If I can, I will send you the despatches, it was the best thing done this war; the force which attacked us was the whole of the Dholpore mutineers. One of the guns taken was the largest brass gun I ever saw; had it been bored according to its size, it would have taken a shot of one hundred pounds weight There was said to be a son of the King of Delhi present; we took his women but what became of them nobody knows, they were not killed One of the irregulars looted a necklace which he sold in the bazaar for £100, he talked about it, and the necklace was recovered; a rich native has offered £4000 for it, but those who are judges say that it is worth £13,000

October 17th. We are now on the way to join the force at Cawnpore; we have got to within two marches of Mynpooree, and the mail leaves today. That I should have the command of the only cavalry force in India, in the field, is what I never expected, as there were two superior cavalry officers in the camp before Delhi, and the reason I got it was this: General Wilson determined that Greathead should have the command of the column, and as Colonels Grant and Custance were senior to him, it was necessary that a junior cavalry officer should be appointed, and as I was there I got appointed.

Your affectionate brother,

Henry.

Cawnpore,
October 30th, 1857.

I will now continue my adventures:—

14th. Marched over the bridge of boats and encamped.

15th. To Etamadpore or Omeidpore.

16th. To Ferozeabad.

17th. To Shikarabad. This day I was sent out with two hundred Cavalry and three guns to Kheirguhr which I totally destroyed together with two other villages, killing a few rascals I caught

18th Halt.

19th. Marched twenty-four miles to Mynpooree. The *rajah* who we expected would fight, fled with his whole force.

20th. Halted to seize all the property we could, and to destroy the place. The native soldiers got most of the plunder, only about two hundred *rupees* worth could be recovered for prize money. It was a curious sight to see the Sikhs plundering the boxes of our ladies, of which the fort was full; half finished worsted work there was in abundance, there were, however, two and a half *lacs* of *rupees* in the treasury which goes to government, as the beast did not fire a shot. We blew up his fort.

21st. Marched to Bewar. Found a *sepahi* and shot him.

22nd. To Gooseangunge. As the advance guard was entering into the town, I observed some fifty men running away; gave chase with Gough's Horse and cut up twelve of them, the rest escaped into the high cultivation where the horses could not follow them; they were *ghazees*, the worst kind of fanatics, and were all armed; many fought desperately. I should have told you that on the 19th Colonel Hope Grant arrived while we were at

Mynpooree and superseded Greathead in the command of the force, but this did not affect me as I still was continued in my cavalry command,

23rd. Marched to Kanoj, which is some two miles off the road. 1 was with the advance guard, and upon arriving near the place I received information from some natives that some infantry and a few horse had been there lately and that they had guns which they had taken in the direction of the river. I sent a message to Grant, informing him of the fact, and asking his permission to ascertain the truth of the matter. He evidently attached no importance to the information; however he sent me word that I might go. I accordingly took one squadron of the 9th Lancers, two corps of Irregular Horse, Probyn commanded one, and two six pounder guns. I own that I did not expect to do anything. A shopkeeper, however, came up and told me that the enemy had got some of his guns over the river and had just left the place.

My two guns worked round the town and opened fire on the enemy's guns which were on the opposite bank, and on my shewing the head of my column the enemy fired on it with grape. Their guns were so badly served that we received no damage, one officer only being slightly wounded on the cheek. I now drew up the cavalry under cover of a wall, and our artillery made good practice at them at about four hundred yards, with tremendous effect. At the fourth round the rascals began to desert their guns. I seized on a native and ordered him to cross the river on pain of being immediately shot. He started off and shewed that the river was fordable, though deep, and that the bottom was hard.

After two more rounds from our side, I gave the word for the cavalry to cross the river which they did beautifully, the wave breaking over the saddle bow. We soon got over, formed, and were down upon the rebels who had deserted their guns and were in full flight. The pursuit was continued for about seven miles until my right rested on the river Ganges into which the remnant of the enemy were driven by Probyn's or Watson's Horse. We killed about two hundred and one hundred more escaped into the high cultivation. This has given me more satisfaction than anything else as it is my own affair, and although

I cannot claim much military merit, still the satisfaction of killing the scoundrels of that fiend, the *Nana*, was so intense, that contrary to my custom, I took a spear myself and stuck a few of them that came in my way.

After it was over I came back to camp with my four guns; one twenty-four pound Howitzer, one six pounder European gun, one three pounder brass, and one iron small native field piece. Grant was delighted, and though as I said before, the enemy were contemptible, in a military point of view, still the river was deep, and all was done in a very clean manner without any mistakes.

24th. Marched to Poora.

25th. Marched and arrived at Cawnpore. (till the 30th October).

CAWNPORE

Here I may say that my cavalry command comes to an end. Colonel Little has arrived from England and has superseded me in the command of the cavalry. As for me I am in a strange fix, I am still officially in the 2nd Dragoon Guards, as the notification has never reached the regiment. I put the case before Grant. As an officer of the 2nd Dragoon Guards I had been put in orders to command the cavalry of Greathead's force. Little was my senior, and as I did not officially belong to the lancers I could not do duty with that corps. Grant solved the difficulty by appointing me to the command of the Irregular Cavalry. However, all this may be changed when Sir Colin Campbell arrives, which will be in a few days.

I had now an opportunity of visiting the scene of that fiend the *Nana's* atrocities. The blood of our unfortunate ladies and children still clings to the walls. Many children were still hanging on a fallen tree when Havelock's column took the town. I myself have got a lock of hair belonging to a lady who was murdered, and also a child's frock; the child could not have been more than one or two years old from its size. These poor creatures were in a small house to the number of two hundred and thirty, all women and children, when the demon sent in a few *chumars*, a low caste of wretched natives, who cut and hacked them to pieces with swords and knives, and any who

The House at Cawnpore where all the Women and Children were Murdered

endeavoured to escape outside were shot down by *sepoys*, or bayoneted. The next morning many were still breathing, and in that state were flung into a well which was filled with their bodies. It was not judged fit to remove them so the well has been filled up with earth and there they rest not unwept, for I could not help shedding tears myself. Yes! I observed to an officer who was a witness to my weakness, if I can weep I can kill also, as I have already done, and if it pleases God to spare me I have not done yet.

I have also seen the place of Wheeler's defence: such a cowardly piece of atrocity was never before witnessed; twenty-four guns playing on the barracks for twenty days. The dastard *Nana* kept firing from about half a mile off, as he dared not attack the handful of Europeans, but although the buildings are so battered very many were not killed by the fire.

> Camp Cawnpore,
> October 31st, 1857.

Tomorrow we march on Lucknow where Outram and Havelock are besieged in the Residency. All communication is cut off, so we really know nothing about the state of affairs within that fortress, except that they have only provisions for about ten days. Sir Colin and Wyndham are to join us tomorrow or the next day.

I will now tell you a little anecdote. I went to see the room where our ladies were murdered and afterwards to the barracks where Sir Hugh Wheeler held out for twenty-two days. A few days before this I had found in the stronghold of a rebel chief, twelve men. Strictly speaking, I ought to have shot them all, and I was much blamed for not doing so. I did not like, however, to kill them in cold blood.

As I witnessed the scene of so much misery, standing in the place where Sir Hugh had fought, I said, "I repent me that I spared them; I will now kill all I come across." My eye caught a large piece of paper as I spoke; it was two sheets of a large church Bible and it contained part of the *Sermon on the Mount*—"*blessed are the merciful, etc.*" I shewed it to Major Turner of the artillery and to my brigade major, Salmond, who were with me at the time. I gave over the prisoners to the civil power, perhaps they will be hanged, I will enquire.

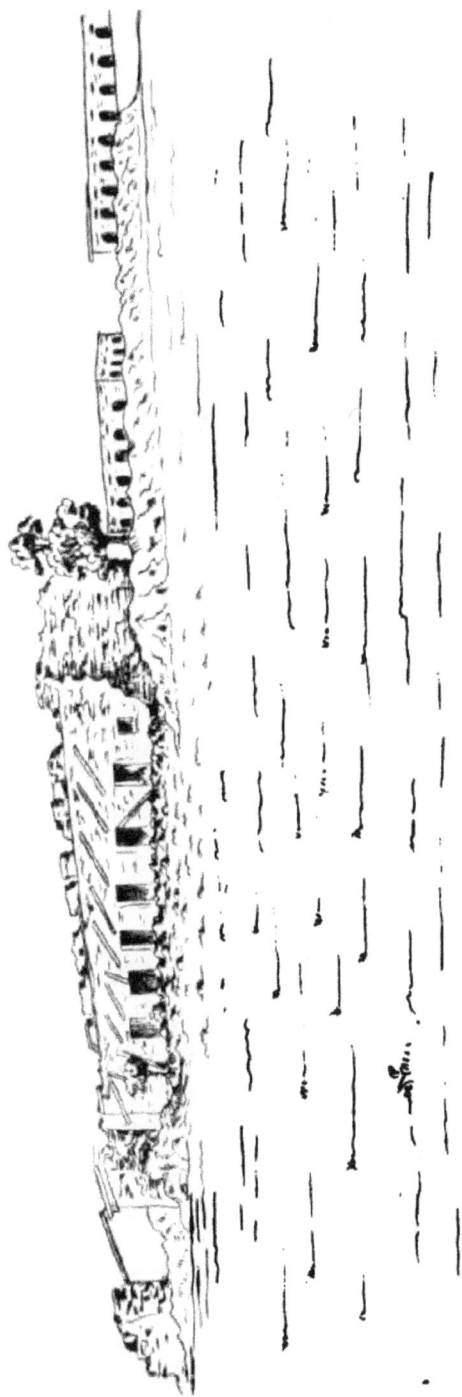

SIR H. WHEELER'S DEFENCE AGAINST THE NANA

Among the ruins I found various leaves of different Bibles, Paley's *Evidences, Illustrated London News,* Homer's *Iliad,* etc., and a lock of fair hair, probably cut from the head of some lady who wished to appear as a man.

Now a word on a subject which seems to press upon your mind. When we burnt the fort, and blew up the magazine of Mynpooree, I found a box of books which I now have. Among them is *Watts, on the improvement of the mind* in which occurs the following passage—

> *Dear and blessed God, hadst thou been pleased in any one scripture plainly to have informed me which of the different opinions about the Holy Trinity among the contending parties of Christians had been true, thou knowest well with how much zeal, satisfaction and joy, my unbiased mind would have opened itself to receive and embrace the Divine discovery.*

That which Watts said of the Trinity, I say of the received Faith of the times. Cannot a man pray to God as a rational creature, as a reasonable being? Must a man believe the Almighty has acted in a most absurd and unreasonable manner in order that he may be saved? I really do not know how I could answer in the next world if the Almighty were to say to me, "How, with the light I gave you, could you believe such things of me?" A national worship and form of Faith is a necessary thing for the unreasoning masses.

30th October. Marched and encamped over the bridge of boats in Oude.

October 31st. Marched to Bushir Serai, fourteen mile& Went with a party of one hundred 92nd Highlanders, one hundred Sikh Infantry and Watson's Horse, to attack a village, but found that the body of the enemy who had occupied it had fled. I surrounded the village with the cavalry, entered it and killed some fifty *budmarches*; lost one Sikh, who was shot. Started at 2.30, returned at 8, very hot.

September 2nd. Shifted camp, and while doing so were attacked by the enemy, a most contemptible rabble. Killed about one hundred, and pitched tents about two miles nearer Lucknow.

(Letters to my wife after we parted.)

Umballa, 18th July, 1857.

I arrived at Umballa yesterday, and start today at 4 p.m., on my way to join my regiment It is of no use deceiving you with good news, when everything is as bad as it can be. Instead of occupying Delhi, we are merely outside the walls.

On the 6th, we lost two hundred and twenty killed and wounded in merely driving the rebels into the city, and young Grant had his horse shot under him. The rule in India is most disgraceful, there is nobody to give orders, so what is to become of it, is impossible to say. The accounts you read in the papers are mere inventions, in order to say something. We now think of holding too many isolated places, there ought to be certain posts told off for the concentration of all Europeans.

Whatever happens, mind and take the advice of William Arnold and follow it, that will be your best chance, for I shall not be able to come to you again, as my first thought must be my duty.

All our officers have been plundered of the greater part of their effects, but I found ours all right in the go-downs. There is a report today that the troops at Noorpore and Kangra, have broken out into mutiny. You should at once make your plans, so as to know what to do in case Dhurrumsala is threatened. Buy a lot of good mules, and endeavour to get some good *palki* bearers in your pay, so as to be off to the hills in case of necessity. You should also have a good stock of provisions laid in for such an emergency.

It is all very well for people to say, pooh! pooh! but the rule is, always to be prepared for what may happen. They disarmed the Indian Light Cavalry here yesterday. Captain —— (that idiot) was indignant, and said he would resign his commission. The brigadier simply told him to fall in and obey his orders. If I had been brigadier, and he had refused to obey orders, I would have had him shot then and there.

God bless you my own dear Mit, and kind remembrances to Mrs. Arnold. An officer has told me that dear Johnny was killed outright, and did not suffer any pain. I will write to you full particulars from the camp, as soon as I arrive.

Your affectionate Henry.

Kurnal, 14th July, 1857.

You see I have got thus far. Send me my pad for my broken leg. All your English letters have been sent on to the camp, I will forward them to you when I arrive. I am going off this evening at 8 p.m. and am now writing in the *dak* bungalow. I went out and visited the graves of General Anson and poor Hallifax. Here is a sketch of the graves. Some jackal has been walking over that of Anson, and has left its footmarks. Alas! alas!

Mr. Lowe, a young officer who is travelling with me, says that he saw our dear Johnny after he was shot He was talking to an officer of the Goorkhas, when a bullet struck him dead. It entered his mouth, passing out through the spine, and of course his death was instantaneous.[3] I will ascertain every particular when I join the camp and will tell you all about it. Kind regards to William and Mrs. Arnold.

Your affectionate Henry.

Camp, Delhi 15th July, 1857.

I have arrived and find myself in command of the 9th Lancers, as Grant is brigadier. Yule has been killed. I went all round the camp and have seen everything. I have ascertained that Johnny was buried just where he fell, with another man. I intend to have his body removed to consecrated ground, and a monument put over his remains as soon as I can get a coffin made. We had a desperate battle yesterday, and have lost 150 killed and wounded. My regiment was not engaged as it was not an affair for cavalry. I have seen Grindall, and he desires to be remembered to you. All our letters have most probably been destroyed in Delhi by these rascally *sepoys*, I enclose those that I have. I am very tired so cannot write more today. I send my love.

Your affectionate Henry.

Delhi, 16th July, 1857.

Send on Elih Buksh immediately, let him travel by bullock train, and supply him with money. I will send you money as soon as I get a bill. We have had no fight since I last wrote, so there is no news of any importance. General Reid is dying and leaves the camp this day. Wilson of the artillery has been appointed to command in his place. I am very badly off without my tent.

---

3. His regiment being at Cawnpore, he joined the army here from Simla, and was attached to the 75th Queen's Regiment.

William Ford dines with me today. Mr Saunders is also in camp. Upton had his horse killed and had a narrow escape. Mind and get somebody to keep my rifles in order, and do not let them get rusty.

Your affectionate Henry.

Camp, Delhi, 18th, July, 1857

You tell me to write long letters, but how can I write about nothing? When anything occurs I will let you know immediately. Now about poor Johnny. Yesterday, finding all things quite quiet in camp, I took six *coolies* with their spades, and started for the field where your brother fell; it is about two or three miles in the rear of our camp. It was 5 p.m. and the sun was just sinking behind a mass of thick misty clouds as I approached the spot where I had previously ascertained that his remains had been laid. I had no difficulty in finding the grave, and after a short time I recognized the decaying form of him whom we loved so well.

I hastily wrapped the body in a blanket, and placing it in a cart proceeded to the burial ground where, finding a newly dug grave, I laid it in consecrated ground, and calling up the chaplain at 10.30. p.m., by the light of my lantern, we performed the last rites over as gallant a soldier as ever died on a battlefield. Two officers of the Rifles, whom I accidentally met, also attended the funeral. He rests by the side of the late General Barnard, and though you, my dear girl, know that he is only taken from us for a time, still we may be excused for mourning over the good and the brave, whom we shall see no more in this world. May God Almighty be merciful to him and take him to Himself.

This morning, the enemy attacked, and the infantry have been fighting all day. We in the cavalry have been saddled up but were not turned out 5 p.m. They are still fighting and news arrived that Crozier of the 75th. has been killed. This attack was led by an old woman, she was wounded in the face and brought in a prisoner. I went and saw her. The fanaticism of these wretches is perfectly ridiculous. I went to the hospital and got some simple dressing for her wound, she must have had a narrow escape as the bullet had cut a large piece out of her cheek.

19th. July. Very bad news has arrived this morning, that Brigadier Wheeler, who was marching to our relief, has been cut to pieces with all his detachment, but I do not think that it can be true, although we have it on good authority. Ford and Saunders both dined with me; they are quite well.

Your affectionate Henry.

Camp before Delhi, 21st July, 1857.

As our baggage has not arrived, you had better ask Arnold to state the case through the commissioner to Goolab Singh, who most probably will try and recover it. Ellis, who left us at Umballa to join the carabineers, died after a few hours' illness. We Were attacked again yesterday, and lost two officers killed. The heat is 100° in my tent, or rather the tent I am living in, as my own has not yet arrived in camp. Sell the pony you do not want, and be very particular in attending to what I require in my letters. I always think of you, and will send you money as soon as I can get a bill, you can borrow what you want for present use. Buy a *janpan* and keep a set of bearers, immediately. I see it takes four days for a letter to go from camp to Noorpoor. I have seen Young, nothing has been heard of Macpherson, but there is no doubt but that he is safe. We are now awaiting an attack, the guns have just opened, so that you see I have no time to write about camp gossip, but merely that which is important. I am going to the front in a cart, as soon as these brutes cease firing, to get a marble slab which I saw lying on the ground, to put over dear Johnny's grave. Remember me kindly to William Arnold.

Your Henry.

Camp, Delhi, 22nd July, 1857.

I open all your mother's letters, in order to get rid of the European envelopes, but defend me from reading them, I enclose you one today. The post is open from Noorpoor and I have received all your letters. We have not been attacked since I last wrote. I send you 600 *rupees*; the order is on the Noorpoor treasury. Arnold will get it cashed for you. There is a great talk of reinforcements, but I shall believe nothing till I see them. My last letter from England is dated 9th June; it came *via* Marseilles, nothing was known at home concerning this outbreak. No tent has arrived. My difficulties are great, no servants, no tent—such is a soldier's lot I was sorry to hear of the illness of Arnold; he will get all right when the rains cease.

Camp, 23rd July, 1857.

I have just come in from the batteries. The enemy attacked this morning and have only now been driven back. Money and Turner, of the artillery, have been hit; Money is wounded in the leg, and Turner was slightly hurt by a shell; Seaton, I fear, is mortally wounded, he appeared to me to have been shot through the stomach, if so, it is all up with him. We in the cavalry were not out, I merely went to look on from the flagstaff. We may have lost twenty or thirty men, but in these affairs, short of your own observation, you can learn nothing certain till the returns come in. I send you a bill for 500 *rupees*, buy a handsome *janpan* and dress your bearers well. Have the *Bara Singha's* horns come to you all right? I wrote yesterday and there is no more to tell you,

Your affectionate Henry.

Camp, Delhi, 25th July, 1857.

I cannot answer all your questions when they are so many, you must recollect that I have a great deal to occupy my mind upon coming into the command of the regiment. I have not yet got my tents, and am living in one of the men's tents with Hutchinson. I picked up a few things I wanted at a sale of an officer's effects, so that I am not so badly off. The little bay horse was taken two marches from Umballa, and then sent back completely broken down; he will most likely have to be fired; it is a great pity. Get some person to write to the Kardar of Basuli about our missing baggage and servants.

Dr. Lawrence, who is attending you, is a son of the celebrated physician of that name, who bought Ealing Park which you know formerly belonged to my aunt, Mrs Fisher. I sent you the *Home News* yesterday, and any letters that arrive shall duly be sent on to you. I think I told you to sell the cream coloured pony for what it will fetch; keep the other, and if you do not want it, you can lend it to your friends.

I was very sorry to hear from Arnold that he is so unwell, cannot Dr. Lawrence do anything for him? I bought six shirts which belonged to a Mr. Walters, who died here of a sunstroke during the attack when Money was wounded; his wound is not so serious as it was thought at the time, and he will not lose the limb. I have got 2,200 *rupees* and send you 600.

I went down to the house of Mr. Metcalf in front of our lines, and got a beautiful slab of marble for Johnny's tomb. I am going to cut the inscription myself. The enemy saw me. I had a cart and six men with Hutchinson, they fired a 24-pound shot at us, which struck the corner of the house. I shall be field officer of the day tomorrow. Everything is quiet in camp today, but it is very wet and uncomfortable. My regiment is in good health and I have only 40 men in hospital. I have got Johnny's watch, prayer book, silver cup, and commission, which I will send on to you.

Adieu.

Your affectionate Henry.

Camp before Delhi, 27th, July, 1857.
We have not been attacked since our last affair, when Money was wounded. It has been raining incessantly ever since so that we are I may say under water which has slightly increased the sickness in Camp; fevers are prevalent, and I have not been well myself, however, today I am better.

I feel alarmed about William Arnold, he must take great care of himself. Ford and Saunders left camp today. Ford is to be employed at Kurnal, and Saunders is to have charge of the road from Alipore to some other place in the rear.

I am very sorry to say that it is all true about Wheeler. He defended himself for twenty-two days, and then ammunition failing, he was compelled to surrender, on condition of being sent to Allahabad or some other place in boats. These villains allowed him and his men to get into the boats and then treacherously attacked them and killed every soul. There are a great many ladies in the power of these miscreants near Cawnpore. I thank Almighty God heartily that you are not of the number, and when you retire to rest, recollect to thank Him for His mercies to us in this sore affliction. Pray to Him, dear Mittie, and you will then be able to bear poor Johnny's loss with greater resignation, looking forward to the time when you, a faithful wife, will meet him in a better place, where there shall be no more sorrow. I wish I could say some comfort to your mother. I will write to her by the next mail.

We have received some very good news. Havelock or some other officer coming up the country fell in with these villains and stormed their camp, killed it is said, 3,000 of them took seven *lacs* of treasure, and seventy guns. Fear nothing on account of us here; the moveable column, under Nicholson, will be with us about the 10th of next month, and with this reinforcement we shall be able to give a good account of anything that can be brought against us. The Nemuch Force, of about 2,000 muti-neers with six guns, joined the enemy yesterday. *Adieu* dearest. My tent arrived all right and now I want nothing. You may send me what you please only I want nothing.

Your affectionate Henry.

Camp before Delhi, 29th July, 1857.
I have received the list of things which you have sent off by Banghy. I hope Isri and our effects have turned up before this. I have pitched my fine large tent and am far more comfortable except from a plague of flies with which our camp is infested. No news in camp. Up to 10 o'clock, I have been employed, with the help of a soldier, in carving the inscription on Johnny's tombstone, and am going to place it over his remains to-mor-row. The marble slab is magnificent and must have been taken from the tomb of some Mahommedan king. No other person, not even General Anson, has such a splendid monument. The slab is six feet long, and the letters are two inches, it is so heavy that it takes six men to lift it, so you see what honours I have paid to poor Johnny, the good, the kind, and the bravest of the brave. I pray Almighty God in his infinite mercy that He will allow us all to meet again when we have done with this wicked and miserable world.

I expect my *bheil-gharrie* (bullock *hackery*) in camp soon, it will be of infinite use to me. We have a mess tent and all belonging to the mess. I go every night and we none of us are disposed to be dull. Supplies constantly come in from Umballa. I told you that I keep no accounts, I buy all that I want at sales and the paymaster pays the bill, never you mind about expense. I will send you enough money to do what you please with. French has turned up from Kashmir, he told me that he knew Goolab Singh had sent two companies of soldiers to punish the villag-ers who had behaved ill to us.

We have heard that six English regiments have passed Cawn-pore on their way up to us, what a desperate smash there will be when they arrive on the other side of the city. Already I see the handwriting on the walls of the king's palace—"*Mene Mene Tekel Upharsin.*" *Adieu.*

Your affectionate Henry.

Note. There is an hiatus here in my correspondence with my wife. Letters have been mislaid, may turn up hereafter.

(*Letters Since Found.*)

Delhi, 2nd August, 1857.

Do not you know that in these times I cannot sometimes find time to write. I have been up all night; we were attacked at 4 p.m. yesterday, while I was field officer of the day. I was fired on while visiting the advanced posts by some half dozen scoundrels who were in ambush. The attack from the city is still going on, it is their Eed, and they seem determined to annoy us as much as possible. My bullock cart has arrived in camp, to my great satisfaction. Weather abominable: everybody feels it more or less. Goodbye.

Delhi, 4th August, 1857.

We have had no attack since the Eed. The rainy weather is most trying to the health, and I have been rather unwell for the last few days. We want a hot sun to dry up everything; beds, linen, tents, &c., all are wet. Nicholson with the movable column will be at Umballa tomorrow, so we shall soon have him here. Today a *cossid* came in with a letter from Havelock, he is at Lucknow after having beaten the enemy well. As soon as he has settled with Lucknow, he will march up here, but we ought not to wait for him, for as soon as the moveable column arrives, we might take Delhi; but alas! we have no man in command who will do anything for fear of responsibility.

This dread of responsibility (the curse of Englishmen) is strong on our first-in-command, I feel that if I had the command, Delhi would be ours in twenty-four hours. Sickness, far more terrible than the enemy, will soon invade our camp, and then with our weak force, what can we do? Despondency, the companion of disease, will rob our men of all energy; far better would it be to lose a few hundreds in an assault, and thus have done with it.

Sir H. Lawrence has been killed at Lucknow, he was wounded, and died some time afterwards, in him we have lost a good man

150

indeed. I ride troopers, having no horses of my own. Hurford is sick, and gone to the hills.

Camp before Delhi,
5th August, 1857.

It gives me great pleasure to see your little letters. I have put up my own girl's picture in my tent, and I take a look at it when I get up and think of her. The English mail has arrived: there is not a particle of news, and they know nothing of the Mutiny at home, it will come upon them like a thunderbolt.

I am adding to Johnny's tombstone, H.E.I.C.S., so that it will now read

CAPTAIN DELAMAIN,

H. E. I. C. S.

Killed in Action,

June 8th,

1857.

Camp Delhi, August 7th.

Elihee Buksh[4] arrived in camp all right last night.

I met an officer yesterday, who told me that he had seen my name in the *Gazette* as transferred to the 2nd Dragoon Guards, which are now on their way to India, so as soon as the notification reaches camp (probably in about a fortnight), I shall have to give up the command of the 9th Lancers. I am told that from that moment, until the 2nd arrive in this country, I shall be cut all allowances, and shall be merely on my Queen's pay of about 260 *rupees* a month. I shall, however, apply to be attached to some other regiment, and have no doubt I shall not lose much.

I told you of the death of Sir Henry Lawrence, I did so on the authority of colonel or rather General Havelock, I saw his letter, he stated positively that he died of his wounds on the 4th of July. Some *sowars* have since come in, and they state positively that Sir Henry is alive and well. People in camp think that Havelock must have written from a false report, I sincerely hope so.

We had an attack yesterday. Browne, of the Kumaon battalion killed, and two other officers severely wounded; our loss in men was very trifling. The villains came out at one o'clock this

---

4. *Syce.*

morning and made us all get up, but they are always afraid to come near. The hatred of these people towards us is something unaccountable; a shopkeeper at Umballa, wrote to the Rajah of Pattiala urging him to make a grand massacre of all the ladies and children in the hills. Howard got hold of the letter somehow, and immediately hung the wretch—splendid thing, martial law. (See frontispiece).

Robertson[5] is in camp, he dined with me last night, I am happy to say his wife is much better.

Camp Delhi,

August 12th, 1857,

I have just received your letter of the 21st July; it must have been detained somewhere, thus you see the reason I knew nothing of Isri having arrived. I was F. O of the day yesterday, there was fighting going on during the whole time. This morning we made a capital attack, and took four guns. I lost two men, killed by cannon-shot at my post; in all we may have lost in killed and wounded, seventy men. I am very tired, and have a singing in the ears, from having been in the batteries. It is, I am afraid, too true that Sir Henry Lawrence is dead.

August, 14th.

I am in great grief at hearing of your illness

I am sorry to say we lost 113 killed and wounded the day we took the guns, I thought at first there were only about 60 or 70.

Today we got our reinforcements in the shape of the 52nd, and part of the 61st, with a Sikh regiment and some guns. There will be nothing done for some time, the heavy siege train left Ferozepore only last Saturday, so that it cannot reach our camp before the 20th.

We have had no rain to speak of now for a fortnight, and we have it very hot, however, I am very well off in my large tent.

Mr. Ellis, the clergyman, joined our camp the day before yesterday.

I hope you have received poor dear Johnny's effects safely, give me notice if they have not arrived, and I will make enquiries.

We may have to march any day, and certainly nearly about the time that Isri joins me with the tent. If this reaches you before

---

5. Capt. A. Cunningham Robertson, 8th Queen's Regiment.

he goes off, let him bring my *tattoo* (the cream coloured one) with him, for I want one sadly, he would fetch 200 or 300 *rupees* here. I will send you some more money shortly, I get 1,329 *rupees* monthly, this is pretty good, if it would only last.

Camp before Delhi,
August 17th, 1857.

Since I last wrote nothing particular has happened; the enemy is quite quiet. We have been reinforced by some 1,200 Europeans, so now we have a respectable force of 4,000 English troops fit to fight tomorrow.

I saw young Edgeworth, and asked him to dinner; he is in the 8th, but does not seem to like it much.

The 2nd Dragoon Guards, our new regiment, left in the *Blenheim* on the 25th of July, so we cannot expect them until sometime in November.

P. S. Since writing this letter I have received the notification of my being transferred to the 2nd D. Gds., I consequently give up the command of the 9th Lancers tomorrow; I merely lose the command allowance, and shall be attached to the 9th to draw pay, but do no more regimental duty. I shall stay in the camp, and do F. O. of the day, and if the regiment goes into action, I shall act as *aide-de-camp* to Brigadier Grant.

Camp before Delhi,
21st August, 1857.

We have had no fighting since I last wrote, but the weather is very muggy and unhealthy.

We were surprised yesterday by the appearance at our advanced picket of a half caste woman, the daughter of an officer. She is a Mrs. Leeson, her preservation has been wonderful. When they were murdering all the European inhabitants at the beginning of the outbreak, she was endeavouring to escape, she had her baby in her arms and two other children with her, a boy of four, and a girl of three years old. She met some *sepoys* who fired at her, the bullet went through the child in her arms, and wounded her severely in the breast. The child was killed, and she herself fell down from the effects of her wound. When she came to herself she found the other two children clinging to her on the ground, a *sepoy* came up, and taking the boy he cut his throat with his sword, he then took the girl and cut her across the face just below the nose, and threw her on the body of the mother. After these wretches were gone, an old man and his wife took her to their house and took care of her; the boy was dead, but the poor little girl lived for six hours. An Afghan then dressed her up as his wife, and got her out of the gate and brought her into our camp. Do these fiends deserve any mercy?

August 23rd.

We have absolutely no news whatever in camp. I am now F. O. of the day, the enemy fire into us every ten minutes, but we are under cover and take no notice of them.

I feel considerably alarmed about William Arnold, I am afraid he must have something very serious the matter with him. If he has to go home, you had better go with him.

The 2nd Dragoon Guards, my new regiment, sail from England on the 27th July, so in all probability they will not be in India for the next three months; I shall therefore, if it please God, go down with you to Calcutta, so take care of yourself, and let me see you with some strength left in you to support the journey.

The great guns were at Umballa yesterday, they will be here on the 29th of this month, and we shall probably take the city the first week in September.

August 25th,

There is no news; everything is quiet but the weather is unhealthy, and many die of cholera, the graveyard is quite full, so that we are now going to mark out another. I have seen a letter from one of the Cawnpore survivors, it discloses terrible suffering on the part of our people, nearly all of whom either died or were killed. The whole of the Europeans with the ladies and children entrenched themselves in the Hospital; they were surrounded on all sides, and the enemy soon destroyed and burnt every portion of the building by means of carcases. The ladies then had no place to go to but the trenches, exposed to a burning sun all day; most of them died, and the rest surrendered. The Nana Sahib, a most desperate ruffian, sent a native woman into the trenches, with proposals for a surrender.

Four officers went out and were well treated; boats were all ready, and the party marched out, no sooner were they in the boats than these villains opened a fire from some masked guns, and they were all destroyed except I believe four who saved themselves by swimming. Nothing is settled about me, and I do not know whether I shall get my pay cut, or not, but I will give you the earliest information when I know myself.

August 28th.
I am attached to the 9th Lancers, and appointed A. D. C. to the General commanding the field force; to keep me in the 9th would not be fair to Drysdale.

The General told me he would attach me to the Carabineers, but this has not been done.

A force, consisting of the 61st Regiment, some Artillery, a squadron of the 9th Lancers, and some irregular cavalry, amounting to 3,000 men, went out under General Nicholson to pick up some guns that were going to our rear. Directly the *sepoys* saw the Europeans advancing, they all bolted, deserting their guns. They fired a few round shot from an old building, and I believe about fifteen men were killed on our side. The 9th Lancers only had two horses struck, and never got near the enemy. These fellows are most contemptible curs; most probably you will see a flaming account of our victory, but what I have told you is the truth.

Jones and Goldie have been appointed to the 2nd D. Gds, our new regiment, by the last English *Gazette*. I have seen the *Home News*, the only copy that arrived in our camp came to Colonel Grant, and he lent it to me, they have only heard at home of the Delhi and Meerut outbreak, and they take it rather coolly; 14,000 men are now on the way out in sailing vessels, and all officers are ordered to join. There is no authentic news of any troops coming *via* Suez. As soon as Delhi falls I shall, if I am spared, come up and take you to Calcutta, when, if I can get leave I will go home with you.

I received two photographic journals by this mail, but I do not know who sent them.

September 2nd,
I have just come off picket as F. O. of the day and have found your letter.

Yesterday, while on picket I was visiting the outposts and saw a shell fall among the men on the stable picket, on riding up I found eight men knocked over and one horse, three have since died; it was an eight inch shell (shrapnel) loaded with 450 musket bullets, the stable picket is where Sir T. Metcalfe used to live, and is the stable on the estate. The men while on picket live in it. There are 300 of them, out of which 200 live in this place, consequently they are packed like a pen of sheep. They lie down and put their fire locks against the wall; there is a 9th Lancer orderly outside, and the bullets went in at compartment No. 3 and did the damage. Now, there is a piece of camp news with a picture of it.

The remainder of the disarmed 5th at Umballa mutinied the other day; they have all been killed.

I am, I think I told you, attached to the 9th Lancers, and made extra *aide-de-camp* in order to remove me from command. I thus lose the command allowance only, Colonel Little will be in India in a few days so I should not have been able to keep the command long. The guns have come nearly into camp; we shall have them by the 4th. we are now sending out an escort for them. This is all my news.

September 4th.

This morning the siege train arrived, 6 twenty-four pounders, 12 eighteen pounders, some eight-inch howitzers, and ten-inch mortars; it will take two days to sort and arrange the different shot, and then we shall get the guns in position, and woe to the vile city.

An Australian steamer has brought in five days' later news from England; 6 more regiments with a large force of artillery are on their way out in steamers; these are in addition to the troops ordered out by the last mail The Jew Bill has been rejected by the House of Lords, this is all the news in the *Extra*.

You will certainly not be able to get away before the very end of the cold weather, as the road to Calcutta will not be open. Lucknow has not yet been taken, and my opinion is that the Delhi garrison will make for that place when we drive them out of Delhi. If the 9th Lancers do not keep the field, or if the force should be broken up, I will come and join you, but it is all uncertain and I cannot at all tell what will happen; your part is to remain quietly where you are and try and improve your mind. Do you go on with your German and French?

Camp Delhi, September 5th,

I see by the dates of your letters that you write every other day, but the post is so very irregular that I sometimes get two in one day and sometimes have to wait three, four, or five days, without getting any.

I believe it is arranged that our fire is to open on Monday and as it may possibly happen that I shall quit the camp as soon as the city falls, you had better arrange your things and send all that you will not want to Mr. Parker; but keep my guns and stag horns, as I am most particular about not losing them. Keep all things that can go by *banghy* with you, but send all heavy things to Mr. Parker so that you can be ready to start off by *dâk* immediately you hear from me. It is possible that I may take you down to Kurrachee by the Indus, or you may have to join our camp if we meet towards Allahabad, but nothing is known at present, and in fact nothing can be known till the result of the attack on the city is seen.

The post has not come in at all today; we have had no rain, but judging from the river it must have been pouring in the hills.

I am sorry to say that cholera is making head again in camp, and all hospitals are pretty full, but this was to be expected at this time of year.

Sir Colin Campbell has arrived in India as commander-in-chief.

Remember me kindly to the Arnolds, I am glad he has recovered.

Camp Delhi, September 7th

I am sorry to say that I was seized with cholera yesterday morning. I am I think now out of danger, but have been in great discomfort. I am so weak, I can only give you a line, and enclose English letters. Nothing else has occurred, you will see that I am put back into the 9th Lancers. We seem to do-nothing, we ought to have been in the city before this.

September 8th.

I just write a line to say I am much better, and hope to be at my duty in a few days. We got some guns into battery last night, but nothing can exceed the timidity of our proceedings, the general is a very good fellow, but his name after this will be ever Fabius.

I still keep very weak, and I am also salivated by the great quantity of mercury I took.

Sarel went out with the squadron the other day, but he never got near the enemy, and no man was touched.

September 10th,
It is no use to talk about the post, everyone knows the bad state it is in. I got two letters from you this morning dated 4th and 5th of Sept.; Nos. 34 and 35, we must bear it, it is one of the consequences of war. I am getting on, but am very weak. All our guns are now in position within 500 yards of the wall, and tomorrow will be a great day. We ought to take the city either tomorrow or next day; the siege may be said to have commenced yesterday, we have lost in the batteries, some 25 killed and 60 wounded, white and black. Poor Goldie! news has come into camp from Bombay that his father and sister have been murdered at Cawnpore, and that his other sisters have been taken away by some *rajah*, I hope it is not true. Orders have just been issued to give no quarter, very unnecessarily, for there never was any intention to give any. The general hopes that the women and children will be spared, my own opinion is that they will not, I am sure our fellows would never kill a woman or child, but my private opinion is that the Goorkhas will kill everything that has life.
It is a very rash and dangerous thing writing on Indian affairs, the only safe thing now is to talk "Napierism."
I am going on as F. O. tomorrow, had it been any other time I should have been on the sick list as I am very weak, but it is utterly out of the question under the present circumstances. I enclose you a bill for 1,000 *rupees* as a present—be patient, dearest, and we will go home together. I will settle with your doctor by letter, do not think about it. You were very good to send money to the Lawrence Asylum, but it is useless, as that establishment must fall unless taken up by government; voluntary contributions are never of any use, such is human nature.

Camp before Delhi,
12th September, 1857.
I am better but still very weak. I came on duty yesterday, and I went to my picket as I thought the city would fall, but now it will not be till tomorrow or next day; unforeseen circumstances arise which upset all calculations. Our batteries opened along the line of wall and very soon silenced the enemy's fire; the bas-

tions are pretty well demolished, and now all that is required is the storming party. I being an *aide-de-camp*, shall most probably be with the general to carry any message that he may think fit to send; there will be a most terrible slaughter. It is a very unfortunate thing that my tent has not arrived, you recollect my instructions to send Isri with the tent, with orders to go to Mr. Parker and request him to inform Isri how he could best get it to camp. It appears Isri brought the tent to Mr. Parker, who told him to go on to the camp, and he would take care of the tent. After all my trouble, to have my intentions frustrated in this way, is very hard; here is the result: I lose 500 *rupees* that I could get for this large tent, and am without the comfort of the small one, this large one being nearly useless for a continuous march. You ought to have told Isri not to part with the tent under any circumstances, however, it may yet arrive in time, but I think it very unlikely; only think, one camel for the tent and Isri on a tattoo would have arrived comfortably by this time, however it is no use talking, it is the old story "I thought" I mean Mr. Parker "thought" it would be for the best. What business had he to think? obey orders, and never think, that is the only rule to get on with.

They talk in the papers of that affair of Nicholson, as the "Battle of Nusufnugger," I was on picket with one of the 61st, and he told me they never discharged their muskets at the enemy, who ran away at the sight of them; all about their charging the guns is utterly false, or rather it was utterly false that there were any men to charge. I will write you an account of the assault.

Delhi, September 13th,

I was delighted to receive your little French letter, it was very well and correctly written.

We kept up a severe fire all day yesterday, and have silenced the great guns of the enemy, except in the Selim Ghur Fort, and the batteries on the other side of the river. I went to the front last night to see, I got within 300 yards of the city walls, but the musket fire was so severe that it was impossible to get on. Dr. Sinclair Smith was going just after me when a random shot—24 pounder—killed his horse, and he had a narrow escape. A great many are killed in the batteries, an officer named Fagan, of the artillery, was killed yesterday. I think we shall assault tomorrow

(Monday). I am still very weak and ill. The notification of my having been put back into the 9th Lancers not having arrived, I do not take command, however, I shall get all the back command allowance when it does arrive.

I do not think it is a good thing being put back into the 9th, however, it may turn out well for me if I could only get one more step.

No news of my tent, is it not annoying? I really should have thought Mr. Parker would have known better. A tent like that would sell here for 300 *rupees*. I am now paying 40 *rupees* monthly for camels for my large tent alone, and with the *klassies* it makes it 60, so my house rent is 50 *rupees* a month, all which would be saved if I had my small tent; and after the minute instructions I gave, how Mr. Parker could have taken it away from Isri I cannot conceive.

The firing just now is very heavy, and the city wall very much damaged. I do not think we shall lose more than 50 men in the actual assault, but afterwards many more will probably be killed, as these fellows will fire from the houses, and thus many lives will be lost in the streets. The days are now very hot as the rains have apparently ceased, however it is cool enough at night. I send you the 1,000 *rupees* that you may have enough money if anything should happen to me.

Kashmir Gate, City of Delhi,
15th September, 1857, 12.30 p, m.

We assaulted the city wall yesterday at daybreak, and are now in possession of nearly all the bastions, but it will be a day or two before we can take the whole city. The Selim Gurh still keeps up its fire and there is a constant rattle of musketry. I have not had my clothes off since the attack; they are defending the house in which I am now writing, against the enemy. These rascals fought well, and our loss is great, but nobody knows what it is, six or seven officers, and a brigadier general mortally wounded. The 9th Lancers had no officer hit, some 40 men, however, were wounded, about six badly. We killed very few *sepoys*, but as we have more work to do, I will not complain till we are out of the wood. We shall perhaps take the magazine and tomorrow Selim Gurh. I am pretty well, considering, and as yet have escaped unhurt.

City of Delhi,
September 16th, 1857.

Since I wrote yesterday we have breached and taken the magazine with very little loss; we may now be considered as firmly established within the city, and a very few more days will elapse before it is entirely clear. We are shelling the palace, but I have no doubt the old fox of a king has long ago walked off. We have not got the Lahore Gate yet. Thus you see the news I have to give you today, differs little from that of yesterday, we are slowly and surely making progress. The women, children, and shopkeepers, who are brought in to headquarters are all spared, but I am sorry to say, a great many were shot in the shops and streets, and the stench in the place is most sickening. I asked after Br. General Nicholson this morning, he is wounded through the intestines, and there is, I believe, no hope for him, he may live forty-eight hours.

Of our Lancers there are about six very bad cases, the rest will recover. There were eight officers' horses hit, Hamilton lost his brown horse, killed by a grape-shot.

There is no news of my notification so I suppose it is lost If I possibly can, when we have got possession of the city, I will come and fetch you to the plains and make you comfortable at Umballa till I can get you home. I am very sorry to hear your cousin also is ill, but now that the rains have ceased I am in great hopes that she and you will soon recover.

City of Delhi,
September 17th, 1857.

I write to you every day because I know you are so anxious although I have little to add to what I said yesterday. We continue to throw shells into the palace and the city generally; we gain ground slowly but surely, and with little loss. The stench of the dead who are lying about the streets makes me so sick that I have quite lost all appetite. Mr. Saunders[6] is in camp and very well. General Nicholson is reported better today though they say he is mortally wounded, the doctors know a great deal but I have often found them wrong in their opinions, do you recollect the boatswain on board the *Omar Pasha?* God bless you, dearest.

---

6. Charles Burslem Saunders, B. C. S.

Headquarters, Delhi,
September 18th, 1857.

There is still hard fighting going on, the mutineers resist most desperately and we have made no progress since I last wrote. This morning we failed at the Lahore Gate, the —th could not be got to advance. It will be some time before we get possession. Sickness increases (3,000 sick), 200 go sick every day, in fact we have much too few men. I can only write a few lines daily, you know I am doing duty as *aide-de-camp* to the general (Wilson).

City of Delhi,
September 20th, 1857.

This morning we blew open the gate of the palace and I went in with the storming party, it was nearly empty, we only killed one man, and shot all the wounded who were left there, so the city may be said to be completely ours. Selim Gurh was also taken without loss, the *sepoy* mutineers have all decamped, and are gone in the direction of Gwalior. Cholera is among us, Greathead of the Civil Service died this morning. General Nicholson's case is hopeless but he still lingers on. I am still suffering from the effects of the mercury I took, and I think it possible that I may get up soon to Dhurumsala to fetch you to Umballa. I have been out all day in the sun and can hardly write.

We have this moment taken the Jumma Musjid, so at last Delhi has really fallen.

Palace, Delhi,
September 21st, 1857.

Headquarters have this day gone into the king's palace. I am now always at the staff mess and thus I am going to remain till my notification comes out. There is not a soul of the enemy to be seen; everything is as quiet as possible, and not a single shot to be heard, therefore, I have not any news to tell you. I feel glad that it is all over, although I think it likely that the Cavalry will go in pursuit eventually. The day the *sepoys* ran away we killed about 70 who were wounded and could not get away; nothing shews more clearly than this the villainy of these rascals, leaving their sick to be killed, of course they loaded all their carts with the plunder of Delhi.

All the inhabitants of Delhi have also departed so that we alone occupy the city. The palace is a magnificient residence looking on the river, very nice and cool.

My small tent has arrived all right.

Moveable Column, outside the city walls
(no date).

I have a great deal to do but will write regularly. The king was taken prisoner and is now in the house called Begum Gurh, near the Lahore Qate; he is guarded. I saw and spoke to the poor old wretch; he is past 90 years old. Three of the king's sons (*shahjadahs*) were taken prisoners with a European, a sergeant-major of some native infantry regiment The king's sons were immediately shot, and the sergeant-major will be hanged today. A moveable column, composed of the 8th and 75th Queens, with a couple of regiments of Punjab infantry, with about 1,000 cavalry including the 9th Lancers, and 16 guns, go in pursuit tomorrow. Brevet-Colonel Greathead commands the whole, and I command the cavalry brigade. We shall most probably cross the river by the bridge of boats and proceed to Alighur, clearing the country till we get to Agra. I am better in health, thank God, and hope to do some good service.

The bodies of the king's sons are lying in the Chandee Choke, a large street, exposed to public view. I feel sick of blood, but we shall have to execute an immense number before we have done.

The number of *sepoys* that went off with some guns (field pieces) was estimated at 8,000, but I believe them to be less in number.

I have left my big tent in camp to be sold, and am marching with the small one.

Ghazee oodeen ka Nuggur,
September 25th, 1857.

I just write to tell you I am well. Yesterday, 300 *sepoys* turned up, concealed in the town, they were of course immediately shot.

Mr. Saunders is in Delhi, he is made commissioner, I believe him to be a very able man.

We have had a very disagreeable march, I got up at 2 o'clock this morning, and my tent has just come up, our mess tent has not yet appeared. We are marching on Bolundshur, but I think it is more to punish the villagers than anything else.

Poor Nicholson is dead, he was a gallant fellow, but of disagreeable manners, over bearing, and violent in language, but he is dead and we will only remember the good he did. Had he lived he would have commanded this column.

I have got a fine force under me, and if we do come on the rebels they will surely repent it.

This is my command: 9th Lancers, 1st, 2nd, 5th Punjab Irregulars, with 200 of Hodson's Horse, in all 5 regiments of cavalry. I am so tired I cannot write more.

Camp, Moveable Column,
Secundra, September 27th, 1857.

We marched from Ghazee oodeen ka Nuggur to Dadree which is a very large place. I received the order to destroy it with the neighbouring village, this I did most effectually by burning it, and then the sappers upset the house of the principal person there, which was *pucca* and would not burn. I found a lot of ladies' bonnets, gowns and shoes, and a large packet of letters, belonging most probably to some persons who they had murdered; all the inhabitants had fled. Today we marched to Secundra, a large village containing, when the rebellion broke out, 10,000 inhabitants, it has been completely sacked by the Goojurs and an immense plunder carried off.

We are within 10 miles of Malagurh where there is a fort with 10 guns mounted; we must settle this off tomorrow. There is a body of 10,000 Goojurs before us so we shall have a great deal of work before we cut them up and disperse them. We get up at one o'clock every morning and march till 7 or 8 so that I am glad to get a little sleep in the day. My health improves under difficulties, and I hope to meet you at Agra. I cannot write more because I am so tired, and indeed a short account of our proceedings on the march will constitute the sum total of all my letters. Recollect I get no news, no papers or reports, we are out of the world.

Bolundshur, September 29th, 1857,
(day after the action).

I have not been able to write for two days and had we not halted today, I should not now have been able to do so. We have had rather a severe fight with the Wulud Ahud and the Nana

Sahib. I was eleven hours in the saddle, the heat of the battle lasted about two hours and a half. I have been all day writing my despatch as you know that I command the cavalry brigade. Poor Blair had the head of his shoulder blade amputated this morning, and if he does not die he will lose the use of his left arm; he ran a *sowar* through the body who cut through his left shoulder before he died. I have taken a severe revenge on the enemy for poor Johnny's death, I enclose you a rough copy of my despatch as I really cannot write much more.

All the villagers are against us, they murdered one of our sick who remained a little behind the column on the march. Of course I went through the town with the lancers. Drysdale, Sarel, Thonger and Blair were wounded and 6 men and 20 horses killed and wounded.[7] We shall blow up the fort of Malagurh tomorrow and advance on Anoopshur and from thence most probably we shall go to Allighur.

Khoja, on the trunk road to Agra.
3rd October 1857,

I am in better health now, and begin to have some appetite for my food, for which I most heartily thank God.

Poor Blair was sent back to Meerut just before we left Bolundshur this morning. The only way I can account for these rascals making such a fight of it is that they were not Delhi *sepahis*, but part of a force which was coming to Delhi. A very dreadful accident happened yesterday. Holmes the engineer who distinguished himself so much by blowing open one of the Delhi Gates and who was to have received the Victoria Cross, by some mismanagement, blew himself up with the fort. He was, of course, blown to pieces, and another European had his legs broken. Young Edgworth was rather severely wounded; Drysdale[8] is very ill from the effects of Delhi, and I should not wonder if he did not recover; his collar bone having been broken, he is *hors-de-combat*. We take, hang, and shoot a great many prisoners. News has just come in that the enemy have seized upon Alighur, but that on hearing of our advance they have since evacuated it.

---

7. Greathead afterwards spoke to me about this affair, he said that it was not cavalry work. I silenced him by saying that it was necessary to storm the town. Of course he should have done so with the infantry, but he did not.
8. He recovered and later became General Drysdale.

You must be very particular not to let any person get hold of the letters which I write to you. Of course you can tell the Arnolds all the news generally, but people with you are so eager to hear particulars that my name might get into the papers, which might do harm with the big wigs, who always, hate to see the truth told to the public before they have prepared the garbled version of the same with which they are in the habit of humbugging John Bull.

We are marching on Agra, and I expect to receive orders to march with all my cavalry and artillery on Cawnpore. Your plans are quite simple—remain patiently where you are till you receive instructions from me. We lost a sergeant by cholera last night My cart and small tent are veritable godsends, I would not take £2,000 for them. I put my tent and boxes in the cart and keep them with me, and thus have a tent pitched instantly, while others have to wait till 9 or 10 o'clock. The weather is getting delightful.

Your affectionate Henry.

Camp Alighur, 5th October 1857.

We marched at two this morning, and on arriving at Alighur we found it occupied by about 400 fanatic Muaselmans, who opened a fire of round shot on my advanced corps of Irregulars. They, like good soldiers, retired by alternate squadrons, when these silly idiots made a sally out of the town thinking that they were bolting.

As soon as I learnt this, being with the main body about a mile distant, I advanced six guns and opened fire on their wretched artillery if such it could be designated. They had ten pieces in all, one three pounder and nine telegraph post ends which they had mounted on carriages, and which would hold a six pound shot at the muzzle. They carried a few hundred yards, of course without any precision.

My cavalry separated, and we advanced on each flank of the enemy, and after a few rounds more from artillery, the enemy all turned tail, when we charged home and got well into them. We may have killed some three or four hundred; a vast number hid themselves in the *khets*, or high cultivation on the sides of the main road. We did not lose a man. I hope that this terrible example will give them a lesson. Greathead with the infantry came up but there was nothing for them to do. I only reached camp again at twelve o'clock having been ten hours in the saddle, and am, of course, very tired.

On my return, I formed the cavalry in skirmishing order and beat up the *khets* on each side the road, killing about a hundred men who were hiding in them, and as I looked on our bloody lances, I thought of poor Johnny and how it had pleased God that I should take vengeance on them. These ignorant wretches imagined we were a small force from Agra. This will do a great deal of good and give them a lesson. We shall most probably halt here tomorrow and then march and utterly destroy Akbarabad which is about eight miles off.

Your affectionate Henry

Gunj, a village on a cross road between
Akbarabad and Hatrass,
October 8th, 1857.

We marched from Alighur on the 6th to destroy a town called Akbarabad. As usual, I went on ahead with the cavalry. When I got within three miles, the dawn was just breaking, so I ordered the four regiments of irregular cavalry to gallop on and completely surround the place. We were very successful, as we thereby surprised all that were in it. The two ruffian brothers Mongol Sain, and Mehen Sain were caught and cut to pieces, with one hundred of their followers. The remainder of our force arrived in about two hours, when the village was burnt, and the Serai of Mongol Sain, was blown up. The beast had five guns in all, loaded with old iron nails as he had no round shot. We halted next day, visiting and burning another village where they had murdered one of my *sowars*.

We shall have a great deal of trouble; news has been just brought in that these rascally Goojers and fanatic Moolvies are collecting again to attack a party of Sikhs which we left in occupation of the town of Alighur. We have sent fifty horse and one hundred and fifty infantry to their aid. The fact is we must mercilessly destroy every Mussulman we find, all are armed against us with battle axes made in their villages and the ends of the telegraph posts furnish them with artillery. These improvised guns will throw a six-pound ball to some distance.

We are now marching on Agra, where it is thought the Dholpore force are coming, but I think they will not do this when they get news of the fall of Delhi.

Your affectionate Henry.

Agra, October 11th, 1857.

I have great news to tell you. Our column was near Akbarpore, some forty two miles from Agra, when we got urgent letters from Colonel Fraser for the cavalry and artillery to come on, by forced marches. Colonel Greathead remained behind with the infantry and I marched on thirty four miles with the cavalry and artillery that night and the. next day, this brought us to Kundowlie which is eight miles from Agra. Being determined to ascertain, personally, how affairs stood as we needed repose, I rode on to Agra, and finding all quiet there, returned, and we halted at that place till four o'clock the next morning.

Colonel Greathead succeeded in bringing up the infantry by putting them on elephants, camels, limbers, carts, etc., and we all marched in and took up our camping ground on the plain towards Gwalior, arriving by nine o'clock am. This ground is about two miles from the fort. Most of the officers went into the fort for breakfast. Colonel Cotton, who was the senior officer, asked me to breakfast with him, but I told him that I must first put out my pickets. He said there was no necessity as he already had mounted pickets all round, and that there was no enemy near. Under these circumstances, I went with him into the fort, breakfasted, and called on several people, when suddenly a report came in that the enemy had attacked our camp. I went out with Cotton and finding a buggy standing there belonging to somebody in the fort, we immediately appropriated it and drove out to the camp with great difficulty, as the road was blocked with carriages, camels and carts, all flying to the fort for protection. Isri, my servant, was by my tent with my horse—all the camp followers had run away, in fact I saw not a soul in the camp except Captain Drysdale, who was on the sick list, having broken his collar bone when his horse was shot under him at Bolundshur. He told me the regiment was formed up in the front.

Colonel Cotton came with me to the front where I found the 9th Lancers all mounted and drawn up ready under Captain Fawcett, I saw some of our Sikh regiments formed into square, and round shot were flying in all directions. I looked in front and saw the enemy's cavalry coming on at the gallop. They had reached our nearest gun and cut up the artillerymen, but they did not keep it many seconds, for I was upon them with the Lancers, on which they all broke and fled, in the greatest confusion, I had mounted Colonel Cotton on one of our troopers, he went to the right and took over the chief command, and, by degrees, all our guns came into action, supported by a battery and the Europeans who came out of the fork. We then made a general advance of all arms, continuing to work on till, having taken two heavy guns on the right, the enemy gave way entirely and endeavoured to retreat.

Cotton then ordered a general pursuit by all the cavalry. I left two squadrons of the 9th Lancers to guard the camp, and pursued the enemy for ten miles up to the river, on the banks of which I halted, having killed great numbers and taken all their guns, baggage and camp; there was an enormous quantity of plunder. I did not get back to camp till six o'clock and feel quite stupid from the effects of the sun. The 9th Lancers lost French, killed; Jones[9] I fear, mortally wounded, and about ten men. I think we shall get great credit for this. Cotton is a good officer and did his work well. I can write no more.

Your affectionate Henry.

Agra, 13th October, 1857.

What can I do in these terrible times? hardly can I spare time to write a word. Your continued illness gives me great alarm, I fear you must have something serious the matter with you, but I hope to have better accounts in the next letter. I enclose a letter from your mother. I opened it and read the first few lines, and saw enough to know that at the time she wrote it she knew nothing of poor Johnny's death.

Our victory was most complete and the cavalry will get great credit, and indeed they deserve it. We have heard that the Dholpore force has utterly dispersed, and part has gone away to Mooltan. Yesterday we got another gun, so that altogether we have taken fourteen. We buried poor French yesterday. Jones is alive, I had sent him with his squadron to be an escort to two guns, the enemy's cavalry attacked him, when his squadron

---

9. He received nearly twenty wounds, but eventually recovered.

charged and defeated them, but Jones himself was surrounded and cut up most fearfully; his bridle arm being broken by a carbine shot, he could not defend himself. I never before saw the enemy charge with such courage. I was glad of our opportunity of charging them in the plain, they were defeated in a second, and the gun they had taken, recovered. I know nothing of our movements, but most probably we shall go to Dholpore and then return to Agra.

They are very slow down country in sending up troops. If we were not halted I could not have written so long a letter, as the fatigues of duty leave me no time, but I always write the important news, so that you may know it first.

There was plenty of plunder, and I have got the chair belonging to the enemy's general who is a son of the King of Delhi. I have also got a bag of silver, *rupees*, bangles and other ornaments, which I gave to the native horsemen, the chair I sent in to a friend in the fort, and you shall have it hereafter. Remember me to the Arnolds.

Your affectionate,

Henry.

Letter to Mrs. Arnold (my wife's cousin).

Camp, Aroun, October 18th, 1857.

My Dear Mrs. Arnold,

You know the Duke of Wellington said—"*a battle is like a ball, we each know the part we took therein, but we cannot know all the parts others may have taken.*" Many thanks for your kind letter concerning my dear wife. I feel so distressed at her suffering that it destroys all the pleasure I should otherwise feel after our great success at Agra. There is a petty *rajah* at Mynpoorie, who says he is going to fight us, my own opinion is that he will run away. We shall most probably be in Cawnpore in eight or nine days, but I do not expect to have any serious fighting till we get to Lucknow. We do not intend to interfere with Futtyghur at present unless they attack ns in the line of march. Since Agra we have been marching without any event happening, except the burning of a village or two. The Agra people were delighted at our having beaten the enemy, they can now get out of the fort without fear. The fellows we polished off there were the Dholpore men.

As soon as the Gwalior force (Contingent) heard of our success, they immediately left the place, and are said to be marching on Cawnpore, so that we may possibly fall in with them. Hoping to hear a more favourable account of Mittie by to-morrow's post, believe me dear Mrs. Arnold, with kind regards to your husband.

Yours faithfully

H. A. Ouvry.

P.S. Colonel Grant joined and took command of the column today, which deprives Greathead of his command, but does not interfere with me as I continue to command the cavalry brigade.

Mynpoorie, October 19th, 1857, 12 noon.

My dearest Mittie

I have just been eleven hours in the saddle so cannot write much. We marched a forced march from Aroun to try and surprise the *rajah*, he however bolted, and we have got nothing but one brass gun. I am very disappointed. The report is now that the enemy mean to stand at Bewar, but I do not believe they will. We shall probably halt here for a day, as the Infantry are completely knocked up.

Now with regard to yourself, it is all nonsense about morphia not taking away the pain, the reason is you do not take enough, an underdose of morphia makes you more restless. When the pain is great take, immediately, half a grain of morphia, and if that does not take effect, take another half grain. Do not be afraid of poisoning yourself, as I tell you that the smallest dose that was ever attended with fatal effects to a grownup person was four grains, so that you are quite safe with one grain. I myself took a grain and a quarter for a dose.

Your affectionate Henry.

Kanoj, October 23rd, 1857.

We marched to Kanoj this morning. On arriving at the camping ground I gained information that some three hundred men with four guns were crossing the Kali Nuddi, about four miles off. I sent back information to Grant who gave me permission to look them up, I took one squadron of the 9th Lancers and two regiments of Punjab cavalry under Watson and Probyn,[10] to

10. Later Sir Dighton Probyn.

171

see what I could do, I had also two six-pounder field pieces. On arriving at the river I found the enemy had crossed over with three guns, and the moment we shewed ourselves, they opened fire on us. My two guns returned their fire at about four hundred yards off with such effect, that at about the fourth round, they began to desert their guns.

Seeing this, I ordered the artillery to cease firing, and advanced the whole of the cavalry into the river which was about four and a half feet deep and a hundred yards wide. We then charged and took all their guns, which consisted of one twenty-four pound howitzer, and one six-pounder field gun which were English, one three pound and one one pound, native. We pursued with the whole of the cavalry, the irregulars taking the lead and the lancers gleaning after them. We may have killed about two hundred, and the right of the cavalry coming on the Ganges drove a number of them into the river, who were all drowned. We took all their ammunition, and the whole force consisting of three hundred infantry and fifty *sowars* are utterly disorganized and most of them killed.

A gallop of fourteen miles after a march of forty yesterday and twenty-four this day has made me feel very tired. We are going twenty-four miles to night, as we have heard bad news from Lucknow, Havelock is besieged in the residency and has only provisions to last till the 10th of September.

God bless you.

Your affectionate Henry

Camp Chauhanpore, 20 miles from Cawnpore,
(no date) between 23rd & 29th Oct. 1857.

I got your letter yesterday, after not hearing for three weeks. I was delighted to see that you had turned the corner, and hope that you will soon be able to go out

I am very sorry that Arnold and his wife both go away and leave you.[11] Why, you will be then quite alone; however, you must do your best and take care of yourself.

We have received very bad news from Lucknow. Outram and Havelock are in a mess, but I think I can clear the road with my cavalry, helped by a little artillery, at any rate we are going to try.

---

11. Their governess and children, however, remained with my wife.

Since I last wrote, I have destroyed the town of a rascally fellow who annoyed the district; I forget his name. His fort was blown up and his village destroyed. He had 800 matchlock men who all bolted, except a dozen who I took in the fort. There are about 1,500 infantry at Cawnpore and more are arriving every day. I was fourteen hours in the saddle yesterday, and have just arrived after a long march, so that, between duty, sleep, and meals, I have hardly any time to write. I have to place all pickets for the safety of the camp, so that after the march, I have often some ten miles to ride.

God bless you my dearest and may you soon get well and be off home.

Your affectionate H. A. O.

Cawnpore, October 29th, 1857.

The Futteghur *rajah* has cut off our communication with Agra, so that the last letters I wrote you have come back to me, and most probably you will not hear from me for some time. I told you of my little affair with his detachment at Kanoj,[12] when I got four of his guns and killed about two hundred of his rascals. Nothing has occurred of any consequence since then. We are to halt here till Sir Colin Campbell comes, which will be about the 1st or 2nd of November, we shall then march at once on Lucknow and relieve Havelock and Outram who are besieged in different buildings. All our officers from England are expected to join today, so we shall be very strong. The 93rd marched in yesterday, and troops of all kinds are pouring up country so that I hope soon to write you word that we have utterly destroyed all opposition.

The Gwalior force of mutineers are said to be near Kalpee with forty guns. I went and visited the scene of the slaughter of our ladies, their blood, hair, and brains still adhere to the walls. Scratched on the walls was the following:

> I have passed many a happy day but never thought it would come to this, Countrymen remember the 16th of July.

I picked up in the house the remains of a baby's dress, I could not help shedding tears when I thought of what had taken place, and I felt an inward satisfaction that it had pleased God

12. This affair of Kanoj was afterwards called "General Grant's victory at Kanoj."

to allow me to be partly an instrument in avenging their cruel deaths, which I think I did well on several occasions with my cavalry, and especially this last time at Kanoj, as those rascals belonged to the very man by whose orders these atrocities were committed. I hope you still continue to improve in health. God ever bless and preserve you.

Your affectionate Henry.

Cawnpore, October 31st, 1857.

We march for Lucknow tomorrow. Sir Colin Campbell and General Wyndham are expected to arrive tomorrow. The 93rd. Highlanders, a splendid regiment, are now in camp, so we shall have 4,000 infantry and 1,000 cavalry with a number of guns. An officer and fifty men of the Royal Artillery have also joined. It is a terrible thing to have the *dâk* cut off, I never hear from you now, and I write only on the chance of your receiving this. We are quite in another climate here, it is terribly hot all day, indeed I believe the climate of Cawnpore is about the worst in India. There is a steamboat on the river close to the bridge of boats. I visited the house defended by Colonel Wheeler and picked up a long lock of hair which evidently had been cut off short from the head of some lady, what suffering they must have endured before they were killed! How thankful I ought to be to God that you were not among them. These are sad times, but God will not punish us too severely. I hope that you pray every night that I may be spared to meet you again.

We may have a severe battle at Lucknow, or we may have nothing to do, it is quite on the cards that these wretches will all run away on the approach of our army. In the meantime we never hear a word of Outram or Havelock who are besieged in the residency.

Bless you dearest, and may God give you health, and a speedy meeting with

Your affectionate Henry

Camp near Lucknow,
3rd to 9th November, 1857.

Halted, awaiting Sir Colin Campbell, who joined on the 9th. We paraded, and Sir Colin said that the cavalry had covered themselves with glory. Sir H. Grant being in command of our force. Sir Colin told him that he should not supersede him, but that he was to continue in the command of the whole force.

We are now off to Lucknow, and here I must break off as some officers who are going home will bring these short notes to you. Of course I will write more in detail after events.

Camp near Lucknow. We are still halted at the same spot waiting for the commander-in-chief who has arrived at Cawnpore. Yesterday I went with a force to Alumbagh, about two miles from Lucknow, where a body of our troops are besieged—one squadron 9th Lancers, two regiments irregular cavalry and a lot of infantry with six guns. We threw in supplies and brought out the sick. The enemy tried to hinder us, but a few rounds from our guns made them all run. Our loss was *nil*, but a very extraordinary and ludicrous accident happened.

I went out ahead of the column with one squadron of the 9th Lancers and two guns. We placed the guns in position in a small *tope* of trees about seven hundred yards from the main road where our column remained, some Infantry were placed to watch our proceedings.

Suddenly we were observed to have sustained a perfect rout, cavalry and artillery rushing back to the main column all mixed up and in the wildest confusion. Fawcett, who commanded the squadron of lancers, was thrown from his horse, and how I myself got out of the scrape I can hardly tell. My horse reared and plunged so that it was a considerable time before I could get him to move on at all. The infantry stood to their arms not knowing what to make of it, while we galloped past, away into the plain. Such a rout was never seen, but nobody could see any enemy in pursuit. Now what do you think was the cause of all this? Why a pendulous bees' nest in a tree. One of the 9th Lancers, Lieutenant Evans, whom we call "*Bashi Bazook*" foolishly stuck his lance into the nest and naturally the bees attacked us with the utmost fury. Many are now laid up with swelled heads and eyes. I got punished about the head and ears and my clothes are full of stings, but I am not much the worse for it.

On actual service with a European enemy, such an accident might have been attended with very serious consequences, however,—all's well that ends well. It is a great lesson never to despise your enemy, a few small flies could do what 20,000 *sepoys* would never have dared to attempt. How little is man,

175

and how easy for the Almighty to thwart all his plans by the most, apparently, insignificant agency! I hope you continue to improve. No letters.

Yours affectionately,

H. A. O.

Headquarters, Nov. 15, 1857,
Martiniére, Lucknow.

Since I last wrote we have remained encamped within six miles of Lucknow. Sir Colin Campbell joined and yesterday we advanced on Lucknow. We came down by Dil Kusha (heart delighting) Park, and the enemy first met us in force near the Martiniére. After we had crushed them by a *feu d'enfer* we went in and took the house, and this is the position we now hold. This day we halt and tomorrow we attack. Yesterday, Wheatfield of the carabineers, attached to the 9th Lancers, Mayne, quartermaster general (brother of the parson), with about thirty men, were killed and wounded. There can be no doubt that tomorrow we shall reach the residency and relieve the garrison. Such is the state of affairs at present.

This day I for the first time again assumed the command of the 9th Lancers by order of Sir Colin. I felt very much my false position as commanding the irregular cavalry, and I took an opportunity of stating the case to Sir Colin who saw the absurdity of my still continuing to be considered in the 2nd Dragoon Guards, when it was well known that my appointment to that regiment had been cancelled while we were before Delhi.

Yesterday the enemy met our men fairly and we beat them off killing twelve of them.

Col. Little who has joined, is promoted to a brigadier and Col Grant is brigadier general.

Young Pickering has joined our camp, he called on me today. I have not received a line from you for three weeks on account of the *dâk* having been cut off. We have left all our tents behind.

Adieu dearest.

Your affectionate H. A. O.

Headquarters,
Secundra Bagh,
Lucknow, Nov. 20th, 1857.

We attacked Lucknow with our whole force under the command of Sir Colin Campbell, on the 16th. We advanced by the Dilhooska Park, which we occupied after a trifling resistance. We then attacked and carried the house which commands the Martiniére, which was occupied by us after an hour's cannon fire. This was our first day's work.

On the 17th we advanced against the Secundra Bagh, which is a large building occupied by 2,000 of the enemy, who defended it with desperation; indeed they had no choice as they had no retreat. We dragged up heavy artillery to within sixty yards under the hottest fire I ever saw, breached the walls and stormed it by the 93rd Highlanders and Sikhs. Every soul within perished, men, women and children. No more horrible sight could be imagined; the dead lay in heaps. Fire was then applied to the sheds, and all were burnt, many alive. Cawnpore has been fearfully avenged. I am sorry for the women and children, but it was impossible to distinguish them in the general massacre. Two days after, some were found alive among the heaps. One man only, got out and was cut down by a sailor. Sir Colin Campbell exposed his life under the fire in a most gallant manner.

On the 18th we stormed and took the mosque and formed a junction with Havelock and Outram. We also took the barracks. On the 19th the whole line of the river was ours and the place was relieved. There was little doing on the 20th, the enemy still holding the Kaiser Bagh and the town.

I do not think that we shall at present occupy the whole place, as our force is too small, but we shall get off our women and sick to Cawnpore. The cavalry lost a few horses by stray shots, but were not engaged as it was no place for them. On the first day I commanded the advance guard and escaped unwounded, which was a wonder, as the fire was very heavy. I really cannot say what our loss is in all, but some twenty officers and four hundred or five hundred killed and wounded may be near the mark.

> *Adieu*, with much love,
>
> Your affectionate H. A. O.
>
> Headquarters, Lucknow,
> November 21st, 1857.

We have not been firing much since I last wrote, merely holding our position to get off the ladies, half of whom went yesterday, and the remainder leave the residency tonight.

I find I underestimated our loss in my last letter we lost forty-one officers and 500 men killed and wounded—ten officers killed.

I am heartily sick of this place, the dead are merely covered with a little earth and the effluvia is most offensive.

You will be delighted to hear that I have been mentioned in the despatch.

Your affectionate H. A. O.

Alum Bagh,
26th Nov. 1857.

I got a letter from you today, and am delighted to hear that you are free from pain and much better. All our communications will soon be restored, and then I hope to meet you once more, as God has spared me from this dreadful Lucknow affair.

There have been eighteen officers buried and upwards of 600 men killed and wounded, 150 of whom are dead. There is no post, but my letters are sent with those of the commander-in-chief by *cossid* (messenger).

This is what we have done since I last wrote. We occupied the whole river front of Lucknow; orders were then given to evacuate our position; we removed all the ladies and children, as well as all the treasure, and then returned without any loss, except an unfortunate cook who was killed by a round shot.

We march on Cawnpore tomorrow, and from thence, most probably, we shall go and settle with the Gwalior force at Kalpee, and the Futteyghur Ragah at Futteypore; after that I cannot say what will be done.

I commanded the cavalry during the relief of Lucknow, as Col. Little was detached to another duty. I covered the retreat with General Outram's force, and I hope to get something for it, as well as some prize money, my share may be some £2,000.[13] If I am killed, you will put in your claim for it. Poor Mayne, the clergyman's brother, was killed and was buried where he fell I have not had a single line from England and I send the last English letter to you. You had better get all your things ready to move at a short notice.

Your affectionate Henry.

---

13. I got nothing, and my prize money was a myth.

Cawnpore, 6 Dec. 1857,

It is some time since I last wrote to you, but till the roads were thoroughly opened it was of no use.

I told you that we got all the ladies out of Lucknow and then marched on Cawnpore where we found things in a very bad state. General Wyndham went out most rashly to meet a larger force of the enemy, and had to retire to his stronghold, after losing his whole camp and the town of Cawnpore, which was taken by the enemy. He lost a great many in killed and wounded, in fact, it is the worst thing that has happened to us since the commencement of the mutiny. All the government stores and ammunition were seized by the rebels. Brigadier Wilson was killed, with Col. Woodford and many other officers.

Thus we found affairs when we returned to Cawnpore, where we encamped on the low waste. After a slight fight every day for three days, they left us in quiet, and we immediately sent off our sick and the ladies to Allahabad, while the rebels were still holding the town. Yesterday, when all our *impedimenta* had been sent away, we went at the enemy in earnest. I never saw such a thing, they never stood a moment, but fled as soon as they saw us striking our tents. The cavalry pursued some fifteen miles and took every stitch they had, including guns and baggage but killed very few indeed, owing to mismanagement as usual. I am very tired and have had nothing to eat all day and had to sleep on the ground at night. Our loss is next to nothing.

Poorah, 10th December. We made a long march under Grant with his division and came up with the enemy at this place at the *ghât* on the river. I got at them with the lancers and killed fifty and the irregular cavalry killed forty more. We took all their guns and did not lose a single man either killed or wounded.

Your affectionate Henry.

Cawnpore, 14th December, 1857.

I have not heard a word from you for six weeks. Your last letter said you were free from pain, but that you could not walk and were only able to go out in a *janpan*. There will, I think, be no more real fighting, it is all up with the Pandies. The last thing we did was to take fifteen guns, as I told you in my last. The enemy always bolted and we lost no men either killed or wounded; but sleeping in the open on the ground has given me pains all over my body, and a bad attack of diarrhoea, which has, I think, to do with my cholera at Delhi, although the attack there was very slight. The doctor says I ought to go on sick leave, which I think I may do as, now the fighting is all over for the present, there is nothing to prevent my taking rest. Get some soldier's wife to escort you and come and join me at Cawnpore.

Cawnpore, December 22nd, 1857.
I have not heard from you at all. I have been laid up for the last three weeks with diarrhoea and rheumatism and have got six weeks' leave to remain at Cawnpore, and if I do not get better I am advised to go to England with other sick. Nothing has been done, and now the fighting is over I wish I was well out of it. I direct this to Umballa as I do not know where you are.[14]

Cawnpore, 27th December, 1857.
Two long months have passed away and I have not received a line from you. Of course I know the reason, but now I should think the roads may be opened. I write on chance only, as they tell me at the post office that they are not open, and this makes me feel very unhappy. Sir Colin lingers for weeks and does nothing, simply because he does not know what to do. A proclamation of an amnesty should be issued and flying cavalry columns sent out The cold weather will soon be over, and then Europeans cannot act without terrible sacrifice of life. Oh, for a younger man at the helm, these old men are all slow!

Here am I at forty-five only, and I feel I am nothing like I was, and besides, as Sir Charles Napier said, I am a Sybarite and cannot sleep on wet ground without getting rheumatism. Sir Colin is nearer seventy than sixty and he had done his work well. War is like love, neither Mars nor Venus will favour old men. Positively I have no news to tell you.

Your affectionate Henry.

Cawnpore, 30th December, 1857.
I have heard on good authority that the ladies at Agra will soon be coming down country, therefore get to Agra as soon as possible. Perhaps I may be able to go to England with you.

I believe Sir Colin Campbell is near Futteyghur, so now the road to Agra must be open. Bless you my own dear.

Ever your affectionate Henry.

---

14. This letter did not reach my wife till the 10th February, 1858.

Cawnpore 31st December, 1857.

I can only reiterate my daily prayer that you will proceed immediately to Agra. I enclose an order for one thousand *rupees* as you may be short of money. I am a little better and if I continue to mend, of course I cannot go home with you, as my regiment is still on service, although the fighting may be done. I was before a Medical Board who decided that I might stay six weeks at Cawnpore to see if I could recover before going to England.

My name has appeared in all despatches, but that is all humbug and nonsense. I have now not received a line from you for three months. I bless you my dearest, such is the prayer of your affectionate Henry.

Cawnpore, January 3rd, 1858.

The roads are now open, but I have not heard from you. I go to the post office daily, but always come away empty. I do not get better and am still very ill. My doctor says that chronic diarrhoea is very dangerous after having had cholera. I am thin and suffer also from neuralgia but my head is clear and I may get over it if I go away to England for a time. With my best love.

Your affectionate Henry.

Cawnpore, January 7th, 1858.

I have just got seven of your letters all at once, some dated two months back. You ought to have been some time in Agra, if you have been able to move. It will be unfortunate indeed if I am obliged to go away without you, as I am very ill, and only fancy, poor Colonel Cotton who was in command at Agra, is dead! No news whatever.

Your affectionate Henry.

Cawnpore, January 8th, 1858.

Sir Colin has walked into Futteyghur without opposition, taking or rather finding fifty guns. I am sorry to tell you that in a slight skirmish at Kanoj, the seat of a former exploit of mine that I told you of, and which was described in the papers as "Grant's Victory at Kanoj." Younghusband, the distinguished irregular cavalry man, was killed. I am very distressed at this and be will be a very great loss to his corps. Love.

Your affectionate Henry.

Cawnpore, January 14th, 1858.

It is decided I am to go to England so I hope to meet you soon, when we can go together. The only news I have is that Outram had a kind of fight at Alum Bagh, the rebels attacked him and he drove them off with a loss, to them, of four hundred. Outram's loss was six wounded, two of whom have since died. You can come and join me here as soon as possible. With love,

Your affectionate Henry.

Cawnpore, January 19th, 1858.

Four *sowars* would be an ample escort for you, as Sir Colin is at Bewar; get some other lady to come with you. I am to be sent, with others, to Allahabad, where I will try and wait for you. Tell Mrs. Anson that I did mention Captain Anson's name to Colonel Cotton, as commanding the 9th. His name will be in the despatch, and he will probably get a brevet majority, so I hope she will be satisfied. I will have a room ready for you.

January 19th. No news, except that Colonel Grant has gone to Umballa, most probably to see his wife, so you may judge that there is very little doing at Sir Colin's headquarters.

Colonel Fraser is old and though he has been a very good man, and is personally brave, still he is now nothing better than an old woman. Have nothing to do with him anymore; send your baggage by bullock train, buy a carriage and come on sharp. Major McPherson I am sure would help you.

I feel quite sorry that you have not got the Sogdollager,[15] you did not say where you had left him.

I look forward to the day when my own girl will be restored to me. I pray God to keep you, comfort you, and sustain you, as He has always done in all your trials, and so long as you remain true to Him, depend upon it, He will never forsake you.

Allahabad, January 31st, 1858.

The days drag on their slow length in this gloomy fort. A dreadful report, for me, has come in, that Sir Colin has stopped permission for ladies to travel, but I do not think he will stop you. He has got cautious in his old age. There is no danger. Remember me kindly to Lady Outram, if she should be near you.

Isri will bring a carriage for you when you arrive. I gave him

---

15. A dog.

thirty *rupees* for himself, and you can give him more if he should want it. Let nothing stop you. The commander-in-chief is an obstinate old fool, who is not likely to give permission for you to travel. If you have got good sense you will listen to me. Do you think I do not care more for you than he does? *take* permission.

I hope you got the letter I wrote, enclosing one for Lady Outram. The East India Company has ceased to reign. It is all up with John Company (*Hogia*) so much the better. Everything here below is a mere question of time. John Company has expired, suddenly, full of years, if not quite full of honours. Let us regard him with a charitable eye. *Requiescat in pace*—let him rest in peace, and may those who succeed him take warning by this Mutiny, and learn to govern with greater ability.

The whole credit of the plan for the relief of Lucknow ought to be put to the account of Outram, while Sir Colin has complacently allowed it to be put to his own. I have now in my possession the plan of Sir James, sent to us before he knew that Sir Colin was coming. The whole thing was done for Sir Colin, with the solitary exception that he attacked Secundra Bagh before he took the barracks, which was a great error on his part, as I will show you from my drawing when you arrive. He would have had much less loss had he followed out Outram's plan.

Your affectionate Henry.

(My wife reached Allahabad on the 10th of February, 1858, and we left India 23rd February, arriving in London on April 9th. Nothing particular occurred during the voyage. On passing through Paris, I had an interview with Lord Cowley, the Ambassador, and gave him information on the state of affairs in India.)

★★★★★★

In June 1858, I returned to India and took command of the 9th Lancers.

Ship *Holmesdale*, off Brighton, June 30th, 1858. We got well out of the Thames the first day, but since we have had light winds, and were becalmed off Sandgate. I could see our house with my small glass, very well. It made me feel very uncomfortable, when I thought that I might have been living there with my girl; however, I look forward to better times.

Mr. Darling who fitted out my cabin never came to be paid so you must find and pay his bill £14 1s. 6d.

We have a very good set of passengers. Lord Hardwicke introduced himself to me as senior officer on board. His son, Lord Royston, is going out to join the 7th Hussars. Half past seven p.m.. Isle of Wight in sight and pilot just leaving. *Adieu.*

Ship *Holmesdale* fifty miles North of Madeira,
July 7th, 1858.

I last wrote by the pilot off the Isle of Wight, since which we have had good luck, a N.E wind, before which we have had a splendid run to Madeira, making good about two hundred miles a day. Nothing has occurred worth mentioning. We have only one lady passenger, a Mrs Lumsden. I have begun a letter, when I shall be able to send it, is another thing.

Off St. Antoni, Cape Verde, July 15th, 1858.

We may probably find a homeward bound vessel to send my letter on to you.

July 18th. You see I write small scraps, from time to time, as you wished me to do. A homeward bound ship passed us in the night; these ships do not like to lose time by heaving to. I feel very melancholy at my separation from you, and I have nothing now to look forward to except your affection for me, in this world. Think always and pray to God for me.

July 21st. I took a stereoscopic view on board, which you shall have one day when I am able to send it.

July 25th. No ship has passed and the wind is against us. I wish I had never left you.

August 1st. No ship.

October 16th. This day arrived at Calcutta, tired and out of spirits. Went to Grindlay and found one letter only from you and one from Peter. I am glad you are all so happy. Grindlay gave me my Insignia of the Bath. I intend to proceed to Cawnpore, immediately, and join the 9th Lancers. General and Lady Outram are not in Calcutta. India is just as it was when I left it. I am glad Peter is going to be married. God bless you and my love to you all.

Calcutta October 21st, 1858.

The mail has been detained for some State reasons, so I am enabled to write again. I am not at all well, I cannot get rid of the pain in my back and I do not know what to do for it, I think it must be gout I have taken my *dâk* and shall most probably be with my regiment at the end of the month, as a railroad is now open from Allahabad to Cawnpore. Send £25 to Mrs T. Campbell and £25 to Fanny Delamain from me. I am afraid they are hard pressed, as Edward lost all his little property some time ago.

22nd October. Just got your welcome letter. Mind you get yourself a handsome piano and continue also to improve your mind, especially with regard to your knowledge of languages. I do not see why you should not get a Latin Grammar just to obtain a slight idea of the language—and continue to pray for my welfare. Buy something handsome for £25, and give it as a wedding present to Peter.

Shergotty, October 21st, 1858.

I intend to write little scraps, from time to time, while they are fresh in my memory. I am going by carriage *dâk* to join the regiment.

At Jugdespore, some few hundred rebels made a stand a day or two ago; a great many were killed and they have dispersed to some hills, where they now are, about three miles from the *dâk* bungalow, where I am now writing. The magistrate sent me a letter telling me that there was no danger on the road as far as Benares, so I am going on alone, except that I have one European soldier servant. Passing Raneegunj, I enquired for Captain Grubbe, but he had left for Calcutta.

Benares, October 28th, 1858.

I arrived here this morning. Colonel Douglas fell in with the rebels near Sasseram, three days ago, he killed some of them and the rest ran away. A stranger would have turned back, but I knew, of old, that after a recent beating, they would not come near the trunk road for some time, so I went on. I found my carriage, which had not been sold when we came home, and I am going to take it with me this morning. We shall have a winter's chase after a scattered enemy, who have crossed the Soane and are coming down towards us. There are very few of them in

185

Oude. Tell Fred I met a man who said he knew him, his name is
—— he looked a snob, so I did not cultivate his acquaintance.

Cawnpore, October 30th, 1858.
Arrived here this evening and found the regiment has the charge
of the old King of Delhi at Chowbeepore, just one march off.
Tomorrow will be Sunday, so they will halt and come in on the
1st November. I passed through Allahabad yesterday. The governor general and Lord Clyde were there, but I did not see either
of them. The 9th Lancers are to give over the old king and go
on to be stationed at Futteypore, which is between Cawnpore
and Allahabad. Anson is sick at the hills; Hamilton and Wilkin-
son are both gone home sick. I am just going to take a buggy
and drive out to the regiment.
Colonel Briscoe, of the 2nd Dragoon Guards, has been sent
home, and Campbell, the other colonel, is dead. Had I remained
in that regiment, I should have got the command of it, without
purchase.[16]

Cawnpore, October 31st, 1858.
We are now encamped on the spot which poor Wheeler defended, and we march in charge of the old king for Allahabad
in a day or two. I found the regiment all rights and am now
very busy getting all my things for service; we march on the
3rd November. General Grant and Lord Clyde are both very
well. How strange it is that those who get anything good always
remain well! Perhaps it may be a good thing for me that I am a
nobody—that is, I have no interest and no .friends to say I have
got merit, or it might keep me from you my dearest, you who
are my real blessing, while all the rest is mere shadow. Pity it is
that knowing and believing this I should feel disappointment
at being out of the ring. God knows what is best for me, but if
I continue in my present sentiments, it will not be long before
we meet again. With my best love to all at home

I remain, your affectionate Henry.

Allahabad, November 15th, 1858.
I can only write a few words to tell you that soon after joining
the regiment, I was taken ill with congestion of the liver, and
have been carried in a *dhooly* ever since. We arrived here yester-

---

16. *Vide* Appendix.

186

day. Two hundred men of the 9th go on with the old king, four marches towards Calcutta, and then return. I march tomorrow with the headquarters of the regiment to join Sir Colin Campbell at Nuzeebghur, some forty miles across the river into Oude. God bless you.

Sultenpore, Oude, November 21st, 1858,
I am a little better, but cannot write without getting a headache, so you must make the best of what I send. I cannot find that there is any enemy to fight. We are going to Fyzabad. This eternal marching is very trying to me, the nights are so cold and the days so hot. ———— has come to grief through shamming sick, his wife has been the ruin of him. Every little place in Oude has its little mud fort. There will, in my opinion, be bands of marauders in India for the next two years, about these parts. I think that all those in arms against us in Oude, have now got to' the borders of Nepal, across the Goomtee. I am much better today and intend to ride tomorrow's march. I am tired of the whole thing for, unless you are in a particular set, there is no hope. I thought the Duke of Cambridge would have been just, but alas! he is guided, by the powers in this country.[17]

Fyzabad, November 24th, 1858.
Three days ago. General Grant rode into our camp, and then passed on to Fyzabad, where we found him this day. Fyzabad is on the Gogra, a very large river. The enemy, some 20,000 or 30,000 *canaille*, occupy the opposite bank and are now firing into us, which I am so accustomed to, that it appears quite natural; it amuses them and does not hurt us. We have established a bridge, with a kind of *tête du pont* on the opposite side of the river. We intend to cross over very soon, and then they will fire off all their guns and run away. We shall pursue and kill a very few, and perhaps take all their artillery; and this again and again. Hamilton left us for Calcutta, and died going down the river, he unfortunately drank very hard.

I am writing this to go by today's post which leaves at 2 p.m. I have just returned from a long march and am tired, so can-

---

17. To show how true this was, I may here mention that long after I had come home for good, I was talking to an old friend, an official at the Horse Guards, and he said that the Duke of Cambridge wished to do what was right, but that it was more than his place was worth, to interfere with Lord Clyde. He told me that the duke had himself said so.

not write much, but will write again after our next affair with the rebels. I wish heartily I was with you, as I am sick of this disgusting service in which no honour is to be obtained. I have nothing more to tell you, but I beg God to bless you my dearest I need not say remember me in your prayers.

Nawabgunj, one march the other side of the Gogra, November 26th, 1858.

Yesterday we crossed the river, attacked, and of course defeated the wretched rabble called the enemy. Their position was a strong one, had they known how to defend it. The quicksands by the river side were most annoying. My leading troop of Lancers got into a quicksand, and a number of guns stuck fast and could not be brought into action. General Grant was in command, and the enemy bolted at the first discharge of our guns. We pursued with some horse artillery and after two or three hours, we came up with some two hundred men, of whom we may have killed about sixty or eighty; the rest escaped into the thick jungle. I have one lancer wounded. We returned at 2 p.m. having started in pursuit at 4 a.m.

The horses were dreadfully knocked up, so we are halting today. I think that we shall now go in the direction of Bairaitch, where it is said that a woman is at the head of a force. In this mutiny, the women have shewn more courage than the men. I am horribly stiff and tired from riding so long, in my weak condition. My lancers have killed very few; it does no good killing these poor wretches and I believe the authorities do not wish any more to be killed.

I was obliged to kill one myself. On coming up with him, he threw away his matchlock, and my orderly tried to cut him down, but could not get at him with his sword, so I was compelled to run him through with my lance, which I always carry, as if he had been spared, he would have possibly shot some of our side.

These poor wretches are certainly failures of nature, what could they have been made for? I repeat, I wish I was well out of it, and no honour to be gained. Unfortunately, however, these wasps' nests must be destroyed. Young P—— has gone away to the hills with liver complaint, I am told he eats enormously and takes no exercise, this is sure to bring on liver complaint in this country.

Camp, Nawabgunj,
Six miles on the Nepal side of the Gogra,
December 2nd, 1858.

We remain encamped in the same place since I last wrote after our fight. Tomorrow, we march in the direction of Bairaitch, and shall in all probability leave bodies of troops at different places, as the moment we move, the niggers come out of the jungle, and then it is the old thing over again. I am a little better, but have no appetite for food.

I received Peter's note in which he says Grant is older than I am, but Peter forgets he had a commander-in-chief to kick everyone out of his way. This is a very pleasant mode of getting on, but I have no ambition left. I see the imposition practised and I see no remedy. I am playing at a game where there is cheating going on, and I intend to play no more. What can be more barefaced than allowing Little to remain, when he has openly avowed his intention of never coming back to India?

The papers are full of the duke's regret at the abuse of the purchase system, and yet he will allow an officer, whom he knows never intends to serve again in India, hang on, in order that he may make more money by selling his commission after the regiment returns home.[18] If any of you can ascertain anything about this, I should like to know. Of course, I cannot sell while we are in the field. The 9th Lancers will not come home this cold weather as we have a winter campaign before us, and after going through this, what prospect is before me?—either to be put in as junior in a new regiment, or upon compulsory half-pay.

We never hear any news and I know nothing of what is going on, and write without knowing when the mail will go out. Indeed there is no post; a dragoon carries our letters to Allahabad. Baker died at Delhi, no person knows anything about his effects. Apply to the Secretary of State for War, that is the proper channel The regiment had left and he must have died in some other hospital.

---

18. Brigadier General Little got the regiment by the promotion of Grant, who lost the 'over regulation' of his commission. He ought to have been gazetted as M. G after his appointment to be brigadier general, as Grant was. *Vide* Appendix.

Camp, Buncipice,
In the Jungle, some 25 miles from Fyzabad,
December 7th, 1858.

It will be no use looking for the names of places, I am now writing twenty-five miles N.N.E., of Fyzabad. After our last affair, we marched to a place called Bangaon, where there is a little fort, which the enemy deserted on our approach. We halted a couple of days and blew up the fort. Yesterday we marched to Mitchligunj, and were taking up our encampment, when a certain Devibukhs (gift of God), whom our men call *Davy Bux,* poured a shower of grape into our advanced guard, out of a dense jungle. It knocked over one artillery horse and carried off the leg of a gunner.

We formed up, immediately, and the infantry advancing into the jungle, under cover of a smashing fire from two troops of horse artillery, the enemy at once broke and fled, leaving two guns which were brought in. From the nature of the place, all pursuit was out of the question; in fact we are on the outskirts of the Terai, that dense jungle which extends from the slopes of the vast mountains of Nepal. We took a number of prisoners, and among them two *sepahis* dressed in the proper uniform of their regiment. General Grant gave them each a copy of the Proclamation of Amnesty and dismissed them to take it to their friends in the jungle.

December 9th. We are now fourteen miles west of our position on the 7th, at a place called Gonda, the *rajah* of which fled, so we had no fight this morning. We shall, most probably, march to Bagram Ghât, the ford across the Gogra on the road from Lucknow to Bairaitch, there we shall meet with the commander-in-chief and attack the Queen of Oude. She has seventeen guns and a miserable rabble of perhaps 10,000 men.

This may finish the war here for the present, but nobody knows or can know anything, for certain, as to other parts of India.

Of course I am in great suspense about the regiment's coming home. Some say we shall come home immediately, that is to say in about two months; others not till 1860. If we come home at once, Little will do me out of the regiment, but I should hardly think they could do such a thing as let him stay on till 1860. Perhaps they might keep on two lieutenant-colonels. I have got nothing for it but patience, I suppose. I am better and can now drink a bottle of beer at dinner.

December 12th. Secora. We marched, and arrived here yesterday and found that the enemy had disappeared. It appears that they have gone to Toolseepore in the Terai. No other news.

Camp, Bulrampore,
December 19th, 1858.

We have been encamped at the above place for the last three days and I see no signs of a move.

We have just had a hearty laugh at mess. When the mail came in, it contained Lord Derby's announcement that the rebellion was now subdued. He ought not to holloa till he is out of the wood. Why! we have 20,000 men with, God knows how many guns, within twenty miles of our camp. I shall endeavour to explain to you how we stand. Lord Clyde is at Bairaitch with 5,000 men, Grant is at Bulrampore, and Rowcroft's column is advancing on the left bank of the Bhoodi Raptee (or old Raptee). Bulrampore is on the right bank of the Baptee, which is a deep river with high banks; the Bhoodi Raptee is the old channel of Raptee, and has little water in it. The Terai is the name of the forest which is found, almost everywhere, at the foot of the Himalayas. Lord Clyde has, it is said, 17,000 (but it is impossible to say to five or six thousand how many) of the enemy against him near Bairaitch.

I think I told you Oude had never been surveyed, but the best map is that portion of Oude which you will find on the trigonometrical survey map of India, which you can buy in London. Get that map, then stick pins accordingly, a pin with a red head for Grant, a blue one for Lord Clyde, etc., and you will have a perfect idea of the present state of affairs in these parts.

Now if we, that is Grant's column, cross the Raptee you will see that the enemy has no escape, it will be beset by Rowcroft on one flank, by us on the other, and will have to fly either to the Terai, or in the direction of the Raptee. There is no living to be got in the Terai, it is impracticable for guns and of course the rebels will be unable to get them over the Raptee, so they are, in what the Yankees would call "a regular fix." They are not *sepahis* but all the scum of Oude, the armed retainers of *rajahs*, thieves and outcasts of all kinds, who having always lived by plunder, will never turn their hand to any honest employment.

191

In my opinion, very few of them will be killed, as the ground is very bad for cavalry and artillery, and when they do run, they run very fast.

That fellow at Nepal—Jung Bahadur (the brave in fight) is beginning to very insolent. I look on a war with Nepal to be quite on the cards, if not now, most certainly in a very few years. The "brave in fight" refused to receive the resident, Colonel Ramsey, and it appears he has since written insolent letters to the governor-general. What an idiot he must be, but so it always is! you know that he who is doomed to fall is first deprived of reason.

You recollect the day my own dearest, when we were out shooting in the cold season, when the rain came on and I took my horse into the verandah of the tent because it was so cold? Well! we have just had another such fall of rain, and everything is most miserable in camp. You are the only gainer as, having nothing to do, I have time to write you a long letter.

Note. Of course the Mutiny had failed; and, indeed, was virtually overcome when Delhi fell.

The sun is out now and it is very pleasant What a desperate pity young Pickering is not with his troop of artillery, which is in our camp, he will be absent from the cold weather campaign.[19]

Brigadier Hagart, of the 7th Hussars, commands our brigade. He is, without exception, one of the best fellows I know and we get on admirably. The 9th Lancers are in a splendid state. I have only eight men sick, and we turn out (that is to say the men) just as if we were at Canterbury. For myself and the greater part of the officers, I cannot say much as regards our "get up," jack boots, *mirzaies*, and helmets of different shapes, is the order of the day and no two are alike. This must be put a stop to directly we are out of the jungle, but I have no right to say a word on this subject, as I set so bad an example myself. When I get my photographic apparatus under weigh, I will send you one of myself as attired for the jungle, and one, the correct thing, in order that you may judge for yourself.

It is Sunday, and I am now going to church parade with the regiment. I shall pray God to bless you, my own dear little wife,

---

19. He was away on sick leave.

and that we may shortly meet. Send photographs, I like them very much; get a good stereoscopic one and send it, let it be daguerreotype and coloured. I know it will fade but it will last some years.

Camp, Bulrampore, December 10th, 1858.
We cross the Raptee at this place tomorrow, and do not go higher up the stream as we ought to do if we wish to destroy the enemy's army, so I now suppose that the intention is for us to join Rowcroft and thus drive the rebels towards the column of Lord Clyde. I, myself, do not approve of the movement, we shall however, most probably get all their guns, of which it has now been ascertained they have a great many. This is the latest news. Goodbye, dearest, and God bless you.

Your affectionate Henry.

Heer, in Gorruckpore, December 27th. 1858.
We did not march as I told you we should, but remained at Bulrampore till Christmas Day when, having heard of the doings of Rowcroft, we crossed the Raptee at the ford by Bulrampore.
——— is generally pronounced to be an incapable of the nth power. He advanced on the enemy who were stationed near Toolsepore, in number about 15,000 or 20,000, mostly rebel *sepahis*, with twelve guns. They stood firm in a fine open plain, but instead of attacking their left, he attacked their centre, so that after a slight resistance to a very feeble and irresolute attack, they retired in good order carrying off ten out of their twelve guns. The main body have gone off to their left, threatening the Gorruckpore district, so we made a rapid flank movement with cavalry and artillery under Grant, leaving our infantry and heavy guns at the ford near Toolsepore.
I must make you a plan in order that you may understand this, unfortunately, I have not been able to get my baggage, so have no paints to colour it, but you can do this easily by putting blue for Grant red for ——— and green for the enemy, then paint the rivers and mountain streams blue and mark the places red or yellow, and put in a red and yellow streak to separate Oude from Gorruckpore, on the dotted line.[20]
On the 26th, we made a very long march of thirty miles, to Boodhi, leaving our heavy guns and infantry behind, under

---

20. These plans are omitted.

Brigadier Taylor, the heavy guns at Bulrampore, and the infantry, sick, etc. at the point near where ———— fought; he had sixteen killed and wounded. Today ———— has joined us at Heer. The enemy are supposed to be somewhere about where we shall march to attack them tomorrow. This is the exact state of affairs up to the present date. I was twelve hours on the march yesterday, so I am going to take a sleep after having written to my dearest The whole of the operations have been deplorable, and will continue to be so, so long as incompetent men are appointed, by private interest. I am better in health than when I last wrote and send my love to you all.

Your affectionate H. A. O.

Camp Bunhownee, January, 9th, 1859.

I take up my narrative from the last letter I wrote. On the 4th we, that is Grant's column, marched to attack the enemy at Kimda Kate, a fort in the jungle at the very foot of the hills. The enemy had fourteen guns and any number of men; (it is impossible to say with accuracy how many). As we advanced we found them drawn up with their guns in position on the banks of a *nullah*. Suddenly they appeared to melt away like a snowdrift dissolving, and when we came up not a soul was to be seen; they had all disappeared into the thick jungle of the Terai at the foot of the hills.

We quickly formed our infantry and advanced into the wood, where we picked up all their fourteen guns, loaded They discharged two small ones, without effect. As following their men into the depth of the jungle was out of the question, we drew off our guns and encamped, and this, without the loss of a man. The guns were captured and the rabble have found refuge in Nepal.

The *begum* and her army played the same part on the approach of Lord Clyde; after a few days' skirmishing they dissolved and have gone either to Nepal or some place near it Lord Clyde is going to leave the field, and has stated that the war is at an end; so it is just possible that the Regiment may come home immediately, but I, myself, do not think so. We shall know our destination in less than a week.

Camp, Chundunpore,

January 15th, 1859.

Since I wrote the first part of this letter, we marched on about fourteen miles, and are now awaiting orders. I have delayed this letter hoping to be able to tell you something, but no news comes. I have improved in health during the campaign, and right glad was I to hear that you were getting so strong. I escaped a most terrible accident out shooting. I went with four or five officers to the jungle, and we came on a spot which the enemy had occupied, there was a large quantity of gunpowder and cartridges scattered on the ground. We began collecting the powder and I had just heaped up about four pounds when a servant lit a portfire and Evans[21] took it out of his hand, the powder ignited and blew up within a yard of me. Evans was right over it, he has lost his whiskers, moustache, eyebrows and all the skin of his face. I only got the heat, but if there had been a little more, we should all have been blown up.

Your affectionate Henry.

Camp, Bulrampore, January 18th, 1859.

We have now been here ten days, and have just heard that we are to march tomorrow for Lucknow, where we shall receive our orders as to our final destination. We have been without a drop of wine for the last week, and all eatables are nasty in the extreme. You may say these are minor evils, but let anyone who thinks so try to live for a month on prison fare, and I am sure he would say that on a good diet a great deal depends. Try some bread made of musty flour, with rancid butter, tough meat of a vile kind, and then tell me what kind of a breakfast you have made; however, it cannot last forever.

My idea is that we shall not come home till June 1860. The rebels have all gone into Nepal, and if we return, they will pour through the passes again and plunder the country. Nobody in high command sent instructions to Jung Behadur, the Nepal general, to hold the mountain passes, and even now we do not do what we ought, *viz*, hold the passes on this side, which could be easily done. The spies yesterday brought in word that the rebels are in very great distress, on the other side of the first range of Sewalik hills. I took a party of lancers and light cav-

---

21. This was the same officer who thrust his lance into a nest of bees.

195

alry and went over one of the passes, it was just practicable for horses. The jungle at the foot of the hills is here very narrow, and the number of mountain ranges between the first and the habitable part of Nepal, is about seven. This section will explain our position, we might easily send a force of infantry over.

Your affectionate Henry.

Camp, Byram Ghât, January 27th, 1859.
I am coming home. The regiment will leave for England, I suppose, about April, but I shall come immediately. We are now within four marches of Lucknow, and when we arrive there, I shall get leave of absence to precede the regiment to England. I shall take my passage in the first steamer that leaves in March, and intend to go *via* Trieste.
I shall be a fortnight at Lucknow to settle my affairs, as well as those of my regiment. Is it not a cruel thing that I should be deprived of my command? If we had not come home, Little would have sold, he had commissioned Steele to act for him about the negotiations, all upset by the sudden ordering of us home. We were to have gone to Lucknow to drill a newly raised corps, but General Grant used all his influence to get us home, and he has succeeded.

Your affectionate Henry.

Lucknow January 31st, 1859.
We are now encamped under a temple at which my picket was firing round shot when we relieved Lucknow. Lord Clyde is here, he is not very well and has been in bed for the last three days, he has never recovered his fall.

Your affectionate Henry.

Camp, Lucknow, February 5th, 1859.
I have got my leave and start for Calcutta on the 14th of February.
Lucknow is much changed, nearly half the city is being utterly destroyed. There will be no chance of its being retaken in a hurry.
General Grant is quite well, and is not coming home at present. Lord Clyde also will not leave his post, though he has been very unwell of late. He ought now to think of himself a little.
I am going to have the old regiment out for the last time tomorrow, after which the men will volunteer to other Regi-

ments. We shall not bring home three hundred men.

Your affectionate Henry.

Camp, Lucknow, February 13th, 1859.

At five o'clock the carriage will be at my tent and I shall commence my journey for home. Last night I asked General Hope Grant and all his staff to dine with me for the last time; they all drank my health and we were very jolly. Before dinner I called and took leave of Lord Clyde, he was very kind to me. He was lately very ill but is now much better though looking very thin.

The last news I have to tell you is that Jung Behadur asked for troops to be advanced into Nepal, while he took the rebels who have fled there, in flank. Accordingly Horsford with a column was sent, and attacked them, taking fourteen guns, without sustaining any loss. As usual, they fired off their guns without any effect, and then, as usual, bolted.

The Rajah of Bulrampore has been allowed to annex Toolseepore, in addition to his former *raj*, on account of his good conduct to us. It will give him £30,000 a year, pretty good this! I am packing up in great haste and can write no more except my love.

Your affectionate Henry.

P. S.—The 9th Lancers leave Lucknow for home on the 17th, and will probably be in Calcutta by the middle of the month.

Alexandria ,March 21st, 1859.

I sail at twelve o'clock this day for Trieste. Only fancy, I found Arnold at Cairo very ill; he had been laid up for three weeks. He had a friend with him or I would not have left him.[22]

Paris, April 4th, 1859.

I arrived in Paris at 6.15 this morning. Isri is with me. I have brought him because I could not do without him, and government paid both our passages. His keep costs absolutely nothing and he is of great use; if he should not suit I can put him in the steamboat and send him back, his fare would only be £13, but I think of keeping him in England. I have dressed him in trousers and he looks so very funny. I am pretty well, and am going

---

22. William Delafield Arnold, fourth son of Dr. Arnold, of Rugby. He subsequently got on as far as Gibraltar, and there died on the 9th of April, 1859, aged 31. His wife died the year before, soon after my wife left her.

to the play tonight and leave for England tomorrow. I sold my photographic apparatus for £25. I shall keep the money to buy another at home, when you can come with me. Thank the baroness for me. When the duke does anything for me then I will believe it and not till then, as I do not put my trust in princes.

Your affectionate Henry.

Appendix

1

With regard to Abraham being a mythic personage—I mean the Old Testament account of him is a mere poetic imagination, on a par with that of the rest of the Patriachs. That there was some real nucleus, which' gave rise to the myth, I have little doubt. The same remark would apply to Moses, the pretty story of Joseph and his brethren, etc. These myths have their parallels among all old nations. We in England, have the legend of King Arthur, with his round table, knights, and frail spouse, all of which are the invention of the poet; and, although King Arthur had a nucleus of genuine history in his myth, such a person as represented by the poets, never existed; and yet, up to a very recent period, King Arthur was considered, generally, as an historic personage. Henry VIII shewed Francis I the very round table at which he sat with his Knights. We know now that all these pretty stories about the Knights of Arthur's Court, Sir Lancelot and King Arthur s wife, were written at a comparatively modern period, long after the petty chieftain, who formed the nucleus of the myth, had passed away.

And so it was with the myths of the ancient Hebrews, they were collected, certainly, after the reign of Saul.

The books called the Books of Moses, were manifestly written at a period when there were Kings in Israel, as any unprejudiced person may convince himself by referring to Genesis xxxvi, 31—"*And these are the kings that reigned in the land of Edom, before there reigned any king over the children of Israel.*" The author of the book therefore knew that there was a monarchy in Israel. How then could Moses have written it?

2

It was on a gloomy day, after I had been reading in Bartrihari, that

I composed the allegorical little sketch in the text. When I wrote it I had Schiller's *Cassandra* in my mind, and felt inclined to adopt his mode of thought.

He wished to have his blindness restored to him during an attack of "*Weltschmertz*," *forgetting* the impossibility of his desire.

The legend makes Goethe on his deathbed cry for "more light." Kusalem discovered that Truth was bitter indeed, and consequently he returned to his beloved *Error*. This question is so plainly put in the two following pieces of German poetry, that I think my readers will pardon me for reproducing them here in an English dress, as German is very rarely understood in this country. They are both entitled—

More Light.

"*More Light!*" *groaned out Goethe, when stretched on his deathbed,*
"*Why comes not more light wretched mortals to speed?*"
"*Because they've too much,*" *replied Nature, "already,*
'*Tis light in excess, that's an evil indeed.*"

'*Tis the dazzling light, shed by Physical Science*
On all the great questions that prey on the mind,
Which dispels that soft twilight to human sight suited
Where fantasy dwells with illusion combined.

Cry rather with Schiller, "restore me my blindness.
And let fond delusion still o'er me hold sway,
Naked Truth's not for mortals, her kisses are deadly.
So come genial Error, I wed thee this day."

"*Ah! no,*" *cried fond Error, "my bed you deserted,*
Allured by the sheen of my sister's cold charms,
He who once she has lured to her icy embraces
Can ne'er again slumber in Error's fond arms."

Fair *Error* spoke the truth for, as Goethe remarked, "*That, if your happiness is a mere dream, you had best dream on—once awakened, you will never slumber again.*"

Now let us return to another view of Goethe's last words,

More Light.

"*When the Angel of Death swooped down on the Sage,*
And the shade of his wings threw a film o'er his sight.
The last trembling accents which died on his tongue,
As his soul took its flight, were for light—for more light.
And well would it be for mankind if they'd profit.

And learn to interpret their meaning aright;
Then ne'er would they fail the great truth to acknowledge,
Humanity's happiness lies in more light"

At the present time, 1892, the German *Kaiser* has taken alarm at the preference which his people are showing for *Satyama*, and he wishes to educate the rising generation to stagnate in the arms of *Pramada*, but his efforts are sure to fail. He might as well attempt to stay the tides of the ocean. The philosophic Teutons have tasted the embraces of the cold but faithful *Satyama*, and His Imperial Majesty will soon discover that—

Wer einmal gekostet Ihr kälte umarmung
Am Busen der Taüschung kann nimmermehr ruhn.

3

My mind was still unsophisticated when I wrote my opinion concerning the Duke of Wellington. I then did not know that all men, whether officers in the army or in the diplomatic service, when they arrive at power or occupy a high position, acquire a second character. Perfectly honourable in their private characters, in their public ones they think there is no disgrace in the *mensonge officieux*. Men in power always fear the truth when it appears inimical to their interests. Lord Clyde and General Mansfield had all their lives agreed to the truth of what I said concerning the cowardice of the *sepahis* in their own minds, but had both publicly asserted the contrary, that is, they supported that which they knew to be false. Lord Clyde said afterwards "God forgive me; it was the only time I ever wilfully lent myself to an untruth in my life." [*Vide* Russell's Diary.]

And while I am on this subject, I would here mention a case of the *mensonge officieux*, which refers to myself, personally. I call it a downright *mensonge officieux*, but a legal friend, laughing heartily after he had read the case said "You must not call it that, it is merely a *petitio principii.*"

Now Schopenhauer has said "When a proposition in which there is no direct certainty is put forward as truth, that constitutes a *petitio principia;*" another expression for this Kuntsgriff is employed by Fichte, he calls it *an absolute postulate*, the plain meaning in English, however, is *lying out of it*, only we must not call it by that name. *Mensonge officieux* is the French euphemistic term, and which is considered perfectly fair in official life.

On my arriving in England, after the Indian Mutiny, I lost my full-pay commission, which was equal to a money fine of £ 6,000. I complained of having had my transfer to the 2nd Dragoon Guards cancelled, by which I lost my "over regulation," but could get no redress. H. R. H. the Commander-in-Chief, however, gave me a staff appointment, as some kind of compensation, but I was persistent, and when I retired, I again renewed my complaint to the Horse Guards, as I had no retiring allowance, and I could not get back the money, even, which I had expended; in short, for my service of nearly thirty years, I got no reward, (except medals, clasp, and Order of the Bath), and, moreover, was out of pocket £3,000. H.R.H. ordered a "Careful Report" to be made on my complaint, and the following is the result:—

Horse Guards, War Office,
28th June, 1872.

It appears that you are not satisfied with the answers already given to you, and you complain that "you were transferred to the 2nd Dragoon Guards without your knowledge and consent, against the rules of the Service, whereby you are ruined in your profession and deprived of your 'over regulation,' which you gave; also that you were 'appointed to a blank Lieutenant Colonelcy in the 9th Lancers when that Regiment had been relieved in India and was on the Home Establishment.'

My answer. [*Where does it appear? certainly not in my complaint This whole paragraph is a mere petitio principii and the writer well knew there was not a word of truth in it, and that the direct reverse was the fact, I complained that I was removed from and not to the 2nd Dragoon Guards, and the very next paragraph proves that the writer well knew what my complaint really was. The Secretary of State for War knew nothing of the Purchase System,, and hence he must have thought I was a fool or endeavouring to deceive him. The writer took words out of my letter without their context. Let any man of honour reflect—how could I have made such a ridiculous complaint?*]

I have received the directions of the Field Marshal Commanding-in-Chief to state in reply the following circumstances:
In June 1857, it became necessary to augment the 2nd Dragoon Guards then about to embark for service in India, and as the 9th Lancers at that time were under orders to return to this country, His Royal Highness, to prevent you from being reduced to half pay, and *according to custom* transferred you to the 2nd Dragoon Guards.

[This is a perfectly correct statement in all its particulars. I was placed in the 2nd Dragoon Guards at my own particular request as well as according to the custom, of the Service, to prevent my being placed on half pay. Why then was my appointment cancelled, whereby I was put back into the 9th Lancers and was actually put on half pay? How then can H. R. Highness consider this to be "only just?" He knows that my exchange was cancelled because my services were wanted for the 9th Lancers.]

During the next month (July), it was decided that owing to the services of the 9th Lancers and 14th Hussars being required during the Mutiny, these corps should not return home.—
His Royal Highness then considered that it *would only be just* to the officers who had been transferred from those regiments to the 2nd and 3rd Dragoon Guards (under the belief that the two former were to be relieved in India by the two latter, which did not take place), to cancel such transfers, and, accordingly, in the *Gazette* of the 24th July, 1857, your transfer and that of some other ten officers to the *2nd* and *3rd Dragoon Guards* were cancelled. By this arrangement you virtually never left the 9th Lancers.

[I ask, who were those ten officers? They were the eight junior lieutenants and two captains, and really only five of these were transferred. Vide Army List.

That might have been just to them, but to me who was senior major in the 2nd, to be put back into the 9th Lancers, and to be degraded a step in rank, it was simply monstrous, as any person who has any knowledge of the purchase system must see at once, I appeal to the Annual Army List of 1857.

Virtually never left the 9th Lancers? All I know is that I actually left the 9th Lancers—gave up the command of the regiment before Delhi, and never joined again until the Relief of Lucknow. Why, I held a command of the whole of the cavalry of the pursuing column, as major in the 2nd Dragoon Guards.]

With regard to your statement that you were appointed to a blank Lieut. Colonelcy when the 9th Lancers had been relieved in India and were on the Home establishment, I am to bring to your notice that you obtained your promotion without purchase, in succession to Sir Hope Grant promoted a Major General, on the 5th March, 1858 and that the 9th Lancers did not return to this country until October, 1859. As *you were then the 2nd Lieut. Colonel of the corps, you* were of necessity reduced to half pay in accordance with the rules of the Service.

[*Of course this 2nd Lieut. Colonelcy was a blank one as the regiment had served its term, in India. "Of necessity reduced to half pay?" then how could His Royal Highness have thought it just to cancel my appointment to the 2nd Dragoon Guards where I was safe from, such reduction, and which was my right by the rules of the Service, as the writer of this report has admitted at the commencement of this "Careful Report," and by which I lost £6000 in the value of my commission? Again, my having obtained my promotion without purchase, was a loss of £2000 to me. My majority was worth £8000 and my lieut. colonelcy in the 9th only £6000.*]

Under the purchase system it is presumed that you were aware that no officer could sell upon the *half pay list* for more than the regulation value of his commission. In your case you received the difference between the price of a cavalry and infantry lieut. colonelcy on your retirement to half pay, *and without waiting for an opportunity when your services* might have been made available, you voluntarily made a direct application to sell your commission, which was then worth £4,500, and the Reserve Fund being at that time able to bear this expense, you retired under the conditions of the Horse Guards Circular memorandum of 16th February, 1861.

[*How could I ever be employed again? I was 67 years old—besides an opportunity did occur, but it was seized upon for patronage and given to an officer who had already sold out of one regiment before, (Col. Shute),*

Certainly, I knew that I could only sell for regulation, but what I complained of was that I was forced into that position by having my majority in the 2nd Dragoon Guards cancelled against the rules of the Service under which I enlisted.]

To make this case clear at one glance it is only necessary to refer to the Army List of July, 1857, and then to compare it with that of August, 1857.

July, 1857.
2nd (The Queen's) Dragoon Guards.
Lieut Colonels.
Wm. Campbell.
Hylton Briscoe.

Majors.
Senior Major—Henry A. Ouvry.
Edw. Ruck Keene."

August, 1857.
9th (Queen's Royal Light Dragoons) Lancers.
Lieut. Colonels.

J. H. Grant, C.B.
Archibald Little.

Majors.

J. Rose Holden Rose.
Junior Major—Henry A. Ouvry.

Note:—My commission as senior major in the 2nd Dragoon Guards was worth £8,000 in the market, but after my being degraded a step by being replaced in the 9th Lancers it was only worth £4,000, and His Royal Highness says that he considered it "only just"

To make this case quite clear to those who are unacquainted with the purchase system, they have only to suppose that I was in possession of a freehold property—a house for instance worth £8,000, and that some despotic power had taken it by force and had given me one worth £4,000 in exchange.

To cancel my appointment to the 2nd Dragoon Guards, was in fact to take a link out of a chain, which of course fell to pieces. When the 9th Lancers returned home there was no Regiment to relieve them, as they had been previously relieved by the 2nd Dragoon Guards, and consequently there was no place to put the supernumerary officers. In fact, the Indian Mutiny, through which I served, was the cause of my losing £6,000 in the value of my commission, and as there is no law to resort to, the War Office has been enabled to deprive me of the whole fruits of my service.

"Uniuscujusque jus potentia ejus definitur."

When I returned there was a Reserve Fund, and the following will show how it has been misapplied.

THE PURCHASE OFFICER, THE CIVIL LIST, AND THE TAXPAYER

This comes of not doing justice, and refusing to redress grievances because we saw no immediate interest in so doing.

Thus wrote Lord Brougham to Lord Grey on an occasion when something disagreeable had happened to the Ministry, and it may be a warning to the present one if they persist in their present oppressive system of injustice with regard to "over regulation" sums, for which the government is clearly responsible.

In his late speech at Greenwich; the prime minister said:

The abolition of Purchase is achieved at a great cost, because when the people of England set about practical reforms they never accomplish them in a niggardly spirit, but their practice is to make generous compensation to those who may have suffered, or may imagine themselves to suffer by them, and in every doubtful case, to adopt the liberal course of action.

This sounds like justice—even more, it pictures that sublime equity which Mr. D'Israeli says is the characteristic of a British House of Commons; but when we come to look to facts, we find that this sublime equity is on]y partial, that it is to be applied merely to those whom it would be impolitic to offend, *viz.*, those on full-pay.

All other officers are to have their "over regulation" confiscated, and are to be turned adrift at a period of life too old to form fresh engagements.

But "over regulation" was illegal, and why should we be called upon to make good, losses which have been sustained in consequence of illegal acts, say the taxpayers?

I say *why* indeed?—but are the taxpayers called upon to do so, that is the question?

It is utterly false to say that the taxpayer is called upon to pay for the "over regulation" of the officers; it is exactly the other way; it is the taxpayer who has robbed the officer, has spent the money, and now demurs to give him back his own. I proceed to prove this by asking who supplied the Reserve Fund; and who took the money of this fund but the *taxpayer* and Civil List.

In the report of the select committee on the Army Reserve Fund will be found as follows:

The existence of this fund has enabled the Secretary of State for War to levy on *his own authority* charges on persons seeking promotion or first appointments in the army, and to apply the proceeds to *public objects* at discretion; and again:—

"Your committee do not doubt that the re-formation of the corps of Yeoman of the Guard, and Gentleman at Arms, and of the Military Train has been beneficial to the public service; *but that consideration does not appear to them to be sufficient to warrant the application to such purposes without the authority of Parliament, of sums received for the sale of commissions in other branches of the service.* The same objection applies to the payments which have been made for half-pay commissions in the artillery and engineers (non-purchase corps).

Every farthing of the Reserve Fund was supplied from the private resources of the purchase officer who has for the last 40 years been the milch cow of the taxpayer.

Instead of the taxpayer being called upon to pay the purchase officers at a great cost, it is the purchase officers who have been called upon, at a great cost out of their private resources, to buy up half-pay commissions in non-purchase corps.

If justice has been done in no niggardly spirit, what is the meaning of the large meetings of officers at Willis' Rooms and elsewhere, to petition Parliament because they cannot get their "over regulation."

The Royal Commission which has lately given in its report on "over regulation" sums says, "The regulations expressly prohibiting the practice of giving over regulation have been *gradually relaxed and finally withdrawn.*

There has been a tacit acquiescence in the practice, amounting in our opinion to a virtual recognition by civil and military authorities.

If this be the case, on what plea then can government refuse to pay back to every officer, at least the "over regulation" which *he gave*, instead of only to full-pay officers whether they gave or not. That the "over regulation" sums were imperative just as much as "regulation" sums, the following case plainly shews:

Certain officers refused to pay the usual "over regulation" and went on the plea that it was illegal. The commander in chief, after expressing his deep regret that so gross an instance of irregularity (in refusing to pay these illegal sums) should have been brought under his notice, and in vindication of the rules and regulations of the service, after having consulted the judge advocate general, announced his intention of submitting to the sovereign that the commissions of all these officers should be cancelled and that they should revert to their former ones.

This was actually done, and an officer who *would* give "over regulation" brought in from another regiment.

Again in another case, an officer who had retired, complained that he could not get his "over regulation" money from the officer who succeeded, *viz.*, £400, and the officer who would not pay was punished by being deprived of one year's rank in the army.

Here we see a commander in chief, backed by his legal adviser, the judge advocate general, punishing officers most severely for not doing what those, who now seek to confiscate the purchase officers' property, call an illegal act

The Royal Commission now sitting act indeed with justice to full-pay officers who retire, they not only give the "over regulation" which they paid, but sometimes double and even treble, while all other officers are refused any compensation at all.

If an officer has sold out and applies for his "over regulation" he is told by the War Office authorities he has sold out and can have no farther claim on the government; if he has not sold out he is told he is past sixty therefore he can have no claim to either "regulation" or "over regulation" the whole of his money is confiscated.

The officer who has sold, says, "I sold indeed, but I did so in order not to have the whole of my property confiscated, but I never got the "over regulation" which I gave with the recognition of the government. After a long service I only received one third the value of my commission, I was placed on compulsory Half-pay so that I could not get the money back which I paid." I get the answer:

"You have been very unfortunate, it is a very hard case, but we will not give you a farthing." And this treatment to old officers is the act of a liberal government, and the prime minister says publicly that "generous compensation will be made to the officer!"

The law of England boasts that there is no wrong without a remedy. That remains to be tried, and if there is really no redress, and if the government and the Duke of Cambridge, in the name of the crown, have the power legally to seize upon a fund supplied by the purchase officers of the army, and to use it to compensate officers in non-purchase corps, and members of the civil list, while some of those purchase officers who supplied the money are denied all compensation from their own Reserve Fund, (notwithstanding that the Royal Commission assembled by order of Her Majesty the Queen reported that the "over regulation" sums were given with the recognition of both the civil and military authorities) then I say that it is a gross malversation, and the legal dictum that there is no wrong without a remedy in England, is a mere myth.

The following orders issued by H. R. Highness the Duke of Cambridge, doubtless upon the authority of the government—for the idea of Her Majesty the Queen whose justice is proverbial, having anything personally to do with them is too absurd for argument—will illustrate what has been observed.

Horse Guards Circular,

25th May, 1861.

Her Majesty having been pleased to approve of a reorganization of the corps of Gentlemen-at-Arms, the purchase of commissions is to cease, *compensation being made to existing interests from the Reserve Fund by the Secretary of State for War.*

And again:

6th August, 1861.

The Queen has been pleased to approve that the purchase of the officers' commissions in. the corps, of the Yeomen of the Guard should cease at the earliest moment possible.

Any officers who acquired their commissions by purchase and are desirous of retiring from the corps, on communicating with the captain, *will receive from the Secretary of State for War* an amount in compensation thereof.

And at the time these orders were issued to compensate officers of the civil list, there was a surplus on that list, (shewn by documents in the House of Commons) amounting to £370,000, which surplus has been constantly increasing.

And this, notwithstanding the Civil List Act, which provides that "if at the end of any year there shall be a saving or surplus in any of the classes of the civil list" it shall be lawful for the Lords of the Treasury to direct it to be applied in aid of charges and expenses of any other class, excepting the fifth or pension class.

To sum up the merits of the whole question here mooted, the case may be thus shortly stated.

The officer commanding in chief acting under the *advice of his legal adviser, the judge advocate general*, pronounces that the "over regulation" is according to the rules and regulations of the service and *punishes severely officers who infringe them.* The Royal Commission lately assembled have reported that the "over regulation" sums *had the recognition of both civil and military authorities*, and still there are officers from whom the government withhold their money, under pretence that the practice was illegal

Compulsory Half-pay

If anyone has a grievance nowadays, he can be quite certain of getting a hearing for it; and if there is anything in his complaint, the public attention will be called to it by means far more ef-

ficacious than the presentation of a petition to parliament—
Times, August 8th, 1857.

Certain officers who had purchased their full-pay commissions
were placed on compulsory half-pay, without any compensation. They
thus lost half, or more, of the value of their commissions; they applied
for compensation from the Reserve Fund, which was accumulated
entirely from money received from purchase officers: but this Reserve
Fund, *supplied entirely by the purchase officers in the army*, was much too
valuable a resource to be frittered away in paying merely just debts and
claims upon it. It formed a very convenient fund for misappropria-
tion by the authorities:—such as compensating officers in the non-
purchase corps—Engineers, Artillery, Military Train,—and for making
reforms in Her Majesty's Household, as the following document from
the Blue-book shows:—

EXTRACT FROM THE REPORT OF THE SELECT COMMITTEE ON
THE MILITARY RESERVE FUND.

1. The Military Reserve Funds comprise what is generally
called the Army Reserve Fund and the Guards' Fund.

2. The Army Reserve Fund appears, under the name of Half-
pay Fund, to have existed sixty years ago.

5. About the year 1850, the Reserve Fund was constituted on
its present basis by the then Secretary of State for War.

8 From returns laid before your committee, it appears that the
sale of commissions in succession, to officers retiring on half-
pay, produced, between 1st April, 1862 and 31st. December,
1866, £338,678, and the difference between the sums received
by retiring officers and those paid by the purchasers £109,379;
the total, £448,057, representing the sum *received by the State
during less than six years* out of the purchase-money *paid by officers* for their promotion in the army.

9. During the same period, £204,881 was credited from the
fund to cavalry officers purchasing their promotion; £46,625
was applied to the reform of the corps of Yeomen of the Guard,
Gentlemen at-Arms, and the Military Train; and £311,599 was
paid, by way of composition of their half-pay, to half -pay officers of the line, the *Artillery*, and the *Engineers, relieving the half-
pay vote*, but not to an amount equal to the composition.

15. Your committee are of opinion that in any case the fund itself should be wound up.

16. Its existence has enabled the Secretary of State for War to levy, *by his own authority*, charges on persons seeking promotion or first appointments in the army, and to *apply the proceeds to public objects, at his discretion.*

But no public monies should be at the disposal of a minister, except such as are annually voted by Parliament as charged on the consolidated fund, and all sums received by public departments (unless otherwise applied by law) should be paid into the Exchequer.

17. *Your committee do not doubt that the reformation of the corps of Yeomen of the Guard and Gentlemen-at-Arms, and of the Military Train, has been beneficial to the public service; but that consideration does not appear to them sufficient to warrant the application to such purposes without authority of Parliiament, of sums received from the sales of commissions in other branches of the service*

The same objection applies to the payments which have been made for the purchase of half-pay commissions in the artillery and engineers.

Money, all supplied by purchase officers, is seized upon by *irresponsible* power, to compensate officers in *other non-purchase* branches of the service, and re-form Her Majesty's Household, and enable a minister to make political capital by presenting a diminished half-pay list.

These second lieutenant-colonels who purchased their places with their own money, apply for compensation from their own Reserve Fund, to which they all subscribed; the Secretary of State for War refuses to listen to them, and sends them away, after some thirty years' service, to face poverty in their old age, and he takes their money to compensate Gentlemen-at-Arms, Yeomen of the Guard, and officers of non-purchase corps.

One gentleman alone of Her Majesty's Household received £8000 of *our money* that has thus been confiscated, as I have shown.

It cannot be possible that Her Gracious Majesty knows that money, coming from the officers of her army or their friends, has been applied to the re-form of her household, and to place her servants on a more respectable footing, yet it is quite true that this has been done in her name, as the following circulars will show:—

Horse Guards Circular,

25th May, 1861.

Her Majesty having been pleased to approve of a reorganisation of the corps of Gentlemen-at-Arms, the purchase of commissions is to cease, *compensation being made to existing interests from, the Reserve Fund by the Secretary of State for War.*

Purchase is to cease—I ask, who received the money which these Yeomen paid for their places?

Horse Guards Circular,

6th August, 1861.

The Queen has been pleased to approve that the purchase of the officers' commissions in the corps of Yeomen of the Guard should cease at the earliest moment possible.

Any officers who acquired their commissions *by purchase* and are desirous of retiring from the corps, on communicating with the captain, *will receive from, the Secretary of State for War* an amount in compensation thereof (from the money supplied by the purchase officers of the army.)

Thus it appears that the above officers purchased their commissions; then it follows that some person got the money—where is it? The Reserve Fund supplied by the purchase Officers is seized upon by the Secretary for War in the name of Her Gracious Majesty.

The Crown sells commissions to its palace officers, appropriates the money, and then reforms the scandal at the expense of the purchase officers in the army, some of whom are, as we see here, mulcted of two-thirds of their property by arbitrary and irresponsible powers, and refused all redress.

How such a state of things should now be in the 19th century in England passes imagination: nothing worse in this line ever happened, even in France, before the great Revolution.

In fact the purchase system was similar to a company in which the purchase officers were shareholders.

The shares went up 100 *p.c.* in the market.

Thus a commission which was at first sold for £6000 became worth £12000 in the market, and of course could not be purchased for less.

The Secretary of State for War was the director of this company, and any money made was the property of the purchase officers.

Under ordinary circumstances, the shareholders had the law to appeal to in case they considered that they had a complaint to make of the conduct of the directors, but in this case it appears that there was "no contract," so that a shareholder had nothing to trust to but the honour of the Secretary of State for War, who has pleaded "no contract" in a late action. I ask, was there no moral contract? Were the Secretary of State for War and the field marshal the commander-in-chief justified in compensating court servants and others out of the large surplus which he had capitalized by the sale of commissions, and which came entirely out of the purchase officers' pockets, while all compensation was denied to some of the shareholders who supplied the money?

It has been urged in Parliament that six millions had been paid to the purchase officers. I ask, how many millions the taxpayer saved during the sixty years that the purchase officers have been serving for next to nothing? Again, if it had been a question of any enormous sum that was demanded by these purchase officers, but the fact is that there were only three or four of them.

How different the case was when men in high positions bad to receive compensation, or in the case of the late hereditary pensions! The compensation given to one of these men, who never paid a farthing for their pensions, would have compensated the whole of the officers who purchased their steps and have been sent empty away,

I think there is something rotten in the state of Denmark!

H. A. Ouvry,
(Retired) Col., 9th Lancers.

4

REMARKS ON THE SIKH WAR

It is very amusing to me, now in my old age, to read the newspaper reproaches on the inconsistency of the Q.O.M. and others, for maintaining opinions which are directly opposed to their utterances of, perhaps, twenty or thirty years ago; just as if every man who is worth anything, has not changed his views and opinions more than once during his life time, if he should have attained to a long period of life, when he may be presumed to have become wiser.

Cardinal Newman wrote and preached that His Holiness, the Pope, was Anti-Christ until he was past forty years of age; after which he went over to the said Anti-Christ, and then preached that between Atheism and Romanism there was no *locus standi*. Every man must be either an Atheist or a Roman Catholic.

D'Israeli commenced his career as a Republican and ended as a red-hot Tory.

It may be said that politicians of his stamp are all charlatans, but some there are who honestly change their views. I know full well that I have changed mine, after having had a more lengthened experience of life.

Now, with regard to the Sikh Campaign to which I have alluded in my letters, and especially with regard to the Battle of Chillianwalla. Nothing occurred there, which has not happened at all times and with all nations, in the course of their wars. British troops, like all others, and especially the cavalry require leading; but if old invalids of seventy years of age, are told off to lead them, the natural consequence follows.

If Lord Gough had not mentioned the occurrence in his despatch, in order to excuse himself, no person would have been the wiser. The men who fought shy were just as brave and sound intrinsically as those who charged home. The fault was in the leading, as Sir Charles Napier told them on parade; want of proper leading led to the unfortunate episode which has been made so much of, but which was, in fact, of not much consequence, and had nothing to do with the result of the campaign.

The very excellent sketch of the battle in my text was made by a young officer the day after the fight, and I have incorporated it in the text, as it is far better than the rough sketch I made myself on the day of the action.

★★★★★★

Those who have read my appendix, will recollect the remarks of Lord Brougham; and now, in 1892, we see the truth of it.

Mr. Stanhope having decreed that officers in the army are to pass an examination in the Latin language, I would call his attention to the following:—

Raro antecedentem scelestum
Deseruit pede poena claudo.

Nemesis comes limping slowly; but she comes inevitably.

I have shewn the iniquities of the old purchase system, which was abolished some twenty years ago. But the purchase officers will not die off quickly enough, therefore faith is to be broken with them. Let any man of honour read the speeches of General Fraser, M.P., in the House of Commons, in which the tyranny of the War Office is fully exposed. The following cutting from the *The Times*, March 17th, speaks for itself—

THE PURCHASE OFFICERS

Sir,—A reference to "Hansard," or to *The Times* of the 11th of August last, will prove to your correspondent "M.P." that my contentions, supported by facts and figures, with regard to this important question—affecting the contentment of an army— were fully brought forward by me in the House of Commons on August 9, on Vote XI, Army Estimates, my first opportunity. I claimed that the subject touched the honour of Secretaries of State for War and the honesty of those who serve at the War Office. My indictment was that the terms and "honour-able pledges" given by ministers when the purchase system was abolished by royal warrant have been flagrantly broken; "M.P." will also see how very meagre was Mr. Brodrick's reply. Mr. Stanhope this year appealed to the chairman against my taking part in the discussion on the Army Estimates, as I had a resolu-tion on the paper.

I certainly mentioned to Mr. Stanhope, in the lobby, that the deputation of service members would approach him, in cour-tesy to himself and to uphold the dignity of his position. On a previous occasion he challenged me for voting for volunteer equipment against the government; I claimed to have voted ac-cording to my conscience. These are the only two occasions on which I was ever lobbied by, or lobbied, a minister. I have tried to prove that I was right in my contention on the 9th of August, by issuing a pamphlet giving some 60 instances, out of scores before me, of alleged grievances, thereby to spread information on an intricate subject, and to draw an attention which the War Minister declined to give in the House of Commons. Any idea that claims for compensation and pension would be made at the expense of the private soldier is preposterous, in the face of the Parliamentary return of May 4, 1871, No. 209, by which it appears that between 1841 and 1871 the sum of £1,712,000 was paid into the Reserve Fund, the whole of which money came out of the officers' pockets, and which was applied to various objects, to the advantage of the taxpayer.

I offer my apologies to "M.P." for submerging him in a deluge, and my thanks to those who, from all quarters of the House of Lords and Commons, volunteer to help to guide the ship through all blizzards into a haven, where inquiry will be granted, and a final decision arrived at without "partiality, favour, or affection."

Your obedient servants
C. C. Fraser.

House of Commons, March 17th, 1892.

Now that the G.O.M. has come into his kingship, it is to be hoped that something will be done. However morally bad it was, at any rate the Purchase System and Long Service gave us a contented body of officers and men, which is far from the case now.

Mr. Stanhope, like all other Ministers of State, was what our German neighbours call, *ein Realpolitiker "sans phrase."* With such men there is no argument, they have one object in mind, and that is, never to pay anything except under the pressure of *force majeure.* Justice, equity, honour, with them are merely idealistic figments. He who goes on such principles is not fit to rule: justice is not a virtue in a ruler; on the contrary, it is a weakness; which fact is so well expressed by a French poet, that I cannot do better than quote his lines:—

La Justice n'est pas une vertu d'Etat:
Quand on craint d'etre injuste on a toujours à craindre,
Et qui veut tout pouvoir doit oser tout enfreindre,
Fuir comme un deshonneur le vertu qui le perd,
Et voler sans scrupule au crime qui le sert.

ALSO FROM LEONAUR
AVAILABLE IN SOFTCOVER OR HARDCOVER WITH DUST JACKET

THE RELUCTANT REBEL by *William G. Stevenson*—A young Kentuckian's experiences in the Confederate Infantry & Cavalry during the American Civil War..

BOOTS AND SADDLES by *Elizabeth B. Custer*—The experiences of General Custer's Wife on the Western Plains.

FANNIE BEERS' CIVIL WAR by *Fannie A. Beers*—A Confederate Lady's Experiences of Nursing During the Campaigns & Battles of the American Civil War.

LADY SALE'S AFGHANISTAN by *Florentia Sale*—An Indomitable Victorian Lady's Account of the Retreat from Kabul During the First Afghan War.

THE TWO WARS OF MRS DUBERLY by *Frances Isabella Duberly*—An Intrepid Victorian Lady's Experience of the Crimea and Indian Mutiny.

THE REBELLIOUS DUCHESS by *Paul F. S. Dermoncourt*—The Adventures of the Duchess of Berri and Her Attempt to Overthrow French Monarchy.

LADIES OF WATERLOO by *Charlotte A. Eaton, Magdalene de Lancey & Juana Smith*—The Experiences of Three Women During the Campaign of 1815: Waterloo Days by Charlotte A. Eaton, A Week at Waterloo by Magdalene de Lancey & Juana's Story by Juana Smith.

TWO YEARS BEFORE THE MAST by *Richard Henry Dana. Jr.*—The account of one young man's experiences serving on board a sailing brig—the Penelope—bound for California, between the years 1834-36.

A SAILOR OF KING GEORGE by *Frederick Hoffman*—From Midshipman to Captain—Recollections of War at Sea in the Napoleonic Age 1793-1815.

LORDS OF THE SEA by *A. T. Mahan*—Great Captains of the Royal Navy During the Age of Sail.

COGGESHALL'S VOYAGES: VOLUME 1 by *George Coggeshall*—The Recollections of an American Schooner Captain.

COGGESHALL'S VOYAGES: VOLUME 2 by *George Coggeshall*—The Recollections of an American Schooner Captain.

TWILIGHT OF EMPIRE by *Sir Thomas Ussher & Sir George Cockburn*—Two accounts of Napoleon's Journeys in Exile to Elba and St. Helena: Narrative of Events by Sir Thomas Ussher & Napoleon's Last Voyage: Extract of a diary by Sir George Cockburn.

LEONAUR

ALSO FROM LEONAUR
AVAILABLE IN SOFTCOVER OR HARDCOVER WITH DUST JACKET

IRON TIMES WITH THE GUARDS *by An O. E. (G. P. A. Fildes)*—The Experiences of an Officer of the Coldstream Guards on the Western Front During the First World War.

THE GREAT WAR IN THE MIDDLE EAST: 1 *by W. T. Massey*—The Desert Campaigns & How Jerusalem Was Won---two classic accounts in one volume.

THE GREAT WAR IN THE MIDDLE EAST: 2 *by W. T. Massey*—Allenby's Final Triumph.

SMITH-DORRIEN *by Horace Smith-Dorrien*—Isandlwhana to the Great War.

1914 *by Sir John French*—The Early Campaigns of the Great War by the British Commander.

GRENADIER *by E. R. M. Fryer*—The Recollections of an Officer of the Grenadier Guards throughout the Great War on the Western Front.

BATTLE, CAPTURE & ESCAPE *by George Pearson*—The Experiences of a Canadian Light Infantryman During the Great War.

DIGGERS AT WAR *by R. Hugh Knyvett & G. P. Cuttriss*—"Over There" With the Australians by R. Hugh Knyvett and Over the Top With the Third Australian Division by G. P. Cuttriss. Accounts of Australians During the Great War in the Middle East, at Gallipoli and on the Western Front.

HEAVY FIGHTING BEFORE US *by George Brenton Laurie*—The Letters of an Officer of the Royal Irish Rifles on the Western Front During the Great War.

THE CAMELIERS *by Oliver Hogue*—A Classic Account of the Australians of the Imperial Camel Corps During the First World War in the Middle East.

RED DUST *by Donald Black*—A Classic Account of Australian Light Horsemen in Palestine During the First World War.

THE LEAN, BROWN MEN *by Angus Buchanan*—Experiences in East Africa During the Great War with the 25th Royal Fusiliers—the Legion of Frontiersmen.

THE NIGERIAN REGIMENT IN EAST AFRICA *by W. D. Downes*—On Campaign During the Great War 1916-1918.

THE 'DIE-HARDS' IN SIBERIA *by John Ward*—With the Middlesex Regiment Against the Bolsheviks 1918-19.

www.ingramcontent.com/pod-product-compliance
Lightning Source LLC
Chambersburg PA
CBHW032054080426
42733CB00006B/269